"Michael Rogers has given the church heaven. With pastoral skill, careful interpretation, and logical force, the ultimate destinies of the soul are portrayed. This engaging book will bless laymen and clergy alike. Highly recommended!"

**Peter A. Lillback,** President, Westminster Theological Seminary

"What happens after I die? Who has not asked that question? And very obviously believers want to know what the Bible says. Michael Rogers in this marvelous book has provided a thorough yet readable treatment of Scripture focused upon the triumph of Christ over sin and death. It is convicting and encouraging, challenging yet attractive in handling what the Scriptures say concerning the matters of eternity. It compiles and arranges what the Bible affirms and reveals yet avoids exotic speculation where the Bible is silent. This book is at one and the same time a great read and a great resource."

**Harry L. Reeder,** Senior Pastor, Briarwood Presbyterian Church, Birmingham, Alabama

"Death is the great modern taboo, the thing which we all fear more than anything else and yet which is rarely mentioned, even in Christian circles. It is thus useful to have available a helpful book on the topic. Michael Rogers here addresses the issue head on with theological care and pastoral concern. This is a thoughtful and sensitive exploration of questions surrounding the afterlife and will repay the time spent reading it. Highly recommended."

**Carl R. Trueman,** Paul Woolley Professor of Church History, Westminster Theological Seminary

"Though death, along with taxes, is for certain, surprisingly little has been written on the subject. And most of what is out there may actually be counterproductive. This book stands in the gap. Filled to the brim with keen biblical insight, sound theological engagement, and warm pastoral care, this book will be your first—and maybe only—stop for guidance on any and all issues related to death. Speaking personally, my family and I have been richly nourished by the pastoral ministry of Michael Rogers for fifteen years. I am delighted to see that wider audiences may now experience his edifying teaching."

**Stephen J. Nichols,** Research Professor of Christianity and Culture, Lancaster Bible College

"After nearly forty years of fruitful pastoral ministry you would expect Michael Rogers to be wise in guiding believers through the challenging question, what's next after this life? In *What Happens After I Die?* those expectations are exceeded. These pages reflect a depth of biblical reflection and practical help through which Dr. Rogers now extends his thoughtful understanding of Scripture to all who will read. What does the Bible say about heaven and hell? How will this world end? How can I be ready? These and many other questions are addressed with skill and Christ-centered hope. This is not dry eschatology; it is biblical truth that both challenges and encourages, enlightens and engages."

**Timothy Witmer,** Professor of Practical Theology, Westminster Theological Seminary; author, *The Shepherd Leader* and *The Shepherd Leader at Home*

"Is it pie in the sky when you die? Or is it seventy virgins? Or both? Or neither? Michael Rogers does an outstanding job of leading a search of the Scriptures to see what is true about the future destiny of God's children—and of everyone else. This book will shape your prayers and your life so that both are more 'conformed to the image of his Son.' I commend it highly."

**Samuel Logan,** International Director, The World Reformed Fellowship

# WHAT HAPPENS
# AFTER I DIE?

# WHAT HAPPENS

# AFTER I DIE?

MICHAEL ALLEN ROGERS

*Foreword by Bryan Chapell*

**:: CROSSWAY**

WHEATON, ILLINOIS

Trade paperback ISBN: 978-1-4335-3302-0
PDF ISBN: 978-1-4335-3303-7
Mobipocket ISBN: 978-1-4335-3304-4
ePub ISBN: 978-1-4335-3305-1

---

**Library of Congress Cataloging-in-Publication Data**

Rogers, Michael Allen, 1949–
   What happens after I die? / Michael Allen Rogers ; foreword by Bryan Chapell.
      p.   cm
   Includes bibliographical references and index.
   ISBN 978-1-4335-3302-0 (Trade paperback)—ISBN
978-1-4335-3303-7 (PDF)—ISBN 978-1-4335-3304-4
(Mobipocket)—ISBN 978-1-4335-3305-1 (ePub)
   1. Death—Religious aspects—Christianity—Sermons.
2. Death—Biblical teaching. 3. Future life—Christianity—
Sermons. 4. Future life—Biblical teaching. 5. Presbyterian
Church—Sermons. 6. Sermons, American. I. Title.
BT825.R596      2013
236'.2—dc23                                              2012028030

---

Crossway is a publishing ministry of Good News Publishers.

| VP | | 22 | 21 | 20 | 19 | 18 | 17 | 16 | 15 | 14 | 13 |
|----|----|----|----|----|----|----|----|----|----|----|----|
| 15 | 14 | 13 | 12 | 11 | 10 | 9 | 8 | 7 | 6 | 5 | 4 | 3 | 2 | 1 |

# CONTENTS

# FOREWORD

*THE QUESTION NEVER GOES AWAY:* What happens after I die? One of the most poignant times I have been asked this question was after the funeral of a young girl, killed in a farming accident. She had only done what many of us raised on farms have delighted to do—ridden the fender of a tractor while her father cultivated a field. For many farming families, this is a way that kids do what "big people" do, learn farming, and spend time with Dad—all at the same time. The family outing turned to tragedy when the tractor hit a hidden ditch and the girl was thrown.

As she fell, her father turned to catch her, but she was already beyond his grasp. Instead, her eyes met his, and she spoke one word: "Daddy." He later said that she did not scream his name in panic or desperation. Instead, she seemed calm and spoke his name only as if saying a loving goodbye. At one level, his daughter's lack of fear comforted the father. He knew his daughter to be a dear Christian, and he believed that, even in the moment of death, her faith had spared her the terrors of the accident. At another level, the daughter's expression of love for her father haunted him.

In her dying, the young girl had reached out to comfort her father. There was no hint of blame or abandonment. The gesture was a reflection not only of faith, but also of the closeness of the family. And now the father felt keenly the weight of his daughter's enduring some measure of eternity without her parents. He asked me, "Won't she be lonely without her mother and me?"

The father believed that he and his wife would eventually join their daughter in heaven, after their deaths. But he struggled with the idea of their child enduring what would likely be decades without her immediate family. He was simply being a caring father in asking what may have seemed like a question inappropriate for the polite and careful conversations that accompany funerals. As a parent, he could not fathom how his child could navigate the unfamiliar streets of heaven or rest "in the arms of Jesus" without her mommy and daddy there.

The simple question that came from such fatherly concern actually represents a host of questions that stretch thought and imagination as we try to grasp profound truths of our faith. The question about a daughter's loneliness in heaven implicitly is also a question about: (1) the nature of our existence prior to and after Christ's return; (2) the timing and effects of our reunion with loved ones; (3) the nature of our relationship with God and others for eternity; (4) the spiritual status, mental state, and maturity level in heaven of a person who dies as a child on earth; (5) the status of the body (before and after Christ's return) of one who has died, especially if the death is disfiguring; (6) the nature of time in eternity, and whether decades on earth are relevant to a heavenly clock; (7) how answers to all of these questions should affect our lives now; and many more related questions.

The answers to some of these questions will readily come to the minds of biblically informed believers; the answers to others have perplexed theologians for centuries; and the answers to a few will come only when Jesus returns to answer them. The difficulty of some of these questions, however, should not make us hesitate to search Scripture to answer those that we can. The Bible addresses the most pressing questions we should have about what happens after we die in order to give us a strong and precious hope, enabling us to face life's greatest challenges and griefs.

The Bible clearly tells us that we will meet again with loved ones who have died in Jesus. We know that after death, we will be with the Lord forever. We know that when we are with Jesus, grief and pain will vanish forever. We know that our spirit will finally be united with an incorruptible body. We know that sin will touch and tempt us no more. We know that evil will be punished and righteousness will be vindicated. We know that Christ's righteousness will be ours. We know that everlasting joy will be ours. We know that our world will ultimately be made new and better. We know that the afflictions we face now will fade in comparison to the glory that will be revealed in us. We know that when our children die, they are safe in the arms of Jesus.

In order to receive the full comfort and courage of these truths, while also not making assertions that would create false hopes, we need to know what Scripture promises and how those promises apply to our lives. *What Happens After I Die?* does precisely this. In these pages we have the double blessing of clear articulation of biblical truth *and* deep reflection based upon decades of pastoral experience. Dr. Michael Rogers brings us both the sound reflection of a mind that has studied the Scriptures for decades and also insightful applications from a heart made tender by pastoring people through generations.

As a consequence of his pastoral experience, Dr. Rogers presses the biblical truth precisely to the issues that are most likely to affect our lives and challenge our hearts. His conclusions are based on rigorous and faithful exposition of Scripture. When he offers an occasional speculation in the light of mysteries Scripture does not fully unravel, he honestly identifies the questions that remain, while still showing how his tentative conclusions are consistent with what Scripture does disclose.

The importance of this book must be measured against the reader's assessment of the accuracy of the sentence that begins this foreword: "The question never goes away: What happens after I die?" More than three decades of pastoral experience confirm the truth of that sentence for me. A father's question about the possible loneliness of his child in heaven has been preceded and followed by hundreds of a similar nature: "Will Dad recognize us when we get to heaven, though we will be many years older than we were when he died?" "When we are in heaven, will my sister still blame me for not coming to her wedding?" "Will my mother finally be able to support my choice of spouse, after we all die?" "Will Jesus forgive the sins that I have forgotten to repent of, after I die?" "Will my father regain his right mind in heaven?" "Will I have to forgive the man who killed my daughter, if God lets him into heaven?" "Will our baby, who died in infancy, be in heaven, and will she love her parents?"

Such questions can perplex us, worry us, and even deprive us of the joy of the gospel, if we don't know how the Bible addresses them, comforts us, and gives us hope beyond the challenges of this life. Thus, as a faithful pastor, Dr. Rogers is careful to take us to the Scriptures to answer these and many more questions in order that each of us may say, "I can live fully and joyfully now because I know what will happen after I die."

Bryan Chapell

# PREFACE

*"NOW I LAY ME DOWN* to sleep, I pray the Lord my soul to keep. If I should die before I wake, I pray the Lord my soul to take." In early childhood that prayer formed both a mantra and a creed; it was the total sum of Christianity I knew. When you think about it, the systematic theology packed into those two sentences is very comprehensive. It is a petition for God's providential care offered in conscious acknowledgment of one's felt mortality, humbling the petitioner and teaching a sense of God's sovereignty over human beings he has made. Here is a great spiritual foundation to build upon. Would that all prayers were as eloquent.

My mother must have taught me the prayer, though I have no remembrance of that. We were an unchurched family until I was six. Nevertheless, this bedtime petition was a fixed ritual well before I began Sunday school attendance as a first grader. The prayer was my entire religious life, repeated as a reflex when the bedroom light was switched off; I recited it with all the discipline of a cloistered monk at Evensong. Looking back, I believe a subliminal element of fear motivated me. That one word, *die*, was conspicuous in this liturgy, like a word wrapped in barbed wire. Could it be that I might not wake to see tomorrow? I was ten before death affected my life, when a boy from my school died in a fire. But the merest possibility of life cut short sobered me. I figured adults who composed prayers probably knew things I did not, so I prayed with fervor about premature death, however remote the chance. Such was my talisman raised against unknown darkness.

People everywhere are hungry to know what the Bible teaches about death and realities beyond. A relative void of sound, Scripture-based preaching on the subject is now filled by a glut of personal experience testimonials, proclaiming near-death visionary experiences. A recent bestseller apparently is based on a preschool-age child who stuns his family with specific facts reported about dead relatives—knowledge he supposedly acquired via a brief trip to the edge of heaven and back. Nothing I can say will keep millions from pursuing eternity based on subjective, mystical accounts. Humanly speaking, I offer no comparable fireworks, only the divine Word of God as it speaks on these subjects—the one iner-rant sourcebook of truth revealed from the mind of God by his Spirit. My entire authority as a death spokesman resides in the Bible. If I stray from it, by all means doubt what I say.

Beginning in fall 2009 and culminating Easter Sunday 2010, I preached twenty-six sermons on death and the afterlife for the congregation of Westminster Presbyterian Church (PCA) of Lancaster, Pennsylvania. Sermon CDs purchased and responses to our radio broadcast indicated I had touched a nerve of interest. I serve a congregation of people who love the unvarnished truth of God preached. My predecessor told me after he retired that what he missed most about worship at Westminster Church was "the quiet rustle of Bible pages" as he spoke—hundreds of folk looked up each reference cited. This splendid Berean congregation prodded me to publish the sermon series. I am deeply grateful to them for prayerful sup-port of my weekly pulpit ministry. Likewise, I should thank members of Valley Presbyterian Church in Lutherville, Maryland, where earlier mes-sages on this material were heard by God's flock in the 1980s.

The order of the material has been revised here from the preaching series, and everything was rewritten and expanded. I first deal with the origin of death as the Bible describes its source and its tyranny. Then we delve into the horrible subject of an unbeliever's fate without Christ—termed the "default destination." Only after probing hell will we explore the shining prospect of heaven. As we do, keep in mind that heaven has, in a manner of speaking, two stages: the immediate state of the believer after death as a soul perfected in righteousness and the ultimate event of receiving a resurrection body, climaxing at the final coming of Christ on the historic "Day of the Lord." One chapter, "Is My Child in Heaven?" was at first two sermons, but is now merged into one chapter. Despite its considerably greater length than the other chapters, I felt it had to be writ-ten as a unified argument.

Preachers generally find it hard to translate pulpit words into written prose for publication. It is somewhat like reducing a movie made in three dimensions back to just two. Sermons that may have been effective when spoken can seem bland in print. George Whitefield complained once that he would accede to a request to publish his sermons if someone could figure out "how to get the thunder and lightning on the printed page." My oral style remains intact, since I seek a conversation with you as a reader. I am quite aware of an autobiographical element in these pages, which I sought to restrain but not eliminate. I hoped readers might journey through my own emerging discoveries as a Christian pilgrim learning about death and life eternal, as I've matured from boy, to pastor, to senior citizen.

My audience is the man, woman, or young person in the pew, ordinary folks who seek biblical answers about their future. This book is a layman's survey of a vast landscape. Thus the academic community will most likely dismiss this volume as simplistic. Every subject I undertake is far larger than what I have covered. Whole books have been written about each chapter topic, and I am frustrated by all the side alleys and interesting details I had to neglect. More detailed discussions would be required at many points if I had been writing for scholars.

For those who do seek a more comprehensive, yet plainly written expansion of these subjects, I heartily recommend *The Promise of the Future* by Cornelis P. Venema.[1] Venema's work is superb—thoroughly biblical and balanced. He also deals with competing millennial views and other areas of general eschatology, which I have studiously avoided in my narrower focus upon the experience of the individual at death and beyond. (If you must know my millennial stance before we embark, it is amillennial, the same as Venema and many of the sources I have cited. I look to the lordship of Christ active today, even before he returns to history, and I view the redeemed people of Israel and today's church as one covenant people of God.) Another fine guide written at the layman's level is *Biblical Teaching on the Doctrines of Heaven and Hell* by Edward Donnelley. Anthony Hoekema's *The Bible and the Future* has been a trusted guide for me since the day it was published.[2]

My hope is that the transformational gospel of Christ crucified and risen will be repeated often within these pages. Every sermon I preach endeavors to present at least the kernel of the gospel of God's magnificent grace in Christ Jesus, as do these chapters. Those who do not already confess him as Lord can certainly read this volume with some level of understanding, but I pray that in doing so, they will realize that apart from trusting in Christ as Lord, their only prospect beyond the hour of their death is catastrophic. But with Christ, hope for the future becomes stunning beyond all description.

When I finished the manuscript, I was surprised to realize how often I had quoted various works of C. S. Lewis. He is, of course, one of

Christianity's eloquent defenders, but he disclaimed being a theologian or Bible scholar. Imagination was his forte, and eternity was never far from his gaze. Colorful imagery makes Lewis's exploration of issues touching heaven, hell, and death unforgettable and usually spot-on within biblical parameters.

I am indebted to Dr. Bryan Chapell for his eloquent foreword. He graciously completed this just as he was transitioning from nearly two decades of service as president of Covenant Theological Seminary, to serve as chancellor. My ministry colleague and friend, Dr. John S. Light, was an ever-present theological sounding board. Dr. Stephen J. Nichols heard this material preached and gave me unique aid in early stages of the move toward publication.

Lastly, I speak with profound gratitude to my wife, Carol, to whom this volume is dedicated. Beloved wife: awesome death now wields only one glittering dagger that gives me real pause—a severe yet temporary separation from you.

# PART ONE

# DEATH'S TYRANNY OVERTHROWN

O LORD, make me know my end
and what is the measure of my days;
let me know how fleeting I am!
Behold, you have made my days a few handbreadths
and my lifetime is as nothing before you.
Surely all mankind stands as a mere breath! . . .

Look away from me, that I may smile again,
before I depart and am no more!

PSALM 39:4-5, 13

Why did you bring me out from the womb?
Would that I had died before any eye had seen me
and were as though I had not been,
carried from the womb to the grave.
Are not my days few?
Then cease, and leave me alone, that I may find a little cheer
before I go—and I shall not return—
to the land of darkness and deep shadow,
the land of gloom like thick darkness,
like deep shadow without any order,
where light is as thick darkness.

JOB 10:18-22

For I know that my Redeemer lives,
and at the last he will stand upon the earth.
And after my skin has been thus destroyed,
yet in my flesh I shall see God,
whom I shall see for myself,
and my eyes shall behold, and not another.
My heart faints within me!

JOB 19:25-27

# CHAPTER ONE

# THE LAND OF DEEP SHADE

☼

*A FASCINATION WITH OLD CEMETERIES* first stirred in me when I was twelve. One Sunday afternoon I joined my maternal grandparents on their errand to prune rosebushes planted beside family graves in the rural western New York village of Griffin's Mills. For two centuries, the dead from the surrounding area had been transported to a level green beside a small Presbyterian church until their memorials stood rank upon rank across acres of shaded ground. If Easter Sunday congregants would have filled every pew at the nearby church, they could not equal ten percent of the deceased human beings whose several thousand granite guardians thronged the lawns. My grandparents pointed out markers representing immediate ancestors, but at age twelve I considered any associations I had with these folks a matter of indifference. While my escorts tended roses, I began an hour of curious meandering—my first ever free time spent in a large cemetery. As a naive adolescent I had no notion that I had trespassed upon a great human convocation until I was startled to overhear their murmurings. The dead testified.

Some of the oldest stones bore macabre carvings of skulls and crossbones, which I associated with the ensign of a pirate ship. Faded letters on mossy limestone quoted Victorian poetry or verses of Scripture no longer easily deciphered. I found crumbling headstones marking a final bivouac for soldiers of both the American Revolution and the Civil War. One Union army private was identified by his military unit, and I deduced that since his death occurred in the first week of July 1863, he could have fallen to a minié ball at Gettysburg.

Calculating from engraved dates of birth and death, I was surprised at how many pre–twentieth-century lives had tragically short spans. I wondered what a fifteen-year-old girl named Eunice might have looked like. What caused her early death in the 1870s? Could her final illness have been remedied by a dose of nonexistent penicillin? Who could tell me the wrenching story of parents with three small markers flanking their own, each guarding a baby that was either stillborn or less than one year old? Why was one particular citizen with the odd first name of Roscoe so prominent in the 1880s that he rated an eight-foot-tall marble plinth? Roscoe dominated the chessboard of stones like a bishop. What did the size of a grave marker signify seventy years later, when only a handful of his descendents might recall who Roscoe was?

The longer I explored, the more questions that cemetery proposed. My grandparents were surprised to find me reluctant to quit my newly discovered world of not-so-silent human dust. Any previous sense I had that my adolescent life would simply continue unendingly was left behind in that memorable hour. Death had asserted many mysteries. Without realizing it at the time, I went from there drawn to one of the famous resolutions Jonathan Edwards composed before he was twenty: "Resolved, to think much on all occasions of my own dying and of the common circumstances which attend death."[1]

Cemeteries still interest me a half-century later, since my calling has taken me to dozens of them as a pastor presiding at burial ceremonies. Three years after that Sunday visit my grandmother was interred in the same plot she tended on that earlier day. My grandfather never guessed that twenty more years would pass beyond his wife's demise until his turn came. He could not have imagined I would be the minister presiding at the grave when his ninety-four-year-old body was laid to rest. Now I sometimes wonder—who among their widely scattered twenty-first-century descendants ever tends those rosebushes on a Sunday afternoon?

In 1999, purchase of adjacent acreage for a building expansion brought the church I pastor in Lancaster County, Pennsylvania, into possession of a hilltop family graveyard situated within a copse of trees two hundred yards from our existing building. Historical society records informed us that forty-three known burials had occurred on that plot across a fifty-year span between the late eighteenth to the early nineteenth centuries, with the last recorded burial being in 1834. Neglect, ravages of time, and vandalism left only a few broken German-language stones to bear witness. On February 15, 2004, our church reopened that ground for its first burial in 170 years. The body interred that day was my father's. Now, many times annually, bodies or ashes of my sisters and brothers in Christ are placed in this earth, adjacent to the dust of early Mennonite settlers. Burial rights are reserved in that lovely hilltop cemetery, in anticipation of a coming day when my own clay will join that of my father and a growing "cloud of witnesses."

## THE ONLY REMAINING TABOO

What awaits us after death? We begin consideration of the Bible's teaching on the subjects of death, divine judgment, and the final destinations of either hell or heaven. Only the last of these topics is normally allowed today in social conversation by obstinately death-avoiding people. Heaven can be discussed, but the conversation usually pursues a harmless fantasy, malleable to any fanciful shape the speaker's imagination devises: "She's dancing on golden streets now, for sure . . ." The heaven most moderns conceive of is a creation of wishful thinking, a spiritual placebo. It tends to be a light-hearted, harmless way of forecasting the inconceivable. After mentioning it, many people realize they only half believe in it. The heaven of popular discussion these days certainly is not proscribed by the dictates of Christian biblical revelation.

Death as God's righteous judgment and an eternal hell are taboos that secular people steadfastly refuse to discuss, except to tell you how much they disdain all thoughts of them. Avoidance of the subject has a long history. Legend says King Louis the XV of France once banned all people in his kingdom from mentioning the word "death" in his presence. Nevertheless, King Louis most assuredly died.

A pastor friend once made a call upon a church member, a woman advanced in years who was fully aware that she was dying of congestive heart failure. As a mature saint resting in Christ this nursing home patient had no illusions about her future. She was brimful of hope as the pastor read Scripture about heaven, and they discussed the believer's future with confidence. However, in the midst of that pastoral visit, the woman's unbelieving daughter entered the room. She heard the conversation and looked agitated but said nothing. The pastor prayed and excused himself to leave. He was surprised to have the daughter follow him into the hallway, where she verbally tore into him with eyes blazing. She said, "How *dare* you talk to my mother about death! We are doing everything possible to surround her with positive encouragement and you come here telling her she is going to die. How dare you!" Not long afterward that lady attended her mother's funeral. Perhaps she blamed that event on the pastor's negative attitude.

No matter how doggedly you avoid the topic, every single person will die. After decades of superefficient operation, that great engineering marvel—your human body—will shut down and cease thousands of functions in a matter of minutes. Your heart muscle will stop pumping and masses of neurons in the brain will switch off. Your body's core temperature will cool and rigor mortis will begin. What then becomes of the unseen essence of you?

Millions seem to think they will continue uninterrupted life upon this earth. At least, they are striving mightily in that direction, running hard to delay facing a terminal certainty. I drive past a fitness and racquet center every day that has expanded its parking lot several times in ten years just to accommodate hundreds of cars parked there daily by suburbanites arriving in Audis, Volvos, and BMWs, eager to tone up their bound-for-the-grave bodies.

John Lennon of the *Beatles* wrote in his song "Imagine": "Imagine there's no heaven . . . No hell below us . . . Imagine all the people, living for today . . ."[2] Lennon's theology enjoys wide appeal: inviting us to live exclusively for right now; supposing we can be carefree and without consequences in this present moment if we look no further ahead. One evening years ago, on the sidewalk outside his New York apartment, a man with a pistol snuffed out Lennon's vain illusion. Despite the efforts of our death-avoidance, those graveyards really do keep filling up. But unlike fitness center parking lots, the cemetery keeps all its occupants for the long term.

It causes strong concern to realize that of all groups, evangelical Christianity has almost ceased to provide a preaching and teaching emphasis on the biblical hope of life beyond death, based in Jesus Christ. Pulpits today are more often dedicated to preaching topical, seeker-sensitive messages that concentrate on how to have a fulfilling marriage, how to manage your finances, or how to implement sound principles of child-raising. How many "seeker" congregations hear much from Scripture about preparing for the hour of death and for eternity? When, for instance, did you last hear a sermon about hell? Richard Baxter long ago urged pastors to preach "chiefly on the greatest, most certain and most necessary truths. Many other things," he said, "are desirable to be known, but this must be known or our people are undone forever."[3]

Countering this trend of neglecting essentials, I propose to carefully examine the Bible's consideration of death across a broad range of texts, Old Testament and New. We shall find that Scripture offers no death-denial or escapism, just clear-eyed realism. God's Word proclaims hope for eternity in a life secured by Christ's great resurrection victory, which effectually changes all who trust in him as Lord over life and death, heaven and hell. Martin Luther once said, "We should familiarize ourselves with death during our lifetime, inviting death into our presence when it is still at a distance and not on the move."[4] By "on the move" I assume Luther meant when it is gathering speed in my direction. Nancy Guthrie adds, "You must look at death while you are alive and see sin in the light of grace and hell in the light of heaven, permitting nothing to divert you from that view."[5]

## DEATH AS A FEARFUL MYSTERY

On few other subjects is the Bible's principle of *progressive* revelation better seen than this one. Many vital Scripture truths were only half-baked after centuries in the oven of Old Testament revelation. Old Testament saints held a hope of an eternal future beyond death that was vague and often sounded contradictory. Israelites lived for generations staring into a tenuous future, with mystery and darkness as dominant characteristics. Only after many centuries did these dim hopes give way to the full-orbed resurrection confidence of the early Christian church. The keystone event of Christ's bodily resurrection was needed before the Holy Spirit could bestow clear images of life after death that we hold to today. Modern Judaism still depends only upon the Old Testament for its revelation of eternity; thus even the most religious Jews in our century are generally more fixated on quality of life issues in *this* present world than they are on hoping for ultimate heavenly reward or weighing a fear of hell.

Job 10:18–22 presents the Old Testament view of death in highly pessimistic tones, from a man of faith. The famous sufferer Job was in a deep valley of depression when he said, "I loathe my life" (10:1)! He pleaded with God to make some sense of his harsh suffering. Yet his challenge to the Lord was so plaintive, it did not appear that Job expected any positive divine answer. He peevishly prayed, "Why did you bring me out from the womb?" (10:18). His birth seemed pointless. He spoke of going to the place of no return, "to the land of darkness and deep shadow, the land of gloom like thick darkness, like deep shadow without any order, where light is as thick darkness" (vv. 21–22). Job used several different Hebrew words for "darkness," piling one upon the next for a suffocating effect. The land beyond death was to Job in his distress a pit of anxiety, chaos, and despair.

The Old Testament testifies to a master destination beyond death called *Sheol* (or "Hades" in the Greek Old Testament): a place where dead souls consciously survive in varying degrees of blessedness, or perhaps in continued suffering. Old Testament texts often depict Sheol simply as a vast gathering corral for all departed souls. The wicked and the godly go side by side into Sheol, although the two groups may have quite different experiences there. Numbers 16:33 refers to sons of Korah who died under God's wrathful judgment: "They and all that belonged to them went down alive into Sheol, and the earth closed over them, and they perished from the midst of the assembly." That picture would lead you to assume that Sheol is *hell*. But Genesis 25:8 appears to have the same destination in mind when it reports: "Abraham breathed his last and died in a good old age, an old man and full of years, and was gathered to his people." Abraham's future prospect was peaceable. Sheol was for him a blissful family reunion.

Other texts confirm the hope of reunion with generations already departed, as when David predicted in 2 Samuel 12:23 that in Sheol he would see his son conceived by Bathsheba, a son who died shortly after birth. Continuous identity with your earth personality also seems to be guaranteed, since 1 Samuel 28:14 describes the other-worldly resuscitation of Samuel, whose form was immediately recognized by King Saul. Job 3:17–19 paints Sheol as a place of rest and relative freedom: "There the wicked cease from troubling, and there the weary are at rest. There the prisoners are at ease together; they hear not the voice of the taskmaster. The small and great are there, and the slave is free from his master."

Sheol—a word used sixty-six times in the Hebrew Old Testament—might be visualized as a great cavern into which all persons are indiscriminately swept. The expectation was that all living men and women should anticipate going there. Psalm 89:48 asks, "What man can live and never see death? Who can deliver his soul from the power of Sheol?" Sheol's location was understood frequently as in the "depths of the earth." One always descends "downward" to Sheol, which probably gave rise to the persistent yet groundless notion of hell being located literally beneath the surface of planet Earth.

On a few occasions Sheol is painted as a prison with barred gates: "They will be gathered together as prisoners in a pit; they will be shut up in a prison, and after many days they will be punished" (Isa. 24:22). Isaiah at least on one occasion visualized hopeless permanency in that dwelling: "They are dead, they will not live; they are shades, they will not arise; to that end you have visited them with destruction and wiped out all remembrance of them" (Isa. 26:14). These gloomy sentences speak of the *wicked* man, the nonbeliever, who placed no hope in Jehovah. God was not praised or thanked by unbelievers in their lifetimes on earth, and so their religion does not change in the next existence. In a better-case scenario, Old Testament people of *faith* who believed God was their Lord looked toward secure rest and peace in Sheol: "But God will ransom my soul from the power of Sheol, for he will receive me" (Ps. 49:15). Divine intervention was required to realize this blessed result. Only God who first gave man the breath of life can by his Spirit restore a life from the depths of Sheol.

The overall concept of Sheol was mysterious to say the least. At times it appeared to be contradictory. It was a place more fearsome than encouraging. Job was not the only godly person who sometimes lost his afterlife confidence while awaiting such a vague future. Yet other biblical witnesses appeared untroubled by the prospect of Sheol's deep shadows. Notwithstanding all fears expressed, total extinction of living persons never seems to be considered. Biblical teaching about Sheol showed that man continued to exist, and that he existed for a purpose.

## AN OLD TESTAMENT SHAFT OF SUNLIGHT

Having painted a gray view of Old Testament Sheol, we nevertheless find Scripture presenting some distinctly positive affirmations on life after death. Prominently, Psalm 16:11 describes "pleasures forevermore" to be enjoyed at God's right hand. David declared that his "whole being rejoices" and "my flesh also dwells secure" (16:9). Familiar bold assertions of eternal security occur in Psalm 23, where David emphasizes every believer's ability to walk undisturbed "through the valley of the shadow of death" and "dwell in the house of the LORD forever." It is easy to see why the beloved Twenty-third Psalm conveys psychological/spiritual confidence in the face of death. Many persons other than gospel believers seize the literary assertions in Psalm 23 as valued supports in times of crisis. Majesty of the language alone carries some comfort to those who may not know the great Shepherd as Lord.

My favorite Old Testament assurance is Psalm 73:24–26, in which Asaph told the Lord, "You guide me with your counsel, and afterward you will receive me to glory. Whom have I in heaven but you? And there is nothing on earth that I desire besides you. My flesh and my heart may fail, but God is the strength of my heart and my portion forever." Asaph possessed a rock of certainty, which he forcibly called to mind after he'd begun to be overwhelmed by a fleeting illusion that earthly health and wealth were the best prizes to covet.

Consider a remarkably positive text, Job 19:25–27. We have all seen iconic calendar pictures where a photographer captures cumulous clouds looming over a country landscape, but one cloud-opening allows sunlight to stream brilliantly down upon green fields like heaven's own floodlight. This could be a visual depiction of Job 19. We can hardly believe the speaker here is the same Job who poured forth dark pessimism in chapter 10. His faith had experienced a complete reversal. He raised himself up to his full height to shout, "For I know that my Redeemer lives, and at the last he will stand upon the earth. And after my skin has been thus destroyed, yet in my flesh I shall see God, whom I shall see for myself, and my eyes shall behold, and not another. My heart faints within me!" This was a premier moment for biblical hope. It is astonishing that in the ancient book of Job, a hope of resurrection so exactly corresponds to salvation forged by our risen Lord Christ, who will give resurrection bodies to his trusting people when he finally "stands upon the earth" in history's last day. Undergirding Job's stunning prediction was the prophetic Holy Spirit; Job did not speak out of his own devices. As a natural man, he could not have been entirely conscious of every shade of meaning in his words as he uttered them. He prophesied matters too wonderful for his own comprehension.

The key term in Job 19:25 is "my *Redeemer*," from the Hebrew word *go-el*. In ancient times, a go-el was a close kinsman who paid all the costs needed to be a material benefactor for a distressed or deceased relative. It was the duty of the go-el to pay any price and exert whatever influence he possessed to restore what his kinsman had lost: property, a good name, or even descendants to bear his name. Boaz is a classic example, taking this role for Ruth the Moabitess, buying future security for her and Naomi when he married Ruth.

Job knew he was helpless to penetrate death's fearsome shadow by his own strivings. He desperately needed a go-el to execute justice for his pitiful losses and to secure his future as a righteous man. The redeemer he described fits the person of Christ exactly: a living Judge who would stand upon the earth. As a man in a miraculously renewed body of restored *skin,* Job expected to shout for joy at the sight of Christ! Momentarily abandoning his own woes, Job claimed in so many words that Jesus the Redeemer would act for him centuries later on history's timeline. Notice that in our text Job spoke of this event in the present tense, as if the matter was already accomplished in his day. "My Redeemer *lives*!" Some biblical critics warn us not to read too much New Testament resurrection theology about Jesus Christ back into this very early Old Testament prophetic passage. I am compelled to side with many others who ask, what *else* are we supposed to think this could mean?

## LEARNING FROM THE OLD TESTAMENT VIEWPOINT

We might conclude that New Testament Christians cannot benefit from murky, inconclusive ideas of existence after death based upon Sheol and written long before Christ and his resurrection. That would be a mistake. One lesson we can learn is that God can use fear, mental confusion, or even terror in the face of death for constructive ends. Every year I hear testimonies from adult applicants for church membership who tell me how they first consciously trusted in Jesus as Lord when they were young children, because at age five or seven they simply were "scared of going to hell." This should never be the total reason a believer seeks Christ as refuge, yet God can use even this childhood fear as a constructive motivator, bringing us into a deeply felt need of his mercy and grace. Fear of death induces us to run toward a refuge. Pouring cold water on this fear as we pass from childhood to adult maturity is not necessarily a spiritual benefit. Here is one reason why Jesus praised childlikeness, a quality adults need to retain: "Do not fear those who kill the body but cannot kill the soul. Rather fear him who can destroy both soul and body in hell" (Matt. 10:28). Children instinctively know right things to fear. It takes a jaded adult to cease fearing God's final judgment, before which we still should tremble.

I have also heard personal testimonies narrating how some crisis of family grief brought folks to face their own mortality head-on. Crisis suffering may induce us to voice despair like Job's wailing in chapter 10. In

DEATH'S TYRANNY OVERTHROWN

some low pit of sorrow the Lord gains our full attention as on few other occasions. He uses the hour when all material securities are undone for spiritual surgery on us. Like Job, in the course of living we acquire a proud self-sufficiency. Layers of stubborn old lead paint must be scraped or burned off our souls, reducing us to a level where God may apply a new primer coat of grace. Job had to taste bitter spiritual bankruptcy before he could learn a new and radical dependence on his God. Similarly, Paul wrote in 2 Corinthians 1:8–9 about an unidentified crisis in his life: "We were so utterly burdened beyond our strength that we despaired of life itself. Indeed, we felt that we had received the sentence of death. But that was to make us rely not on ourselves but on God who raises the dead." God stripped both Paul and Job of all self-reliance. They exhausted self-based alternatives. Figuratively, at the bottom of a pit of despair, these believers discovered uncompromising trust in God as Redeemer.

A second useful lesson from the Old Testament view of death is the reminder not to build our own imaginative constructs about life after death based on wish-fulfillment or pure speculation. The shape of eternity beyond the grave is no "Gumby" figure we can manipulate to suit our whimsy. A thriving book industry exists today with authors conjuring images of heaven based on totally subjective claims taken from "near-death" experiences. These autobiographies may provide interesting novelties, and many of their authors are probably sincere about their experiences, but they carry no inherent authority for truth or objective reality. We must seek right concepts of eternity based only upon the solid ground of Holy Scripture.

Job's shining trust in a redeemer who would give him a share in historic resurrection came from God's special revelation. Looking to the Bible alone, we will discover that many details we might like to know about the vast future remain mysterious. We must shun the strong temptation to fill in these gaps by our own devices. However, the big picture is no conundrum. God has revealed a sufficiency of knowledge about eternal reality. Deuteronomy 29:29 declares, "The secret things belong to the LORD our God, but the things that are revealed belong to us and to our children forever." Although we are not told everything, God has told us *enough*. So, just as we were taught in kindergarten to color within the lines, the Bible must be our guide in these matters instead of subjective, autobiographical claims.

Third, Christians can take confidence from knowing that in his early epoch of Bible history, Job received a prophetic insight of the same risen Christ we must trust today. We will see in coming chapters that God has ordained a great division to occur among all people at Christ's throne on history's conclusive "day." Your place in that final judgment will be determined before your hour of physical death, based on where you stand with Jesus the Redeemer. Dying in a sure knowledge of him means everything! Some people are so foolish as to think they may be the *only* human beings not in need of this unique Savior to resolve their soul's dilemma.

Jesus Christ—the Redeemer of whom Job prophesied—transacted atonement for the sin of his believing people, shattering death's leg-irons. Because of Christ, we are not consigned to an Old Testament future shrouded in gloomy uncertainty. Every man and woman who ever lived either will answer to a perfectly holy God without Christ as Redeemer-Intercessor, or be assured of his or her mediation by trusting in Jesus before our bodies rest in the cemetery.

Our declaration can be: "*I know* my Redeemer lives!" Christ shall stand upon the earth in the last day. In my own renewed flesh, my resurrected eyes will see him. This prophecy shines splendidly out of deep shadows.

Therefore, just as sin came into the world through one man, and death through sin, and so death spread to all men because all sinned—for sin indeed was in the world before the law was given, but sin is not counted where there is no law. Yet death reigned from Adam to Moses, even over those whose sinning was not like the transgression of Adam, who was a type of the one who was to come.

But the free gift is not like the trespass. For if many died through one man's trespass, much more have the grace of God and the free gift by the grace of that one man Jesus Christ abounded for many. And the free gift is not like the result of that one man's sin. For the judgment following one trespass brought condemnation, but the free gift following many trespasses brought justification. For if, because of one man's trespass, death reigned through that one man, much more will those who receive the abundance of grace and the free gift of righteousness reign in life through the one man Jesus Christ.

ROMANS 5:12-17

*CHAPTER TWO*

# DEATH'S UNIVERSAL REIGN

☼

*AT ONE TIME IT WAS* a common theatrical practice to debut a Broadway musical by opening the show in a city outside of New York, like Boston or Toronto. There the show was on trial while the director, writers, and cast worked out the bugs. Songs and dialogue could be cut or rewritten and new material inserted in the interest of polishing a show into a hit. It seems the idea was that if the show was destined to be a flop, at least this would be discovered in a quieter venue, removed from the glare of Broadway's bright lights and world-class theater critics.

## DEATH CAME BY SIN

When God made the first man in his image and "breathed into his nostrils the breath of life" (Gen. 2:7), it was the pinnacle work of his Spirit (Ps. 104:30). It is a safe assumption that the Lord did not create Adam and Eve as the epitome of all that was "very good" in creation only to turn around and capriciously sentence them to *die*. No artist labors over a masterpiece planning to consign it to a pile of trash at the curb a week later. We may presume from the Creator's intention of making mankind for unique fellowship with him that God gave Adam and Eve biological and spiritual potential to enjoy delightful relations with him without death's tragic interruption being a necessity.

What is death, anyway? Is it a colorless, odorless gas that accumulates in our atmosphere until, after eight decades of daily absorption, its toxins asphyxiate us? Could it be a cancerous anomaly imprinted on everyone's DNA, preprogrammed to wreak cellular havoc, the way a computer virus takes down your hard drive? Automobiles occasionally come under a recall notice when the manufacturer discovers a mechanical flaw that causes an accelerator to stick or the steering wheel to lock in one position. Is death a secret manufacturer's defect in our human fabric from which there is no recall?

## DEATH IS NOT OF NATURAL ORIGIN

In the movie *Forrest Gump* the main character declares, "My mama says dyin' is just a part of livin'." This may be appealing folk philosophy, but according to God's Word, the sentiment is absolutely wrong. Death is no friendly escort coming to take each human being home from the party in the waning hours of life's pilgrimage. It is more like a Viking raid on a Medieval English village, arriving at dawn: they come to rape, pillage, and plunder. As scripted in Genesis, death's debut in history was not simply the way things naturally *are*. And death's entre to human society did not occur on the sly, the way a terrorist might enter the United States via a tunnel under the Mexican border in the dark of night.

Death appeared as God's inevitable judgment upon rebellious human sin. To really understand its debut in human history, think of several movies that have been made from the fictional story of *King Kong*. A foolish theatrical promoter brought the huge ape Kong in chains to present him to audiences on a New York stage. The monster broke loose to rampage the theater and the entire city, finally roaring defiance to airplanes from atop the Empire State Building. Similarly, death is an ogre leaping upon center stage in Eden with a bellow of God-defiance. The appalling intruder invaded the heart of man-to-God and God-to-man fellowship. Strangely, it looked as though death began quietly, as a lie insinuated into Eve's mind. Genesis 3, however, reports that as soon as Adam joined Eve in defiance of a divine command, death broke down the lovely garden's front gate and its effects were irreversible: first claiming the human soul and eventually our bodies as well. That clap of doom is still resounding.

A capsule summary of sin and death from Romans 5:12 and following verifies that every unborn human being was affected. Paul depicted Adam, a real man of history, as the culprit who brought death crashing down on us. Then the apostle introduced Jesus Christ, the God-man also dwelling in history, who by divine grace brought forth a corresponding gift of eternal life, affecting not all persons, but "many." Romans 5:12–17 analyzes death as inescapable reality for everyone because of Adam, while eternal life is a gift imparted to many people, in Christ.

The worldview of materialistic naturalism presumes to have no difficulty explaining death's origin. Forrest Gump's view says death is a razor blade in place of a toy hidden in every box of Cracker Jacks, that each man's apple comes with a resident worm. Naturalism claims every mole, hawk, and human comes with a bar-coded expiration date, because, for reasons unknown, our living cells will not endlessly replicate themselves.

As I watch a lioness tear at the throat of a galloping wildebeest, I realize that every *National Geographic* documentary I have ever seen preaches the evolutionary viewpoint that death is a natural event in a so-called "circle of life." This circle may be small and tightly drawn for a motherless seal pup on the Arctic ice floe with polar bears nearby. It could be drawn larger for a bull elk that endures twenty rutting seasons by asserting lordly dominance over his fellows, trumpeting defiance to all comers. Yet it is only a matter of time until the elk has his turn to be a rotting carcass for wolves—when sun-bleached antlers and a sightless skull bear mute testimony that he lived at all.

Despite the dominance of materialism as a worldview, some scientists occupying the cardboard castle of Darwinism actually admit that a mystery is at work in death. A few are bold enough to say they do not perceive any clear organic cause rendering death *necessary* for an organism like man. Since highly efficient armies of our leukocytes skirmish effectively for decades with harmful microorganisms in our bloodstreams, why could this defense network not continue protecting at least some human bodies for five hundred or a thousand years, instead of a mere eighty or ninety? Scripture testifies that the earliest patriarchs, including Adam and generations beyond, did pile on birthdays until no cake could possibly hold all their candles. Why not us? What unwinding of my inner mainspring makes my death a biological *requirement*? Perhaps the answer is not found in biology, after all.

In the Genesis creation account, man first inhales God's own Spirit-breath, positioning us in clear distinction from plants and animals: "Then God said, 'Let us make man in our image, after our likeness. And let them have dominion over the fish of the sea and over the birds of the heavens and over the livestock and over all the earth . . .'" (Gen. 1:26). Millions reject this cosmology, shrugging it off as a mere literary symbol or mocking it as a myth. However, if you trust Genesis as God's inerrant Word, it is truth to be reckoned with.

Since God made man in his likeness—with unique capability for divine fellowship—and since God cannot die, the Lord planned for us to have limitless lives in which to enjoy him. Does it make sense that death be viewed as a failure by the omnipotent God who spoke the universe into being? If divine image bearers were made to be "like" God, why must we die, as if we were of no more significance than a cornstalk, a mosquito, an amoeba, or a squirrel?

## SIN'S CRASHING DEBUT

Romans 5:12 states, "Just as sin came into the world through one man, and death through sin, and so death spread to all men because all sinned." That reiteration of a Genesis 3 principle argues that human death never was merely a natural phenomenon. (Whether plants or animals ever died before Adam's fall is a sidebar discussion, often debated with more heat than light. Since we know many simple organisms live only hours or days, it seems quite logical that these creatures also routinely died in Eden before Adam sinned. But agreement on this subject need not determine one's biblical orthodoxy.) For humanity at least, in one historic hour death made an ugly entrance. We may wish it were only a badly written, poorly acted theatrical production that would have been judged unworthy of reaching the big stage for long-term performances. However, the Adam and Eve show debuted under Eden's bright lights. And the drama has never closed since that long-ago premier.

Genesis depicts a *spiritual cause* for human death, with secondary biological effects. Even if other living creatures or plants did expire by natural causes from the beginning, neither spiritual nor physical death could have touched Adam apart from our deliberate rebellion against God. Death at its core was an irreversible rupture in the man/God relation, an ultimate divine judgment upon sin. In Genesis 2:17 God warned, "In the day that you eat of it you shall surely die." The man trespassed into forbidden territory. He was deceived to imagine he could gain greater godlike stature by crossing a line that defined God's distinctiveness as Creator vis-à-vis man the creature. Satan the master liar misled first Eve and then Adam to think they might experimentally tiptoe only a step or two into the Holy of Holies where God dwelt, merely to look around. They did not plan to touch or disturb anything in that sacred room. They thought they'd get a good look and not leave any incriminating fingerprints, while satisfying their curiosity as to why this space was rigorously roped off from human intrusion.

"When we decided to be our own saviors and lords," Tim Keller declared, "everything in creation broke. Our bodies broke. The world broke. Life broke."[1] Adam's trespass was catastrophic because it willfully crossed a boundary between dependent human creaturehood and the independent lordship of the Most High God. Helmut Thielicke concluded, "Death in the biblical sense is not the death of man the mammal, but the death of man who wants to be God and who must learn that he is only man."[2]

## HUMAN SOLIDARITY WITH ADAM

From sin's debut onward, Scripture teaches that God has dealt with all mankind in terms of two representative heads: Adam and Christ. Adam was our first federal representative. His action in Eden was *my* action, the same way the United States ambassador to Japan stands in the place of every citizen of the USA when he negotiates a treaty on behalf of our country. Adam was told that if he obeyed God, he would reap wonderful blessings in the bountiful creation (Gen. 1:28–29). Adam would have not only sustenance, but a meaningful career in Eden's management; and he would discover abounding sweetness in the enjoyment of God's world. If he disobeyed, the alternative would be calamity. Thus, death was not created by God. It is better to understand death as the antitype, or dark side, of God's superb blessings promised to the man and woman. We in Adam decided to investigate this antitype, and we reaped a howling whirlwind.

The congregation I serve as pastor built an addition adjoining our previous worship building. Because the new structure conforms to more stringent fire codes than the old, building regulations required installation of an automatic fire door hidden in the ceiling of the main hallway connecting old building to new. Activation of alarm sensors for heat or smoke will cause a heavy steel door to lower as a fireproof barrier. Adam never guessed that God's prohibition against taking fruit of the tree of the knowledge of good and evil would work like this barrier. The security door came crashing down to seal off God's inner sanctum from Adam's violation. Forever afterward, unfettered access to intimacy with God was closed. Some will protest, "But his specific disobedience was only eating forbidden fruit from a tree. How trivial is that!" It might as easily have been a hundred other actions had God chosen to draw the line elsewhere. The particular act itself is not critical. The issue of man's fall was premeditated human disobedience—something we all know about, beginning as toddlers.

A seventeenth-century children's reading book called the *New England Primer* had rhymes for children to memorize corresponding to letters of the alphabet. For *A*, it stated "In Adam's fall, we sinned all." From Adam's fall, sin and death took up residence in every human life. We can hardly call this unfair, because we act or think in terms of real sins each day. But if we think that all we do is to copy Adam's sin, we will follow a species of theology championed by Pelagius, who believed Adam was the first sinner and the worst thing you and I do is to mimic his bad example. But in fact, even the *miming* of Adam is condemnable. Once when I was about six years old I came home to repeat in the presence of my parents a piece of vulgar doggerel I had heard an older boy say on the school bus. I had no clue to what the words meant; I only thought it was clever to repeat something an older boy used to trigger laughter from his pals. I was stunned by my father's swift and negative reaction. I stood condemned that day for being an ignorant, unwitting copyist.

Adam was more than the first sinner with a long line of copyists following him like a Pied Piper. The Augustinian viewpoint understands Scripture to say we all actually sinned in Adam's defiant act. You and I were fatally wounded because we were *present* in the person of Adam, our representative head. Romans 5:19 declares, "By the one man's disobedience the many were *made* sinners." Former TV newsman Walter Cronkite came to fame in the 1950s on a program that dramatized various historic events in short plays. He took the audience into the action of one great event. At the close, Cronkite intoned the show's trademark line: "And *you* are there!" The apostle Paul assumed the entire human race was incipient in the loins of Adam when he sinned. You and I were present in Eden. Acting in Adam, we became God-defiers. The same logic is found in Hebrews 7:9–10, where it is argued that all priests of Levi actually paid a tithe to God via Melchizedek, since they were present in the body of Abraham their ancestor who offered that gift. The fall was not only about imitation, but just as truly about our *participation*.

We wonder: how could it possibly be fair for Adam's one historic disobedience to be counted against us? I must ask you in response, how is it fair for the righteousness of Christ to be counted on your behalf? Those who rail against heaven with fist upraised by shouting the first question must consider the second question as having equal validity! We have no natural claim to the righteousness of Jesus if we disclaim an inheritance from the disobedience of Adam. Earth's great blessing of justification by God's grace through faith in Jesus Christ becomes a believer's possession by the same logic as death falling upon us in Adam's revolt.

## DEATH'S REIGN OF DISASTER

Romans 5:14 bluntly announces next that "death reigned." Sin invaded humanity and brought a foreign dictator to tyrannize us. Suddenly, everywhere we turn, this tyrant's forces menace us with keen-edged weapons of destruction. His intelligence network probes our innermost thoughts. We can keep no secrets; he insinuates his dictatorship into every recess of the mind until it seems he knows us better than we know ourselves. Thus, the ages-long totalitarian reign of death has led to more individual and collective woes than the political tyrannies of Nero, Hitler, Stalin, and Bin Ladin rolled into one dreadful bundle.

Spiritually, death causes ultimate *separation* between the human soul and the human body. What could be worse than to know that the very connective tissue where divinity joined the Spirit of God to our humanity can be torn asunder? To reach for the door of access to God and find it is locked from the other side? This same disruption sealed our bodily demise, although physical death did not occur immediately. "Thus all the days that Adam lived were 930 years, and he died" (Gen. 5:5). Adam kept the funeral director at bay a very long time before his heart and respiration stopped—but he might as well have completed his funeral prearrangements the same day he rebelled in Eden—since from that moment, an open grave beckoned to him.

Consequences of original sin unreeled in a tangle of social and relational effects for humanity. Collectively we may call this "total death." Sin and death did not very long pose as two middle-age "church lady" visitors sitting politely in humanity's front parlor with hands folded in their laps. These two became howling banshees breaking up the furniture, setting fires, and splashing graffiti on every available wall. The death which God's Word announced in Genesis 3 was a phenomenon impacting every dimension of what it means to be human. Genesis 3:17 declares that God's curse upon Adam would be manifested in great difficulty experienced in scratching a living from the earth. Crop failures, drought, famine, unemployment, human slavery, labor unions that prey upon the members' pension funds—every possible form of economic injustice is indirectly traceable to the initial reign of sin and death. Next, interpersonal strife entered the human family: two sons of Adam clashed in such a way that one murdered the other and then denounced all responsibility for his brother. Bitter competition and warfare broke out in succeeding generations. Before Genesis 4 closed, Tubal-Cain was forging weapons of bronze and iron, while Lamech boasted he would have vengeance seventy-seven times against any man who wronged him (Gen. 4:22–24).

Every nuance of human relationships we might expect to enjoy now hears a potential metallic clank of death's chain. Friendships go sour under death's shade. Counseling services could be located on every street corner and would not begin to stem the tide of our epidemic relational distresses. Death plants thorny hedges around joyful relations of parent and child until by teenage years our own progeny may seem to resemble our worst adversaries. Death brought the pain of childbirth so that even the thrill of human procreation is pain-scarred. Complex cellular horrors of cancer followed, along with Lou Gehrig's disease, autism, strokes, and wasting dementia.

Scoffers make light of the Bible's allegedly simplistic picture of Adam causing all this trouble merely by partaking forbidden fruit. But the act of eating a specific food in defiance to a known command of God must be understood as no less a deliberate assault on authority than Confederate artillery opening fire upon Fort Sumter. Mankind's spiritual union with God was bombarded the moment our puny will rebelled against One all-sovereign Will. If this plunge into spiritual anarchy is not solved, the inexorable gravity of our spiritual death drags us all the way into hell. What is hell, if not an existence where separation from God is unchangeable by any power within us?

Annie Dillard pictured mankind's extreme post-fall vulnerability, as if we were creatures walking upon a wide open prairie totally exposed on all sides to depredations of a skilled hunter who turns out to be God. She wrote, "In the open, anything might happen. . . . There is no reply in clear terrain to an archer in cover. Any copperhead anywhere is an archer in cover; how much more so is God! Invisibility is the all-time great 'cover.'

. . . And we the people are so vulnerable. Our bodies are shot with mortality. Our legs are fear and our arms are time. These chill humors seep through our capillaries, weighting each cell with an icy dab of non-being, and that dab grows and swells and sucks the cell dry."[3]

## A BELIEVER'S SOLIDARITY WITH CHRIST

This has been a very gloomy message so far, though it was essential to draw the whole dismal picture, in order to first understand the spiritual origin of death's catastrophe. If the grace of God in Christ had not stepped in with a decisive alternative, then spiritual and physical death would have been the final word spoken about each man and woman ever born. Now we can speak about the rest of Romans 5—for thank God—his grace did intervene.

The Puritan Thomas Goodwin wrote, "In God's sight, there really are only two men in all of human history: Adam and Jesus Christ. These two have all other men hanging from their girdle strings."[4] John Stott concurred: "Here then are two communities, one characterized by sin and guilt, the other by grace and faith . . . the former is in Adam and the latter in Christ."[5] Christ is a federal head on behalf of *some* human beings just as Adam originally was for *all*. Paul argued in Romans 5 that salvation authored by God's grace enters our history as Christ radically changes a believer's entire position with God. Notice the "how much more" logic occurring twice in verses 15 and 17. Paul said if death could force the whole mass of human beings into a grim parade away from God, how much more can God's power cause persons who trust in Jesus as Lord to make a one hundred eighty degree turn. Christ redirects us into a whole new procession, leading us all the way back home to God.

Now instead of death reigning over every human being, Romans 5:17 says certain persons can "reign in life" in Christ. A Christian's physical body still must die; that portion of sin's penalty cannot be avoided. However, that is not the catastrophic part. The total death condition is cancelled when we trust in the blood of Christ shed for us. Because he died on our behalf, my soul need not expire for crimes Jesus already died for. That would be redundant. There is no double jeopardy before a perfectly just God. We can be restored to the Father's embrace of fellowship and sonship while we still breathe on earth. At our physical demise, our souls may part from our bodies, but they shall not be separated from our heavenly Father.

## A FREE GIFT, NOT LIKE THE TRESPASS

Note how Romans 5:15 takes pains to say the "free gift" Christ offers is "not like" the trespass of Adam. Definite contrast distinguishes them. Adam's sin at first included everybody without exception. But Romans 5:15 says Christ's gift of life "abounded for *many*." "Many" is a group potentially quite large, yet it includes less than everyone present. I could state, "Twelve hundred people attended our two worship services this morning, and many were women." That cites a distinguishing characteristic for some not shared by all. Paul's designation of redeemed persons as "many" parallels Bible nomenclature of "the elect" used elsewhere.

Another way two groups of humanity in Adam and in Christ are not alike, is that one group receives a dreadful *wage* they earn, while the others get a splendid *gift* which cannot be earned. Romans 6:23 summarizes, "The wages of sin is death, but the free gift of God is eternal life in Christ Jesus our Lord." There is no great mystery about who is included in the group of "many" people. They are all "in Christ." They are "those who receive the abundance of grace and the free gift of righteousness" (Rom. 5:17).

## PARTING OF THE WAYS

The sober reality, therefore, is that right now, each of us is in one of two conditions. Either we remain where we began—helplessly caught up in Adam's huge procession because we were born following him like zombies. Or by God's grace we have joined many who have already been consciously transferred by faith "into Christ"—new heirs of eternal life. Martyn Lloyd-Jones said, "There are only two groups of people in the world today—those who are of the world and those who belong to Christ. In the last analysis there is no other division or distinction that has the slightest importance or relevance."[6]

Do not fall for the lie that says death is a natural conclusion of life. It is not what our Creator intended, though he remains sovereign over it. Death is a profound spiritual judgment of God against sin that we committed once in Adam, and we continue in this sin every day. So you may choose to spend all your life's energy among a death-denying culture that belongs to Adam. If so, you will emphasize youthfulness and pursue vigorous bodily health as the key to life and will refuse to think about death, hoping that your ignorance can prevent it from happening. Or, by your faith in a risen Lord, you may join the *death-defying* family of Christ.

Because the Son of God went to a cross as your substitute and stood under his Father's judgment, death's sting of wrath is removed for you and many others who by God's electing grace are his possessions forever. Romans 8:23 depicts our present situation: "We ourselves, who have the firstfruits of the Spirit, groan inwardly as we wait eagerly for adoption as sons, the redemption of our bodies." True enough—we must pass through physical death. However, the fatal soul-sting of death is gone for us because Jesus took it all in himself! A Rottweiler death-bite strikes our bodies, but we passionately long for what is just on the other side of that brief moment of fear.

No wonder legend has it that some Christian martyrs told their captors just before the sword fell on their necks: "You can kill us, but you cannot *hurt* us!"

Now in putting everything in subjection to him, he left nothing outside his control. At present, we do not yet see everything in subjection to him. But we see him who for a little while was made lower than the angels, namely Jesus, crowned with glory and honor because of the suffering of death, so that by the grace of God he might taste death for everyone.

HEBREWS 2:8-9

Since therefore the children share in flesh and blood, he himself likewise partook of the same things, that through death he might destroy the one who has the power of death, that is, the devil, and deliver all those who through fear of death were subject to lifelong slavery. For surely it is not angels that he helps, but he helps the offspring of Abraham. Therefore he had to be made like his brothers in every respect, so that he might become a merciful and faithful high priest in the service of God, to make propitiation for the sins of the people. For because he himself has suffered when tempted, he is able to help those who are being tempted.

HEBREWS 2:14-18

*CHAPTER THREE*

# DEATH'S POWER DESTROYED

☀

*THERE IS A PECULIAR SECRET* you would have to learn if you sought to know me well. It sounds absurd, but I'll just say it and you can think whatever you want—I once *died*. It was 1957, and I was an eight-year old boy. I solemnly assure you this is true. My death occurred more than a half century ago, and that event has made all the difference in how I live my present life. It also began my Christian outlook upon a vast heavenly existence I have yet to experience.

No, I am not about to reveal a so-called near-death experience following a car accident in which I floated above my body and saw dazzling angels beckoning. That kind of thing is the complete antithesis of what this book is about. If I had experienced that, I would claim no authority for it. Instead, I claim the identical experience Paul spoke about in Galatians 2:20: "I have been crucified with Christ. It is no longer I who live, but Christ who lives in me. And the life I now live in the flesh I live by faith in the Son of God, who loved me and gave himself for me." The day I put my entire trust in Jesus as Lord, the gospel of grace says my heavenly Father saw me as though I had actually died with Christ on his cross, and all my sin was covered in the perfection of Jesus, my substitute. So in June 1957, just after my eighth birthday in earth years, I died and was reborn into a new standing with my ever-living Savior, who makes all the difference for me, in time and eternity.

## AFTER A FIRST DEATH, NO SECOND

The really fearsome aspect of death is the spiritual judgment which, if one is left unchanged, will render any person a castaway from God's presence. The Bible calls this the "second death"; it is also called spiritual "perishing" of the soul that awaits unbelievers after their body has died. The terminology comes from Revelation 20:6: "Blessed and holy is the one who shares in the first resurrection! Over such the second death has no power." The first spiritual death and your first resurrection are part and parcel of the new birth of trusting Jesus as Lord, also called regeneration. Once this new life takes root, the second death is cancelled. After that, your physical death amounts to a mere change in forwarding address. Your soul goes right on living in union with Christ, and your body anticipates ultimate resurrection. "Therefore, if anyone is in Christ, he is a new creation" (2 Cor. 5:17).

You cannot trust appearances registered by your eyes as you study our present material society. A mere visual evaluation tells you death is firmly in charge over all earth's people. In our last chapter, we observed that Romans 5:14 told us that "death reigned." Every appearance of present human society tells you that death truly is the reigning power. News reports describe car wrecks, plane crashes, warfare, murder, acts of terrorism, and senseless school shootings. One industry that seems entirely recession-proof during a bad economy, with worldwide demand for its services undiminished, is the funeral business. Based only on visible appearances, we might ask, if the cross of Jesus was a conquest of sin and death, why are we still subjected to satanic powers that were defeated and put under Jesus's feet?

The writer of Hebrews was concerned about this problem in Hebrews 2:8. He wrote, "Now in putting everything in subjection to him, he left nothing outside his control. At present, we do not yet see everything in subjection to him." Is this doubletalk? Does Christ actually *reign* right now over Satan's rival power, or not? It appears that death is on the throne. Fear of death brazenly dominates millions, and the unbeliever has good reason to continue being terrified of a spiritual second death that will seize him beyond this lifetime.

There is an unseen dimension we will view only when it is emblazoned on the skies at Christ's great return. The Christian who is under God's mercy in Christ learns once and for all that there is no reason to fear death, because its worst threat already fell upon Jesus. The cross and resurrection smashed the tyranny of death for believers. Christ sacrificed himself for our sin and was raised in Easter triumph. Therefore, for every Christian the awful devastation of spiritual death has itself already died.

## JESUS, BORN TO ENCOUNTER DEATH

Death's shadow lay deep upon mankind before Jesus came. People even wondered if God comprehended their great dread of the grave. And if he knew, did he *care*? The Greeks invented an array of mythical gods and goddesses. A common characteristic of these fictional deities was an elitist attitude of *apatheia*. As the word sounds, these imaginary divine beings were apathetic to human suffering—living in a realm set apart from us and not even pretending to care about mortal problems. The Greeks saw it as a virtue that their gods never condescended to be soiled by our woes. These superior beings would not consider letting the soles of their feet touch sordid human affairs. "Incarnation" would have been unthinkable to Greek gods and goddesses. Not so for the one true God of the Bible, who both cares about man's death-dilemma and acted in amazing power to reverse the consequences. The second person of the Godhead condescended to be born as a human baby, having a direct encounter with human death as his foremost goal in his incarnation.

Early Christian scholars sought Scripture's balanced understanding of the incarnational wonder of Christ as perfect union of God and man. Some explained the mystery by a heresy we call Docetism—a notion that Christ was like a phantom, a pure Spirit who only *appeared* man-like. This made the incarnation into divine play-acting. Jesus looked "as if" he were hungry, bleeding, or groaning in pain, but we knew he could not really be, since such low human characteristics would demean God. The docetic idea is unbiblical; Greek philosophy was in the driver's seat, not Scripture. Nowhere do we read of Jesus the apparition. Instead, the purpose of God becoming man in Christ was to confront in flesh and blood the most horrible moment of the human condition: a gory and painful death. Worse still, his death would be by official execution, promoted by the leadership of Israel, God's own people.

Jesus the eternal Son took upon himself a body capable of dying. Being fully God and man, he moved unswervingly toward the cross as the pivotal event in human history. All four gospels make it clear that Jesus was attuned to a private destiny only he understood at the time. Disciples called him to go off in this direction today or to take up their agenda tomorrow, but Jesus obeyed his inner compass, fixed upon a distant horizon where a cross made of Roman lumber was as good as built on the hill of Golgotha from before time began. Jesus lived out what the prophet wrote: "Therefore I have set my face like a flint, and I know that I shall not be put to shame" (Isa. 50:7). In John 10:18 Jesus declared: "No one takes [my life] from me, but I lay it down of my own accord. I have authority to lay it down, and I have authority to take it up again." Jesus always knew he was born to die. Nothing could deter him from fulfilling a historic appointment.

Christians learn that the eternal condemnation of death we deserve, we do not receive, and the salvation we receive in Christ, we do not deserve. Hebrews 2:9 declares: "By the grace of God [Christ] might taste death for everyone." The verb reporting Jesus "might taste death" was not intended to minimize his full immersion in it. Tasting sometimes indicates only an experimental sampling of food on the end of your tongue without ingesting its bitter poison. However, in this Hebrews 2:9 usage, it means a full-fledged experience. Jesus plunged into death; he was slow-roasted in the curse of death, although he had no sin. To encounter death head-on was the prime reason God's Son was born in flesh.

## CHRIST THE VICTOR IN A DEATH DUEL

The doctrine of Jesus's atonement has many sides to it, like a huge diamond capable of being viewed by its various individual facets. Often we speak of the atonement of the cross in terms of "satisfaction" for various divine requirements of justice. Or we may use the Bible's language about "ransom" from the slavery of sin. We might discuss Christ's "redemption" that buys back what was lost. And we should explore biblical pictures of Jesus as the substitutionary, once-for-all "sacrifice" who appeased the Father's wrath, in our place. Each image correctly shows an aspect of our justification with God. All are accurate, scriptural concepts describing the achievement of the cross, and these meanings overlap harmoniously.

But one facet of the atonement not so often discussed is the military conquest Jesus achieved. Some theologians name this snapshot of the atonement, Christ the Victor. The image is as true a portrayal of the cross as the others, but with special emphasis on how the death of Christ conclusively crushed the head of Satan, fulfilling Genesis 3:15. He met Satan as if two great champions squared off in combat.

Granted, very little seen in the historic drama at Calvary appeared as if Jesus were a warrior engaged in combat; and far less gave any evidence that he won! He was spread-eagled on a cross, hands and feet nailed in a fixed position. He was humanly powerless through hours of a cruel execution. Death was allowed to seize God-in-flesh, but not to hold him permanently. Acts 2:24 declares: "It was not possible for him to be held by [death]." Jesus, who to all appearances seemed a victim, really was conqueror, as his resurrection proved. The combat that mattered was spiritual, and it took place entirely out of our sight, in heavenly realms and hell's deepest dungeons. His victory in that realm was announced on the cross by the words "It is finished" (John 19:30). The conquest finally became visible to chosen resurrection witnesses. One fine Easter hymn trumpets an end-of-battle theme: "The strife is o'er, the battle won. The victory of life is won. The song of triumph has begun—Hallelujah!"

The Bible claims that the death of Jesus was God's masterstroke of military strategy. Jesus was a Trojan horse, rolled into Satan's walled stronghold, who then overthrew the eternal condemnation of death from within the fortress, on behalf of all who trust in him. It seemed a most unlikely battle plan, but by the wisdom of God it was a brilliant tactic.

Hebrews 2:10 calls Jesus the "founder" of our salvation. That Greek noun can also mean "champion." Perhaps this illustration is not worthy of sublime subject matter, but I think about a Sylvester Stallone *Rambo* movie—the one in which he is dropped into the jungle of Vietnam, armed only with a knife and his bow and arrows, on an errand to singlehandedly destroy a Vietcong prisoner of war camp. Rambo freed several emaciated, hopeless American POWs from bamboo cages, men who thought they had been forgotten by their country. Winning a single-handed victory against great opposition, Rambo led these victims to freedom.

Jesus announced in Luke 11:21–22: "When a strong man, fully armed, guards his own palace, his goods are safe; but when one stronger than he attacks him and overcomes him, he takes away his armor in which he trusted and divides his spoil." That was a decisive prediction of the cross. Satan was the powerful king in a fortified palace, and he guarded priceless stolen treasure—the souls of men and women bound to languish in his dungeons. Unlike Rambo, Jesus Christ did not enter death's main stronghold in superhero style, spraying bullets or hand grenades in all directions. He did it by *dying*—since that was the only way a man could penetrate that castle. He emerged on the other side alive and carried off the barred gates of death like a second Samson stealing the city gates of Gaza in the night (Judg.16:3).

At the cross, an apparent victim won a victory in which all believers share. Colossians 2:15 declares that Christ "disarmed the rulers and authorities and put them to open shame, by triumphing over them." Thus we read in Hebrews 2:14 that Christ in his death also "destroy[ed] the one who has the power of death, that is, the devil." Jesus was the stronger man who, after entering the death domain, forever after prevents his own people from being held there. Now as believers enter death, we pass immediately *through* what once was an impassable labyrinth. For people belonging to Christ Jesus, death is never more a locked dungeon—just a gray tunnel with broken gates all the way along.

## CLAMOROUS FEAR QUIETED

Knowing all this—that Christ has changed our position before God and removed the judgment called second death forever—still God's adopted child in Christ may foolishly and unnecessarily cling to qualms and fears about physical death. We all can identify with filmmaker Woody Allen, who famously quipped, "It's not that I'm afraid to die. I just don't want to be there when it happens."

A scorpion bites once and injects all its poison into a victim. What Scripture calls the "sting" of death is spiritual condemnation. The second-death sting went into Jesus Christ at the cross. Therefore, believer: do you accept his victory over second death as your own? If you do, our text in Hebrews stresses the unique sympathizing heart of our Savior. Since he was one of us as a man and endured death himself, who better can communicate transforming encouragement to us, comforting our remaining fears of death? Hebrews 2:15 declares that he died to "deliver all those who through fear of death were subject to lifelong slavery."

The *process* of death remains intimidating, even if its ultimate penalty is cancelled. Who but Christ will best hear our cries and fears about death? Jesus as our merciful and faithful High Priest is "able to help us" like no other. In the novel *To Kill a Mockingbird*, the character Atticus Finch says, "You never really understand a person until you consider things from his point of view, until you climb into his skin and walk around in it."[1] Jesus knows our death-fear because he wore our skin!

I have stood at hospice beds and literally heard what some call the "death rattle" of someone's last few strangled breaths. No one should call this experience a trifle. It is not. A week before I wrote these words, the mid-sixties-aged father of a church member simply did not wake up one morning. As a fervent believer in Christ, he was in the Savior's embrace before his wife realized she should make a futile call for an ambulance. We all would wish for that so-called "easy" death, but that quiet passage is no entitlement to Christians or anyone else.

Another death occurred only days after, and it was calamitous in its circumstances. At a construction site across the road from our church facility, a twenty-seven-year-old worker was caught in the collapse of a ten-foot-deep trench. Only the geographical proximity of this accident brought him to my attention—he died two hundred yards from the office where I studied for a sermon. By the time I knew of his death, television news cameras had arrived. Without knowing the victim personally, the rare manner of his death made it hard for me not to imagine his last moments of panic. His brain surely told his arms to swim out from under tons of earth descending upon him, but those arms were securely pinned—much like the arms of Jesus. Who can bear to dwell on this young man's last conscious seconds as he gagged to death on a face full of dirt before his shouting comrades could dig him out. This unfortunate fellow human being was someone's son, someone's friend. I pray he might have been a child of God, trusting in the death and resurrection of the Lord Jesus. If so, once his last moments of mortal fear ended, death had done its worst to him. I only wish I knew whether this were so.

## A JAIL WITH A BROKEN LOCK

I was not kidding when I began this chapter by claiming that I died along with Christ when I trusted in him as a boy fifty years ago. Paul said in 2 Timothy 2:11, "If we have died with him, we will also live with him." Charles Spurgeon elaborated: "Those who die daily will die easily. Those who make themselves familiar with the tomb will find it transfigured into a bed. . . . Let us live as dying men among dying men, and then we shall truly live."[2]

Nothing in the universe can separate a Christian believer from the power of God exerted for us in Christ (Rom. 8:38–39). Apart from knowing this death-defeating Savior, people are still locked up and trembling before eternal judgment, which they have good reasons to fear. But Christian, why would you linger around weeping and fretful in a jail cell sealed only by a broken lock?

John Chrysostom was an early Christian pastor who lived from AD 350–400. At one point in his ministry he observed elaborate moaning and crying going on at Christian funerals. As a pastor he considered this as a deep contradiction of Christian hope. So Chrysostom mounted his pulpit to ask his congregation, "Why all this crying and groaning? What could be more unseemly for loved ones of a man who is crucified to this world and risen with Christ, than to wail in the presence of death?" He further exhorted, "Those who are worthy of being lamented are those still living in their fear; who tremble before death with no sure faith in resurrection." Then Chrysostom the preacher concluded with words that frame my prayer for you. He told his Christian flock, "May you die, *unwailed*!"[3]

For I delivered to you as of first importance what I also received: that Christ died for our sins in accordance with the Scriptures, that he was buried, that he was raised on the third day in accordance with the Scriptures, and that he appeared to Cephas, then to the twelve. Then he appeared to more than five hundred brothers at one time, most of whom are still alive, though some have fallen asleep. Then he appeared to James, then to all the apostles. Last of all, as to one untimely born, he appeared to me also.

I CORINTHIANS 15:3-8

For if the dead are not raised, not even Christ has been raised. And if Christ has not been raised, your faith is futile and you are still in your sins. Then those also who have fallen asleep in Christ have perished. If in Christ we have hope in this life only, we are of all people most to be pitied. But in fact Christ has been raised from the dead, the first-fruits of those who have fallen asleep. For as by a man came death, by a man has come also the resurrection of the dead. For as in Adam all die, so also in Christ shall all be made alive. But each in his own order: Christ the firstfruits, then at his coming those who belong to Christ. Then comes the end, when he delivers the kingdom to God the Father after destroying every rule and every authority and power. For he must reign until he has put all his enemies under his feet. The last enemy to be destroyed is death.

I CORINTHIANS 15:16-26

CHAPTER FOUR

# BECAUSE HE LIVES

☼

NOVELS WRITTEN BY CHRISTIANS FOR which Christianity is integral to the plot are inclined to be wooden at best and dull at worst. An exception is Paul L. Maier's *A Skeleton in God's Closet*.[1] Well versed in archeology, this New Testament professor plotted a diabolical hoax in which archeologists uncover the first-century burial tomb of Joseph of Arimathea in his hometown of Ramah in Galilee. Concealed beneath the floor of that tomb is something scientists stumble upon: artifacts and a first-century scroll in a sealed jar which testifies that an adjacent stone ossuary box contains physical remains of Jesus of Nazareth. The long-buried document claims that his body was stealthily moved to this location by Joseph of Arimathea on the evening of Good Friday before the garden tomb in Jerusalem was sealed off by Pilate's soldiers. This of course means the tomb found empty on Easter morning actually never held a body except for a brief time, until several women who accompanied the dead Jesus to that place had departed. Then Joseph the aristocrat and disciple had the lifeless body of Jesus moved to his other personal tomb, in Ramah, where allegedly it rested for twenty centuries.

Up to the end of the novel it really does appear that the bones of Jesus had been found. Every test at the highest level verified the authenticity of artifacts no one had been looking for and almost everyone wished had remained unknown. The reader is made to reckon with the implications of this discovery. No matter how much society still desires to believe in a Savior who rose from his grave, it no longer seemed possible. I should not tell more in case you would decide to read the book. I will only say that by the end of the tale, Jesus lives, after all.

When we affirm the Apostles' Creed, we say, "I believe . . . in the resurrection of the body and the life everlasting." Those two facts are inseparable; you cannot have the second without the first. In chapter 3, we saw

Scripture's claim in Hebrews 2 that Jesus was a champion defeating death in a bold raid upon its stronghold. He was the one-man Navy SEAL team landing at Osama Bin Laden's secret lair in a surprise raid of lightning efficiency, taking the Evil One out of commission. Concentrating on the victory of the cross in the previous chapter, I gave little attention to the second epic cornerstone of Jesus's victory: his resurrection. This is now our prime concern.

First Corinthians 15 is Paul's full elaboration of the consequences of Christ's resurrection for all who trust in him. Without the bodily resurrection, the death of Jesus on Calvary would be of no effect. If he did not rise in power on Easter morning, all our hope in him is no more substantial than a wisp of smoke, for death still holds him.

## ALL OUR EGGS IN ONE BASKET

Our hope of eternity stands or falls with the resurrection accomplished for the body of Jesus and applied to us. With dogged persistence, millions of people today believe they will claim eternity based on God's positive moral evaluation of their behavior. They suppose that "good" deeds earn heavenly bonus credits, and the goal is to pile up more good behavior than evil until the scales tip favorably for you. Such notions persist although the biblical gospel absolutely denies them. In biblical Christianity, attaining eternal life is based on nothing a human being does. Heaven's front gate never swings under the influence of human merit or moral entitlement. Hope of eternal life is 100 percent a miracle of God's grace.

Romans 1:4 states that Jesus Christ was "declared to be the Son of God in power according to the Spirit of holiness by his resurrection from the dead." He was God's Son before the resurrection, but without this grand miracle we would have no certification of that fact. Paul in 1 Corinthians 15:3–8 stressed that evidence and testimony of Jesus's resurrection was passed to him from earlier apostles. These eyewitness facts will stand up in a court of law where proof beyond a reasonable doubt is the standard for a verdict. You surely have heard Easter Sunday sermons relating this evidence that demonstrated why the empty tomb simply cannot be explained away. Christian apologist Josh McDowell wrote years ago to say that this clear evidence "demands a verdict."[2] Author Frank Morison's classic *Who Moved the Stone?* was God's instrument in my Christian life to build a sound foundation of reason beneath what I already believed.[3]

Resurrection facts like these build a castle of evidence: (1) The grave clothes were arranged just as he dropped them; (2) The Roman guard detail was overwhelmed in its security task by frightening manifestations; (3) Enemies who had everything to gain by simply producing a dead body could not do so, and they resorted to a flimsy cover-up story; (4) Hundreds saw the form of a man recognizable as Jesus; (5) He ate food and appeared to be entirely in character with his former persona; (6) Radically transformed lives of eleven depressed, confused disciples bolster a tight case, leading to a conclusion that explaining the resurrection by means other than its straightforward gospel narration is more problematic than accepting the Bible's verdict that "he is not here, but has risen" (Luke 24:6). To have faith in the risen Jesus is no blind leap in the dark. This supernatural event is grounded upon reliable historic proofs and logic. We can be surer that this event occurred as reported than we are able to know many relatively recent historic events. (Shall we discuss what really happened in the Kennedy assassination, anyone? Maybe we can talk about the shooter behind the fence on the grassy knoll . . .)

It cannot be maintained by an honest mind that the church invented the resurrection. Quite the contrary, the resurrection was a catalyst for an explosion of faith in the first-century church. If God could raise Jesus from the dead, he must have all power over death. Peter's first sermon in Acts 2:36 declared that by the resurrection "God has made him both Lord and Christ, this Jesus whom you crucified." So apostles went into the world as resurrection witnesses.

The glorified Lord appeared in a vision before John to say, "Fear not, I am the first and the last, and the living one. I died and behold I am alive forevermore, and I have the keys of Death and Hades" (Rev. 1:17–18). By fulfilling his resurrection and by his subsequent miraculous ascension to the Father's right hand, Jesus was awarded the seat of sovereign authority over all affairs in heaven and earth. Paul concluded that either Jesus is raised or everything we believe is a lie and a delusion. Take away the reanimation of Jesus, and death proves to be stronger than God; Christian faith is then a colossal futility. All the eggs of our hope for eternal life really do rest in a single basket, called Easter.

## THE FIRST-FRUIT PRINCIPLE

Now we look to 1 Corinthians 15:20–23 for the "so what?" aspect of resurrection logic. The miracle of Jesus raised by God's power was not once and done; it was more like the first crashing chord opening of a grand Beethoven symphony. The bodily resurrection Jesus experienced is capable of being reproduced in any number of God's people from first-century Easter forward; it is the sole miracle of past history in which you and I can participate today. The Christian's fate is not just a shadowy survival of death, but a robust expectation of the Apostles' Creed's call for "the resurrection of the body and the life everlasting."

First Corinthians 15:20 asserts that "Christ has been raised from the dead, the firstfruits of those who have fallen asleep." Saying someone has fallen asleep is a biblical euphemism indicating Christians whose bodies died, who were known to be united to Christ while alive and thus still are so. Their "sleep" is not literal, and their passing is not permanent. To say they "sleep" now is a figure of speech touching upon a body still in the grave while the conscious soul is in God's presence, waiting for what an old spiritual song calls a "great waking up morning."

The term "first fruit" in 1 Corinthians 15:20 originated with Israel's Feast of Weeks, a harvest festival in which a priest waved a shock of wheat in the air to symbolize hopes for an expected harvest. The resurrection of Jesus is a prototype—the initial mold out of which millions more bodily resurrections could be cast. A flood of other resurrections will pour through that Easter breach God opened in death's barrier. Recalling a principle we emphasized earlier, the resurrection of Christ is seen as a *federal* act: Jesus was the representative of many others. Jesus promised disciples in John 14:19, "Because I live, you also will live." God decrees that the resurrection of Jesus is endlessly transferrable.

First Corinthians 15:22 says every human being dies because of Adam; it never concludes that every human being lives because of Christ. Instead, it says that all persons who are "in Christ" obtain his life. Notice the historic order of resurrection in verse 23: "Each in his own order: Christ the firstfruits, then at his coming those who belong to Christ." Pause over the phrase "*those* who belong to Christ." Who is included? Can we *know* if we are among these people? A good place to seek an answer is John 6:39, where we read a prediction by Jesus: "And this is the will of him who sent me, that I should lose nothing of all that he has given to me, but raise it up on the last day." By his sovereign will, God mysteriously foreordained who is included in the great company of those to be raised in Christ—a vast number of elect souls known to the Father and the Son. They were said to be given as a total company from the Father into the care of Christ the Son (John 17:6). And we are told that the Son will not fail to resurrect a single one of this company entrusted to his caretakership. John 6:40 gives a further identity mark to these people: "For this is the will of my Father, that everyone who looks on the Son and believes in him should have eternal life, and I will raise him up on the last day." John 6:39 left a mystery element in God's election concerning *who* exactly shall be resurrected, but verse 40 provides a highly practical way to identify this group—their present-world identity badge is depositing all their hope in Christ the Son.

We may have a good approximate knowledge of who belongs to this "invisible" church of the elect, although only God knows the case perfectly. The elect are all persons who claim this risen Savior with a sincere profession of faith. God's mysterious grace in election causes Spirit-sponsored awakening of a dead sinner's brain, heart, and tongue to verbalize faith in Jesus. Resurrection faith inevitably will become audible as each one "confess[es] with his mouth Jesus is Lord and believe[s] in [his] heart that God raised him from the dead" (Rom. 10:9). You and I exercise what seems in our estimation to be our entirely free human choice, to speak up and to lay hold of God's miracle gift; but Scripture peers backstage to discover that our testimony of faith in Jesus had an eternal prelude. The Spirit of God was involved in the process of drawing me toward belonging to the one risen Lord.

## WE MAY LIVE A NEW LIFE

Furthermore, this resurrection power of God is not merely scheduled for a final historic rising of our bodies in the last day when Christ returns. That final consummation of personal resurrection can seem far off and unreal. Every Christian already *has* a resurrected life. Romans 6:4 declares, "Just as Christ was raised from the dead by the glory of the Father, we too might *walk* in newness of life." The Holy Spirit of the triune God resides in a believer now. Romans 8:11 is the capstone text for this matter: "If the Spirit of him who raised Jesus from the dead dwells in you, he who raised Christ Jesus from the dead will also give life to your mortal bodies through his Spirit who dwells in you." The same Spirit who awakens us to believe in Christ remains in residence as God's down payment and seal of what will one day be fabulously complete (Eph. 1:13–14). The first stirring of what is yet to be—our graduation into new bodies with Christ—is underway now, evidenced in the gradual transformation of our minds and step-by-step renovation of character, words, and action. All this happens slowly but surely, in our still-sinful but redeemed bodies.

Therefore "the Christian's calling is a heavenly calling; it comes from heaven and reaches out towards heaven." Paul Helm continues, "All aspects of our lives, not only those that are customarily referred to as 'spiritual,' but the social and cultural as well, have significance because they are woven in as part of the divine calling which will end for the believer in heaven. So heaven is not an excuse for taking it easy, it is a reason for renewed effort. . . . Our lives on earth, despite the seeming randomness of what befalls us, the nasty surprises and setbacks, is purposive. And it is not necessary to forsake the earth to find purpose."[4]

## NO LONGER INCREDIBLE

In Acts 26:8 Paul challenges the skeptical establishment of his day: "Why is it thought incredible by any of you that God raises the dead?" God's resurrection miracle that opened the tomb to raise the body of Jesus will impact weak clay-people. Our God specializes in resurrecting what is dead and powerless. Peter wrote in 1 Peter 1:3–5 to Christian disciples: "According to his great mercy, [God] has caused us to be born again to a living hope through the resurrection of Jesus Christ from the dead, to an inheritance that is imperishable, undefiled and unfading, kept in heaven for you who by God's power are being guarded through faith for a salvation ready to be revealed in the last time."

Have you consciously stepped out of imprisonment to death in Adam into new life in the living Lord Jesus? If you're not certain, you may call on Christ today and say, "Lord Jesus, I am dead and powerless. Give me your miraculous new life. Then continue to be at work in me by your Spirit, today and forever." He will answer that prayer.

Once you do know Christ in this bond of living hope, you can endorse these words from Blaise Pascal, scientist and disciple of Jesus: "Without Jesus Christ, death is dreadful, it is repugnant, it is a terror of whatever is natural. In Jesus Christ it is altogether different. It is amiable, holy and the joy of the believer. Everything, even death itself, is rendered sweet in Jesus. It was for this he suffered. He died to sanctify death and suffering to us."[5]

*PART TWO*

# THE DESTINY OF UNBELIEF

For God did not send his Son into the world to condemn the world, but in order that the world might be saved through him. Whoever believes in him is not condemned, but whoever does not believe is condemned already, because he has not believed in the name of the only Son of God.

JOHN 3:17-18

# CHAPTER FIVE

# THE DEFAULT DESTINATION

☼

*AT THE OPENING OF FYODOR* Dostoyevsky's classic novel *Crime and Punishment,* Raskolnikov, a penniless Russian ex-law student, murders an elderly pawnbroker to steal her money. Raskolnikov tells himself this old woman was not important, so no one will miss her or search for her killer; but then he is forced to murder the woman's sister to avoid discovery. He still believes he will face no ultimate consequences. However, Dostoevsky gradually shows the relentless outworking of judgment upon a supposedly hidden act. As you guess from the title, punishment inevitably pursues this criminal. The young man stood condemned from the moment of his hidden crime.

We now continue exploring what comes after death by examining the Bible's treatment of the subject of divine judgment in hell—a topic unpleasant to anyone and abhorrent to millions. Most of human society marginalizes hell, and even gospel believers would gladly leave it alone. We prefer to act as if it did not exist—or possibly that it is only a concern for openly evil persons. Surely hell need not concern *me.* However, hell has long been a prime doctrine of Bible-based Christianity. Evangelicals have classically upheld a high view of Scripture inspiration and authority, with hell vividly taught as an outworking of the character of a just and holy God. If you take the Bible seriously, you must reckon with many things God has revealed about hell as a just destiny for unbelief.

## EVANGELICALS USED TO PREACH HELL

Classic Christian faith endorses justification by God's grace received through faith alone. Persons are born again for salvation, removing them from their prior dwelling under eternal condemnation. To be meaningful, this divine redemption requires rescue *from* a catastrophic loss, the reversal of a devastating misfortune otherwise sure to befall us. So while orthodox evangelicals do not relish preaching on hell, a fundamental assertion of it cannot possibly be extracted from biblical data available to us. It shouts for interpretation. It is a cornerstone doctrine. Until comparatively recent times, you might disclaim belief in hell, but you always knew that in doing so you were stepping outside of fully orbed evangelical faith.

Enter megachurch pastor Rob Bell. In late 2010 he sent tremors through the younger segment of the evangelical community with publication of his book *Love Wins*. His thesis is that God loves all people far too well to ultimately destroy anyone by his wrath. This was hardly a novel notion; Rob Bell says nothing that was not proposed long before him by classic nineteenth- and twentieth-century liberalism. Relying on the goodness of the Lord (while ignoring vast tracts of inconvenient Scripture), Bell posits that divine love will somehow in the end conquer all obstacles of the human will and presumably save everyone. Yet Bell has confused many people by denying that this makes him an advocate of universal salvation. Bell wants to promote the breadth he apparently reads into John 3:16, even if it means excising John 3:18, by borrowing Thomas Jefferson's selective Bible scissors to do it.

Our principal aim here is to know what happens after death according to Scripture. So we must devote four chapters to considering the worst news that could possibly be told to humanity before we can rightly give attention to the grand good news about heaven. It is not improved Bible exegesis or interpretation that produces changes in contemporary thinking set against hell. It is the spirit of the world and the man-centeredness of our time. People deny hell on the basis of their own irrational presuppositions. "Truth is being abandoned, not because it is shown to be false but because it is felt to be unpopular and embarrassing."[1] The change from accepted positions of classical Christianity has come about, as David Wells notes, "not because of new light from the Bible but because of new darkness in the culture."[2]

## THE DESTINATION MILLIONS FACE

In John 3, an intelligent Jewish leader named Nicodemus came to Jesus with a tremendous misconception. He did not know it, but Nicodemus needed Jesus to teach him that heaven is not obtained by praiseworthy deeds, religious zeal, or social prestige. The same huge misconception is held today by millions of non-Christians and badly informed would-be

Christians. They believe heaven is the common destination of most human beings, except for a minority of true rotten apples—the worst cruel and abusive humans whom God must, of course, consign to hell: ax murderers, pedophiles, genocidal dictators, and such. Few would claim to actually know such a tragic, hell-bound personality. The assumption is that you'd have to visit a maximum security prison to interview anyone who is certainly headed for hell.

You can hear evidence of this misconception when you go to almost any funeral. Someone will piously declare, "Oh, at least now he is in a *better place.*" This is the cliché of all clichés. I hear this sentiment spoken over nearly every single man or woman who dies, including wife-abusers, pornography addicts, corporate robber-barons, inveterate liars, and outspoken haters of Christ. Funeral homes are prime places to hear the doctrine propounded that says heaven is for everybody and salvation is achieved by the mere act of dying. Honestly, it often makes me want to ask the one speaking, "What makes you so sure? Perhaps he is in a place that is horrible beyond your worst nightmares." Of course, politeness restrains me from being so blunt, and my wife has given many sharp tugs at my elbow to subdue words she knows very well could be on the end of my tongue.

The broad assumption is that hell is only for *other people.* Yet the Bible's teaching is unequivocally that no one stands upon neutral ground regarding an eternal destination. A spiritual law of gravity operates by which souls naturally descend, and can only ascend if a divine influence reverses their course. By default, everyone has already chosen a final abode and will proceed there unless their progress is interrupted. Contrary to popular assumptions, the destination universally chosen is not God's heavenly dwelling. In fact, "All we like sheep have gone astray; we have turned—every one—to his own way," concludes Isaiah 53:6. A further declaration about all of mankind is in Romans 3:10–11: "None is righteous, no, not one; no one understands; no one seeks for God." Surely, not all those bland funeral home pronouncements about "a better place" could possibly be in sync with biblical doctrine.

## UNNATURAL BIRTH BY THE HOLY SPIRIT

When Nicodemus met Jesus, this religious leader knew very little, for all his education and social standing. In John 3, Nicodemus represents human-based religion groping around in total darkness, waiting for God to shine forth true light. His understanding of his future beyond death was shackled to Old Testament ideas based in Sheol. Happily, we know that later Nicodemus helped reverently claim and bury the dead body of Jesus (John 19:39). He apparently became an authentic Christian disciple and ended better than he began.

Let us briefly consider the first part of John 3 and its teaching on the new birth, before we look closer at verses 17 and 18 as our crux of concern. Jesus took charge of the Nicodemus interview by telling him, "Unless one is born again he cannot see the kingdom of God" (v. 3). The original Greek can mean either "born again" or "born from above"; the two are synonymous. This is a second birth, with its motive force in God's supernatural power. A divine seed of life is implanted where before there was only spiritual deadness. First Peter 1:23 declares that we must be "born again, not of perishable seed but of imperishable, through the living and abiding word of God." Jesus expressed it as: "That which is born of the flesh is flesh, and that which is born of the Spirit is spirit" (John 3:6).

People are generally fascinated with new birth. You've noticed, I'm sure, that if someone brings a newborn baby into a crowded room, nearly every woman present wants to enfold that small miracle into her arms and coo over it. New life has a potent fascination; the same child at age eight will not arouse nearly the same interest. The new spiritual birth we are required to have is entirely God's sovereign work, performed by his Spirit—in that sense it is *unnatural*—not derived from anything in us or any impetus from this present world. It comes entirely from "above," no more ours to manipulate than our first biological birth was our decision. We cannot give it to ourselves; you only "hear its sound, but you do not know where it comes from or where it goes" (John 3:8). Once it is conceived in us, it will not be long before we are aware of it. A woman may not realize the exact moment she becomes pregnant, but she will discover it soon enough. However, it should be clear from John 3:3–8 that we initially are bystanders to the conception or first stirrings of this new birth. To give new life is the prerogative of God alone.

Don't ever become so blasé about your life as a Christian that you forget—whether you were conscious of it happening in the moment or not—that God sponsored a miraculous spiritual rebirth in order for you to begin trusting Jesus as your Lord. You did not become a Christian by a process of logical reasoning and unaided choice. According to

2 Corinthians 5:17, only God working by his Spirit conceived your spiritual birth and brought you forth as a whole "new creation." God wrought a total change of the soul, awakening and quickening us to become interested in Christ and make a trusting response toward him. In Ezekiel 11:19 the Lord stated:"I will remove the heart of stone from their flesh and give them a heart of flesh." First John 3:14 calls this transformation passing "out of death to life."

In John 3:3–8, God's gift of a new birth is discussed as the work of the Spirit, occurring sequentially before the act of faith by which we respond is even mentioned (in 3:15–18). The phrase "whoever *believes* in him" is a consequence of God's new birth in us; new birth never results from a man's faith. Our faith to trust in Christ as Lord is hardly different than a drowning man's desperate hand, reaching to grasp a life preserver thrown by another. Does the one thrashing in the water gain special credit for responding to a rescue initiated by others? Of course not! All praise goes to the rescuer, whose concern and timely action threw the lifeline, literally saving a doomed life. So a new birth is God's sovereign gift. God's salvation comes to any person through an *unnatural*, heaven-sent birth of faith in Christ—a work of the Spirit. Only miraculous intervention like this new birth can stop the course of a man or woman otherwise traveling toward condemnation.

## REMAINING IN UNBELIEF

My office computer is connected to several network printers. One is a modest laser printer located on the desk beside me. Two others are fast, high quality printer/copiers in the nearby administrative office, useful for color printing or for high-speed production. My computer software is configured so that the more limited printer next to me receives all print documents unless I deliberately change the instructions, sending a document to another printer. My laser printer is the default printer; pages travel to it by a natural path, unless redirected by another command.

Do you recognize the Bible's teaching on the *default* destination of all human souls, unless interrupted by God's rebirth of faith in Christ and turned to a new way? Most people do not. John 3:17 said, "God did not send his Son into the world to condemn the world." He did not have to condemn us, for the world had already found an effective way to condemn itself, through mankind's universal and deliberate fall into sin. Therefore, the default path for human souls is being "condemned already." John 3:18 could not be plainer: "Whoever believes in [Christ] is not condemned, but whoever does not believe is condemned already, because he has not believed in the name of the only Son of God." You can see why verses 17 and 18 are the part of John 3 no one much enjoys hearing about.

What does this truth say to those folks I overhear in funeral homes, muttering their worldly and often misinformed incantation, "He is in a better place"? John 3:18 tells them it is very possible that the place occupied by a recently departed soul is a prison of condemnation under the authority of the same God that individual ignored or openly rejected throughout a lifetime.

Many still persist in imagining that failure to actively look to Christ means you stand on *neutral* ground. They tell themselves they have not committed a decision either for or particularly against Christ, so how could their "nondecision" be eternally harmful? Please get this: the Bible never confuses unbelief with innocent neutrality! Unbelief is in fact the worst of all sins. God's explicit verdict upon it is "condemnation." No less than ninety-eight times John's Gospel uses the word "believe." To remain in unbelief instead of believing in Christ is not merely unfortunate; it is spiritually fatal. Bishop J. C. Ryle wrote, "No sin is so great, so damning or so ruinous as unbelief. In one sense it is the unpardonable sin. . . . Nothing is so provoking and offensive to God as to refuse the mighty salvation he has provided at so mighty a cost, by the death of his only begotten Son. Nothing is so suicidal on the part of a man as to turn away from the only remedy which can heal his soul."[3]

Who determines that natural default destination? *We* do. We're born that way; wired for God-rebellion. This is why Jesus said in Matthew 7:13–14, "Enter by the narrow gate. For the gate is wide and the road is easy that leads to destruction, and those who enter it are many. For the gate is narrow and the way is hard that leads to life and those who find it are few." The word "few" in this context indicates definite exceptions to a broader norm. God did not institute the default destination. God loved ruined sinners in this world so much that he sent his Son into the world not to condemn us, but "to seek and to save the lost" (Luke 19:10). Be sure you hear John 3:18 clearly. It does not merely say unbelievers will be condemned *someday* at a final accounting before the throne of Christ. Those who do not consciously believe in the Son as Lord of all *are* condemned "already"—right now. Your sins are an elephant that will not stop sitting on your chest, for eternity.

Some will wonder, "Preacher, what motivated you to talk about this hellfire and brimstone subject? What a negative message you are giving here!" A common way of turning aside serious consideration of divine judgment is to deflect it by mild humor. People joke, "I'd prefer to go to hell since my best friends will already be there." This joker tells himself that since he has avoided serious thoughts about hell by a lame gag, he can avoid thinking about it for a long time. Is there any better demonstration of a biblical "fool"?

I must ask the person who faults John 3:18 as being too negative: Do you consider a Maine lighthouse to be a negative statement as it shines its bright beam into the night, warning ships to avoid wreckage upon a rocky coastline? Do you consider a convention of oncologists who pool research and present papers on the grim morphology of various cancers to be entirely negative—devoid of life-saving benefits?

Incredibly, John 3:19–20 argues that people are not just neutral about the light of Christ; the situation is worse—they actually *despise* it! God's light of truth exposes so many ugly things in mankind, people will shun him at all cost, preferring to hide in the shadows. This means that anyone who makes shipwreck of his soul bears full responsibility. Therefore, God "sends" absolutely no one to hell against his will. Eternal misery results from a lifetime of wrong choices. The person living in continual unbelief wants nothing else, and accordingly, he gets nothing else. C. S. Lewis put it succinctly: "There are only two kinds of people in the end: those who say to God, 'Thy will be done,' and those to whom God says, in the end, '*Thy* will be done.' All that are in hell choose it. Without that self choice there could be no hell."[4]

## HELL PROCEEDS FROM THE BIBLICAL GOD

"If mere human sentiment, generosity, and social tolerance (the dominant gods in our day) held the final votes about the doctrine of eternal condemnation and punishment, the Bible's view of hell surely would find few defenders."[5]

Hell must never be spoken about in a flippant way by the Christian. Only with profound reluctance should we speak of this terrible prospect, with fear and trembling. However, we dare not suppress the awesome witness of the Scripture and become accomplices in the condemnation of others to eternal misery by our silence. Hell is the expression of God's wrath which is necessary to comprehending his love and grace. Hell is part of "the warp and woof of the Christian message, part of its very fabric. It cannot be cut out without causing all the remainder to unravel."[6] Paul Helm further said, "The plain fact according to the Christian gospel is that men and women are not automatically destined for heaven, but that there is for some a place of punishment without relief. It is those who are without Christ who are without hope (Eph. 2:12). They are bound for that place where all hope must be abandoned. And such a fact is as much a part of the overall Christian message as is the biblical teaching about assurance, joy and the love of God."[7]

## NO CONDEMNATION IN CHRIST

In conclusion, I ask a serious personal question: Do you know today that you cherish the light of God seen in Jesus Christ, as John 3:20–21 speaks about? Does your heart rise with joy to think of the wonder of God's Son, the Lord Jesus, sent to redeem you? If you answer yes, the reason can be only that God by his Spirit has given you spiritual *rebirth*, because mankind does not naturally love him. You are now and forever free from God's condemnation. Romans 8:1–2 promises: "There is therefore now no condemnation for those who are in Christ Jesus. For the law of the Spirit of life has set you free in Christ Jesus from the law of sin and death."

People in most of Europe and in Britain, Canada, and the United States, where the light of the gospel of Christ has shined for centuries, are the souls in the greatest peril. Today in these lands it seems that unbelief flees from Christ's light and clings to the pits of darkness, as though people are saying, "Christianity, leave us alone; we love our revelries, our perverted, unbridled sexual lusts, our intellectual conceits, our sleek technology and material idols. Stop your incessant preaching at us and your condemnation of our pet pursuits!" God will give these people their wish. He will leave them without his fellowship, for eternity.

Remarkably though, in scores of countries in Asia, Africa, and South America, where the midnight of false religion has prevailed for centuries, God is turning on spiritual lights of new birth. Every day, thousands who never before saw true spiritual light are abandoning superstition and error and leaping toward Christ, as they discover his gospel truth stirring in their lands. ☺

You need not slide headfirst into the default disaster of eternal condemnation. The gospel searchlight is shining today. Take your stand with Christ. Come into God's everlasting light, where there can be no condemnation for you.

Because I have called and you refused to listen,
  have stretched out my hand and no one has heeded,
because you have ignored all my counsel
  and would have none of my reproof,
I also will laugh at your calamity;
  I will mock when terror strikes you. . . .

For the simple are killed by their turning away,
  and the complacency of fools destroys them;
but whoever listens to me will dwell secure
  and will be at ease, without dread of disaster.

**PROVERBS 1:24-26, 32-33**

For if we go on sinning deliberately after receiving the knowledge of the truth, there no longer remains a sacrifice for sins, but a fearful expectation of judgment, and a fury of fire that will consume the adversaries. Anyone who has set aside the law of Moses dies without mercy on the evidence of two or three witnesses. How much worse punishment, do you think, will be deserved by the one who has trampled underfoot the Son of God, and has profaned the blood of the covenant by which he was sanctified, and has outraged the Spirit of grace? . . . It is a fearful thing to fall into the hands of the living God.

**HEBREWS 10:26-29, 31**

# CHAPTER SIX

# THE STRANGE DISAPPEARANCE OF HELL

☼

*LEGEND SAYS THAT MANY YEARS* ago an unnamed princess belonging to the British royal family once attended Sunday worship with her family at an Anglican cathedral. Exiting the service, the princess greeted the bishop who had preached the sermon. Apparently his doctrine had muddied the plain meaning of his text, causing the royal daughter to inquire, "Is it true, bishop, that there is a place called hell?" The bishop answered "The Scriptures say there is; and the Church of England has always believed this." The young lady probably spoke with more youthful spunk than royal discretion in her next remark: "Then why, as God's spokesman, did you not tell us so today?"

Hell is more easily talked around than talked about. The bishop in question probably found it easier to speak of something like "ultimate existential consequences" than to specify the plain concept of *hell*. Polls taken in the USA consistently show that more than 70 percent of Americans say they believe in the existence of some form of a hell after death. Yet fewer than 6 percent estimate they personally have a real chance of going there.[1] We are good at avoiding personal implications of this awesome reality. The moment it comes to mind, our instinct is to divert our thoughts in a more pleasant direction.

If there truly is "good news" of gospel redemption in Christ, it must signify true escape from catastrophically bad news. We asked in the previous chapter, what is the destiny for the unbeliever? Since human beings are naturally born "dead in trespasses and sins" (Eph. 2:1), John 3:18 declares that anyone who has not been born anew by grace to trust Christ is "condemned already." Spiritual separation from God's favor and other devastating consequences of being unredeemed are mankind's default destination. How could it be otherwise and God remain just?

## WHERE DID HELL GO?

In our times, use of the word "hell" is widely accepted in daily conversation so long as you are telling a joke or cursing. But whoever wants to deliberately dwell on this as a serious theme? Hell is a dreadful topic for conversation. David Lodge wrote, "At some point in the nineteen-sixties, hell disappeared. No one could say for certain when this happened. First it was there, then it wasn't. . . . On the whole the disappearance of hell was a great relief, though it brought new problems."[2] Martin Marty added, "Hell has disappeared and no one noticed."[3]

As I preached on the subjects of death, hell, and heaven for a lengthy series of messages, I became aware of a family that began attending our services, brought by a neighbor. Later, after becoming a member of our congregation, the husband of this new family told me the odd motive that had drawn him to return to us after the first visit. He said, "I figured that in this day and age when sermons usually are deliberately aimed to please the audience, any preacher who announced he was going to preach on the theme of hell for a month straight at least needed to be heard. The sheer novelty of what you were doing was not to be missed." We have no difficulty understanding why the liberal interpreter of Scripture would omit any mention of hell—he thinks it is false. It is far harder to understand how or why it has nearly disappeared from the vocabulary of the typical evangelical pulpit.

## REPROBATION MEANS "TO PASS BY"

Here is a key question people often ask: "How can a good God send anyone to hell?" They feel this objection poses a hard conundrum which totally undermines the Christian system. But in actual fact, the question proves nothing and is one of the easiest I get to answer from time to time. For God does not send anyone to hell. *You* send yourself!

Chapter 3 of the Westminster Confession of Faith addresses a subtopic under divine election that is properly called the doctrine of reprobation. Some choose to see reprobation as the "dark side" of election, since it treats the fate of the nonelect—those not called to eternal life. Some scholars defend what is called "double predestination": the notion that God exercises an active decree actually and firmly forbidding some from his kingdom. They are the ones with some explaining to do. Many of us believe it is more biblically correct to discuss reprobation as a *passive* action by God—a choice he simply does not take up, for his own mysterious reasons. The Confession declares this summary of the Bible's doctrine: "The rest of mankind, God was pleased, according to the unsearchable counsel of his own will, whereby he extendeth or witholdeth mercy as he pleaseth, for the glory of his sovereign power over his creatures, to *pass by*, and to ordain them to dishonor and wrath for their sin, to the praise of his glorious justice."[4] Romans 9:15 is a key supportive text, as it cites Exodus 33:19: "I will have mercy on whom I have mercy, and I will have compassion on whom I have compassion." Also, 1 Peter 2:8 says, "They stumble because they disobey the word, as they were destined to do."

As a practical illustration, many who were not among the gifted athletes in their middle school days will testify of a wound to the adolescent psyche inflicted every time sides were chosen for gym class teams and they were among the last to be taken. No one forthrightly stated, "I reject you." Team captains were never so confrontational. The sting of shame arose from being repeatedly passed over, until you were the very last student to be taken for a team. Choosing you was no longer a preference but a necessity because no others remained.

I always emphasize the words "to pass by" when teaching chapter 3 of the Westminster Confession. I do not suggest that this wording unties every knot of intellectual struggle that vexes our minds over election and reprobation. However, church fathers who wrote the Confession were making it plain that human beings are rushing along a path of determined rebellion against God under their own steam. All the Most High needs to do for anyone to be condemned is to "pass by" that person. God presses no one toward hell against his will. He simply does not *change* your predetermined direction!

Scripture depicts God's love and delight in granting any soul election to eternal life. Reprobation, on the other hand, brings God sorrow: "I have no pleasure in the death of the wicked, but that the wicked turn from his way and live" (Ezek. 33:11). The Bible lays blame for reprobation at the feet of the unrepentant sinner.

Yes, it can be argued that even the Lord's failure to act is still the assertion of a divine choice or decree. But the frequently asked question of why God would "*send* anyone to hell" is already answered. The sovereign God *need not send* anyone in that calamitous direction; he never does! Even when discussing "hardening of the heart" by either Pharaoh or King Saul in the Old Testament, close study will show that the man first caused his own hardening, and then God withdrew, to let him be hardened more. If a holy God never exercised one single positive decree to choose a single man or woman for the gift of eternal life by new birth and justification in Jesus Christ, he would still be entirely just. No one could demand a further accounting from him.

People without Christ absolutely are not forced toward a torture chamber by some deranged prison guard named "God," who arbitrarily plucks every third person from a line to march them off to the gas showers and afterward has their lifeless bodies trundled to the crematorium. Election is an active decree of God, while reprobation is passive. The elect are caused to believe by the grace of divine regeneration; the reprobate is never caused to disbelieve—he does this himself. The elect are chosen by love; the reprobate is passed over. Election is never deserved; reprobation is totally deserved because of sin and unbelief. Election is about grace; reprobation is the consequence of perfect justice.[5]

I am frequently confronted by persons who ask: "What about 2 Peter 3:9? That verse says, 'The Lord . . . is patient toward you, not wishing that any should perish, but that all should reach repentance.'" Questioners sometimes imagine that Peter said it was God's true intent to save everyone without exception, but too many souls just will not cooperate with him. Most people who wield that text as a magic wand which they suppose tears down the doctrine of election are not intent on promoting universal human salvation as an alternative. They merely struggle with the fact that realism says many are evidently lost, and 2 Peter 3:9 implies God takes no pleasure in that. Peter's statement that God was "not wishing" points to his revealed will in a general manner, not his original creation intent before the fall. Loraine Boettner helpfully summarized, "The word 'will' is used in different senses in Scripture and in our everyday conversation. It is sometimes used in the sense of 'decree' or 'purpose,' and sometimes in the sense of 'to desire' or 'wish.' A righteous judge does not will (desire) that anyone should be hanged . . . Yet at the same time he wills (pronounces or decrees) that the guilty person should be thus punished."[6]

The final comprehension of a divine decree of election and reprobation remains shrouded in the mystery of grace, and we will not untangle it in this lifetime. Things shift into clearer focus once you accept the Bible's teaching that our own intransigent unbelief sends us down the slippery slope to hell. God may unexplainably pluck you from this destiny, interrupting your self-destruction. Nevertheless, all he needs to do is to "pass you by," and your own free fall of sin will carry you to final destruction. Reprobation is God's passive decree. You cannot lay any blame for it at his feet. The right question is never, why do some go to hell? The question we have to ponder is, why should even *one* determinedly hell-bound soul ever be saved? Considering this will bring us to Christ in worship and thanksgiving, not angry vexation. We can be sure that election and reprobation will bring greater glory to God, as his grace and justice are vindicated in the end.

## PROVERBS SPEAKS ON GOD'S WRATH

At the moment of death, souls who belong to Christ enter his blessed presence to await a resurrection body at his final coming and the consummation of all things. Correspondingly, souls of unbelievers begin to experience regret and anguish. At the final judgment, they are cast into irremediable ruin as the inevitable outcome of wrong choices. Scripture teaches that those who have lived in enmity against God shall find themselves forever cut off from his blessed presence, left to dwell in the consciously felt awareness of his wrath. Rather than face this truth, the kinder, gentler twenty-first-century perversion of Christianity heard too often in our time subtracts the wrath of God, and you are left with what Richard Niebuhr caustically labeled fifty years ago as "a God without wrath who brings men without sin into a kingdom without judgment through the ministrations of Christ without a cross."[7]

I could have selected dozens of Old Testament passages to illustrate the biblical roots of this doctrine; I purposely picked the unlikely text of Proverbs 1:22–33. The word "hell" does not appear in Proverbs 1, but the foundation principle of its existence is clearly stated. The chapter is a plea from the voice of "wisdom," calling the unwise to heed vital advice; "in the markets she raises her voice" (1:20). Wisdom personified in the Old Testament can be compared to the voice of Christ in the New Testament, since Jesus the Son is wisdom incarnate. In Proverbs 1, wisdom's voice is ignored in the busy marketplace. The call is very audible, but her pleas are rejected. In verse 26 God says he will "laugh at your calamity," referring to those who have ignored wisdom's entreaty. Verse 31 then declares, "They shall eat the fruit of their way, and have their fill of their own devices." And the conclusion drawn in verses 32–33 is that "the complacency of fools destroys them; but whoever listens to me will dwell secure and will be at ease, without dread of disaster."

Proverbs 1 need not mention the word hell, nor depict flames or wailing souls. The Bible's steely logic of God's historic appeal to unbelieving humanity is found here. A choice must be made when divine wisdom offers life-giving knowledge of the Lord our God. How long will fools ignore her in self-imposed deafness and rush forward like lemmings to plunge together over a cliff? God promises calamity will come like a tsunami wave, sweeping the ignorant off their feet. In this, the Lord takes no delight. Fair warning is given, and personal actions have consequences. Therefore each sinner's ruin can truly be laid at his own door, because he spurned every offer to escape. This same logic is found in John 3:18, where we are told that the unbeliever is "condemned already, because he has not believed in the name of the only Son of God." God sent his Son as Wisdom incarnate into the world, so people may turn to him and live. Those who will not hear Christ's call of gospel grace go to the destination their self-determination demands.

## NO NEUTRALITY FOR CROSS-TRAMPLERS

Now consider a parallel New Testament text, Hebrews 10:26–31. Here is a more explicit message. The author of Hebrews imagines people who, upon hearing preaching about Christ, initially pay it some nominal attention. Then they go on to spurn Jesus and his cross! The inspired author was incredulous as he asked, "How much worse punishment, do you think, will be deserved by the one who has trampled underfoot the Son of God, and has profaned the blood of the covenant by which he was sanctified, and has outraged the Spirit of grace?" (Heb. 10:29). The truth of Christ was not only available to these people, "they *received* the knowledge of the truth." This indicates some formal acknowledgment of the gospel from these hearers, but no heart-deep devotion, no true life-transforming faith. Continuing to rebel against God in this situation brings disastrous consequences.

Non-Christians may argue that they have not insulted God or trampled on his Son—they really think they are "neutral" about Christ. In human society, neutrality often can be a virtue. Switzerland is lauded for having maintained a neutral stance through two major European wars broaching her borders. That seems admirable. However, the Bible allows for no neutrality in ultimate things. You either belong to Christ, or you are against him. Unbelief might seem, in one's estimation, to equal at worst a charge of involuntary manslaughter following a death by traffic accident; but to a perfectly holy God who has presented abundant knowledge of himself in his Son, unbelief is premeditated murder in the first degree.

## HELL IN JUST ONE GOSPEL

We could look into a lengthy series of texts about hell as discussed in many biblical books from the Old and New Testaments. For now, we will look at the gospel of Matthew, where Jesus states many of the hardest things about this subject in all of Scripture.

First, he spoke of a hell that is a real place. In his Sermon on the Mount of Matthew 5–7 (the body of teaching many people assess as Jesus expressing his gentlest and most noble thoughts), Jesus spoke about the "hell of fire" and being "thrown into hell" (5:22, 29). Later, he called Pharisees children "of hell" (23:15) and challenged them as to how they expected to escape from going there (23:33). Second, Jesus taught that hell is ruled over by God: "Fear him who can destroy both soul and body in hell" (10:28); and in Matthew 25:41, "He will say to those on his left, depart from me, you cursed, into the eternal fire prepared for the devil and his angels." Third, Jesus spoke of hell involving utter rejection by God: "And then I will declare to them, 'I never knew you; depart from me, you workers of lawlessness'" (7:23). Matthew 13:40 pictures unbelievers gathered to be burned up in a bonfire like so many discarded weeds. In Matthew 25, believing "sheep" are separated from "goats" of unbelief, which "go away into eternal punishment" (vv. 32–33, 46). Fourth, Jesus taught hell involves real and lasting pain. In Matthew 8:12 he said that unrighteous men would be "thrown into the outer darkness. In that place there will be weeping and gnashing of teeth." And further, "It is better for you to enter life crippled or lame than with two hands or two feet to be thrown into the eternal fire" (Matt. 18:8). As difficult as that catalog sounds for the anti-hell crowd to explain away, it is not even everything Jesus spoke on the topic in the single gospel of Matthew!

People sometimes inquire whether we ought to imagine that a biblical hell contains real *fire*? The concept of horned devils with pitchforks in red flannel long underwear and caverns full of rising flames with belching brimstone is a bit too much for the most devout imagination. Probably the best way to answer the question is to understand that "fire" is used in Scripture as a literary metaphor. But instead of downplaying the issue by knowing the fire could be nonliteral, we had better conclude that the *reality* to be faced in hell will be worse than any metaphorical fire! The reality outperforms its symbol. In hell, one will encounter the glory, majesty, and absolute holiness of God whom Hebrews 12:29 calls "a consuming fire." Hebrews 10:31 says, "It is a fearful thing to fall into the hands of the living God." If you insist on facing God unprotected, without the borrowed shield of Christ's righteousness, you might as well undertake a parachute drop to the surface of the sun in your bathing suit.

Again, I am not seeking to trace numerous references to hell in Paul's epistles, the general epistles, or the book of Revelation. Some further details will emerge in the next two chapters. Suffice it to say the doctrine of hell is fully embedded in both Old Testament and New Testament Scripture. If it happened that the Bible contained nothing about hell, God could not be just or the one who justifies. Christ would be no deliverer, since no deliverance would be required by us.

## HELL IN HISTORIC CREEDS

Major creeds and confessions for at least nineteen centuries, plus writings of all the great orthodox theologians of the church agree on this doctrine. The Athanasian Creed from around 500 AD stated: "At Christ's coming, all men shall rise in their bodies and those who have done evil will go into everlasting fire." The Apostles' Creed, existing in its present form since the late fourth century, apparently did not always contain the phrase stating that Christ "descended into hell" upon his death. Evidence seems to show this was a somewhat later addition. Interpreters like Calvin regarded that phrase as describing Jesus's intense spiritual sufferings on the cross. However, all who recite the Apostles' Creed do say, "he ascended into heaven and sitteth at the right hand of God the Father Almighty; from thence he shall come to judge the quick and the dead." So there can be no doubt of divine judgment for unbelief affirmed in the Apostles' Creed.

The Westminster Confession 33.1 states: "God hath appointed a day wherein he will judge the world in righteousness by Jesus Christ, to whom all power and judgment is given by the Father." WCF 33.2 continues, "The end of God's appointing this day is for the manifestation of the glory of his mercy in the eternal salvation of the elect, and his justice in the damnation of the reprobate, who are wicked and disobedient. . . . but the wicked who do not know God or obey the gospel of Jesus Christ shall be cast into eternal torments and punished with everlasting destruction away from the presence of the Lord and the glory of his power."

The Heidelberg Catechism, the Thirty Nine Articles of the Church of England—you can consult the entire roll call of classic Reformation creeds of Christendom. A hell of punishment for unbelief was found time after time, until modern theology began rewriting some creeds.

## WHY WILL YOU DIE?

The United Church of Canada is a denomination of several million members, known for rather left-leaning theology. In 1997, the *Ottawa Citizen* published an interview with the current moderator of that denomination. The Right Reverend Bill Phipps stated, "The divinity of Jesus or the reality of heaven and hell are irrelevant. I don't believe Jesus was God, but I'm no theologian. I have no idea if there is a hell and I don't think Jesus cared either."[8] Here is a minister who testifies boldly that he has abandoned Christian faith, if he ever held to it. He ignores the Bible and tramples Christ underfoot with reckless abandon. (One thing he got correct was his assertion that he was "no theologian"!)

You come to expect this sort of nonsense from extreme liberal Protestantism, but a greater problem today is general de-emphasis on the terror of hell by conservative evangelicals who profess to preach the gospel of the cross. Hell can easily fade out of the picture just by preachers' failing to mention biblical doctrine that might be culturally distasteful, or by not selecting the hard texts in which divine justice and ultimate punishment occur. By simple neglect, the doctrine falls by the wayside, and people hardly notice it is gone.

What did Jesus experience in our place on Calvary, if not disastrous waves of divine wrath for human sin? On his cross, the perfect Son of the Highest was subjected to the torrent of hell for our sake. Devaluing the hell described in Scripture robs the historic cross of its profound meaning. Men talk little of hell because they estimate they have only a little sin, and thus they need only a little savior. When you are dumbstruck by a great, overwhelming sense of sin, knowing you are "condemned already," you will seek a great Savior and realize that without him you will fall prey to appalling destruction at the hands of a tremendous God who merits reverence and awe!

De-emphasis of hell and judgment in the twenty-first century surely is not based on new discoveries in the text of Scripture that impugn what the Christian church has always believed. The problem is not new light shed from the Bible, but new and more determined works of darkness within our culture. Men love darkness and flee the light of truth. The doctrine of hell rips right through the emperor's-new-clothes fabric of a man-centered viewpoint. It portrays a holy God to whom we are finally accountable. However, the same Bible that announces this so-called "bad" news tells us that this marvelous God sent his only Son to rescue millions, giving his life to pay our penalty in his innocent blood. How can anyone possibly preach this hard doctrine of Scripture in any attitude except brokenness and with real tears overtaking us? The reality of hell crushes pride, arrogance, or boasting. Redemption by the cross is all of God's grace. So we plead with this generation:"Why will you choose to die, when God offers eternal life?"

You may recall that as December 1999 approached, the Y2K scare had millions thinking we faced major societal catastrophe as the year 2000 dawned. On December 31, 1999, at Tenth Presbyterian Church in Philadelphia, Dr. James Montgomery Boice led a midnight communion service, which concluded just as January 1, 2000, was being ushered in. At the Lord's Table, Dr. Boice said words to this effect, to members of a beloved congregation he had pastored for more than thirty years: "I ask you to understand that your problem tonight is not whether your computer will work tomorrow. Our great common problem is—we all are going to *die*. You will come to stand in judgment before God! And if you do not come to him trusting in the death of Jesus Christ as your atonement for sin, you will be condemned forever." Those present that night testified that after this charge, a deep solemnity filled that Philadelphia sanctuary as people received the Lord's Supper at the dawning of a new calendar century.[9] Who could have guessed that Jim Boice would himself enter the presence of his great Savior less than six months later? As he spoke that December night, undetected liver cancer was multiplying silently in his sixty-one-year-old body.

I am confident that Dr. Boice is with Christ in glory today. But do you realize that in the time required to read this chapter many thousands of earthbound souls have breathed their last and entered eternity? Each one either is with Christ or has been forever excluded from access to him. I ask you right now to prayerfully consider the words of Hebrews 2:3: "How shall we escape if we neglect such a great salvation?"

The rich man also died and was buried, and in Hades, being in torment, he lifted up his eyes and saw Abraham far off and Lazarus at his side. And he called out, "Father Abraham, have mercy on me, and send Lazarus to dip the end of his finger in water and cool my tongue, for I am in anguish in this flame." But Abraham said, "Child, remember that you in your lifetime received your good things, and Lazarus in like manner bad things; but now he is comforted here, and you are in anguish. And besides all this, between us and you a great chasm has been fixed, in order that those who would pass from here to you may not be able, and none may cross from there to us." And he said, "Then I beg you, father, to send him to my father's house—for I have five brothers—so that he may warn them, lest they also come into this place of torment." But Abraham said, "They have Moses and the Prophets; let them hear them." And he said, "No, father Abraham, but if someone goes to them from the dead, they will repent." He said to him, "If they do not hear Moses and the Prophets, neither will they be convinced if someone should rise from the dead."

LUKE 16:22-31

# CHAPTER SEVEN

# WHAT JESUS TAUGHT ABOUT HELL

☼

*MY YOUNGER SISTER ADORED THE* movies of Shirley Temple. This meant that in my adolescence if I wanted television entertainment, sometimes I had to watch Shirley's cute blond mop of curls bouncing as she tap-danced her heart out in movies like *Rebecca of Sunnybrook Farm*. In that film, Shirley's character, Rebecca, had a serious talk with a girl named Emma Jane. Rebecca said she had planned to become a missionary some day "to save the heathen from going to hell." But she revealed she had changed this career choice, because, she testified, "It's not as though the heathen really need me. I'm sure they'll come out all right in the end. They'll find God somehow." Emma Jane asked, "What if they die first?" Rebecca replied, "Well they can't be blamed for that, since they don't die on purpose!" Shirley Temple was more gifted as a tap dancer than a theologian. Many might chuckle at the missionary philosophy of a cute little girl. Yet her idea about eternal blamelessness for blind unbelief remains a pragmatic but unbiblical view widely endorsed by the masses.

## WAS JESUS MORALLY DEFECTIVE?

In the last chapter we mentioned how the subject of hell as a destination for human unbelief is de-emphasized in the church today, either purposefully or by neglect. Now we face the remarkable fact that no Bible spokesman places more stress on hell as the final consequence of God's judgment of condemnation than Jesus. God's Son was the great theologian of hell. The Christian should not consider it strange that Christ has more to say about hell than anyone else. "The one who tells us most about hell is the only one who can save us from it. What more could we ask? . . . The person sent to warn us is the person who can deliver us."[1]

I have already skimmed a handful of texts in Matthew. There we heard Christ's words about hell forged in iron. It is not practical for us to closely study all the words of Christ on this subject. Jesus was the one who compared hell to the Valley of Hinnom near Jerusalem (also called "Gehenna"), a huge public rubbish dump where dead bodies and trash burned in continually smoldering fires; thus "Gehenna" took hold as a name for hell. Jesus also compared hell to a prison and to outer darkness. It was he who likened hell to "a fire" at least twenty different times.

Twentieth-century scientist and outspoken atheist Sir Bertrand Russell claimed, "There is one serious defect in evaluating the moral character of Jesus—the fact that he believed in hell! I do not myself feel that any person who is profoundly human can believe in everlasting punishment."[2] Russell was bolder than most people who, instead of labeling Jesus morally defective, simply ignore the Lord's clear emphasis on this hard topic. Note that Russell tells us that his rejection of Jesus on this subject was based entirely on what he (Russell) personally "feels" must be true. In his purely subjective view, anyone who promotes Jesus's views on hell must be considered less than human. Keep this in mind, because anyone's cavalier rejection of the doctrine of hell in the New Testament requires them to believe exactly what Dr. Russell maintained. It means concurrently denouncing the prime spokesman who taught more about the harshest dimensions of hell than any other voice of biblical authority. New Testament scholar Leon Morris summarized, "Why does anyone believe in hell in these enlightened days? Because Jesus plainly taught its existence. He spoke more often about hell than he did about heaven. We cannot get around this fact. If we are serious in our understanding of Jesus as the incarnate Son of God, we must reckon with the fact that he said plainly that some people will spend eternity in hell."[3] The credibility of Jesus himself as a spokesman for truth is called into account when it comes to this doctrine. Will you hear him or cast off his teaching because it is painful and you don't happen to like it?

## THE RICH FOOL, IN HELL

A premier text about hell from the mouth of Jesus is Luke 16:19–31. The wider context of its teaching is the abuse of wealth. Yet when describing the other-worldly setting of this teaching, Christ expanded the doctrine of hell. The passage is about a rich man who played the ultimate fool by luxuriating in his wealth, ignoring true faith in God and service to humanity, until he found himself in hell for his godless selfishness. The passage seems much like a parable, but it is not specifically called that. In this text, Jesus's primary intent was not to describe details of the unbeliever's afterlife, but the Lord does end up giving us an insider's view of hell, encapsulating important details of what is taught on this subject elsewhere.

From the Son of God we learn that the ultimate destination of unbelief is ruled over by a sovereign, just God. "The Judge and Ruler over hell is God himself. He is present in hell, not in any form of blessing but in his unsheathed wrath. Hell entails eternal punishment, utter loss, rejection by God, terrible suffering, and unbearable pain. The duration of hell is endless."[4] Spiritually, hell is an irreversible dead end; enduring it involves never-ending regret.

We find that just as surely as Christ-believing souls leave this physical body to immediately enter joyful bliss with God their Savior, the lost person enters a terrifying estate of woe, beyond anything imaginable. And it could have been avoided.

## TWO LIVES AND TWO DEATHS

The unnamed "rich man" and a beggar named Lazarus were polar opposites in earthly life. (This man named Lazarus is not to be confused with the friend Jesus raised from the dead in John 11). They lived in close geographic proximity, yet were worlds apart in all other ways. The rich man could have been featured on a once-popular television program, if the title of the show could be revised to be *Lifestyles of the Rich and Clueless*. Wearing purple cloth signified that you had wealth close to the level of royalty—the equivalent of driving a Rolls-Royce Silver Cloud. Selfish extravagance was the rich man's obsession. The idea that his wealth might bring with it greater social responsibility through charity of a type practiced in modern times by Andrew Carnegie or Bill Gates was unknown to him. Literally at his gate every day was the unwelcome sight of a miserable beggar with dogs licking open sores on his body. The daily goal of the beggar was to fight off those dogs to get at the rich man's garbage. The beggar was neglected by a culture that had no social safety net for poor or disabled persons; he was helpless to improve his wretched existence.

These two men were opposites in faith. This is inferred by Jesus, though not directly stated, since no beggar goes to heaven just because he is poor. It seems Jesus intended to indicate the beggar's faith in God by naming him Lazarus, which means "God is my helper." Though we might tend to view the rich man as a total agnostic, he was at least an ethnic Jew by birth and likely a nominal follower of Israel's religion, since he called Abraham "father."

Extending the comparison, these two men became opposites in the hour of death. Concerning Lazarus, verse 22 simply states, "The poor man died and was carried by the angels to Abraham's side." No mention is made of a funeral. It is not hard to imagine his useless body being tossed on Jerusalem's smoldering Gehenna rubbish heap. However, we may suspect that the rich man's coffin was banked with flowers donated by influential friends. The Rotary Club and the city council were represented at his wake, and the funeral procession had at least six matching Cadillac limos. His tomb was constructed with the finest Carrera marble.

These two men, as Jesus sketched them, forever remained opposites. Instantly at death, everything about them was dramatically reversed; social and spiritual status was turned inside out. A more dramatic reversal of fates than what Jesus painted in a few strokes in Luke 16 would be hard to imagine.

## IMMEDIATE HELL FOR UNBELIEF

We will later show from Scripture that all believers in Christ are promised an instantaneous experience at death that may be called "immediate heaven." God's Word says we shall not obtain the fullness of our resurrection bodies until Christ's final return in history and his last judgment. But without interruption, following our last breath, Christian souls gain the sure promise of "away from the body and at home with the Lord" (2 Cor. 5:8). Here in Luke 16, we discover the opposite of immediate heaven. We could name the refuge of *unbelieving* souls the "immediate hell." From his burial in verse 22 to stunned awareness of a new dwelling entirely unlike his grand mansion, the rich man detected no passage of time. His lost soul flew from the lap of mortal luxury to an experience dominated by two unhappy words: "torment" (Luke 16:23) and "anguish" (16:25).

People wonder: Is the torment and anguish primarily physical? Perhaps mental? Spiritual? Maybe all three? The sufferer himself blames it on "this flame" (16:24). In God's Word the reality of fire in hell is consistently a symbol of divine wrath. Hebrews 12:29 tells us, "Our God is a consuming fire." If you would define the fire of hell, look no further than God himself. Hell is not a prisoner of war camp built beyond God's reach. God reigns in hell as he does in heaven, yet he offers no one there his fellowship, or his pity, nor does he extend them any mercy. God's one rule governing hell is his perfect justice. Paul Helm declared, "Hell is not the result of the petulant temper of a capricious and unstable God, but of his strict and exact justice."[5]

This one-time rich man is in severe distress of soul. It is "anguish" to be denied the slightest shade from the protective umbrella of God's grace. Every person alive today benefits from what we call "common grace" as God withholds various potential misfortunes all human beings fully deserve for their unrighteous deeds. A blaspheming farmer gets as much rain on his crop today as a godly neighbor. However, in hell, even the least of God's common blessings and goodness disappears.

We have no true estimate of how entirely disastrous our fall from grace has been. John S. B. Monsell penned his 1863 hymn, which declared, "My sins, My Sins! My Savior! Their guilt I never knew, till with thee in the desert I near thy passion drew. Till with thee in the garden I heard thy pleading prayer, and saw the sweat drops bloody that told thy sorrow there." The amazing depth of Christ's agony at his cross shows how radically our deceitful hearts offend our holy God. A Christian believer is one who has realized this. By deep repentance and faith in Christ, we are graciously absolved of great guilt. But the unbeliever can only expect his initial encounter with this wrath after death, when no shield is available. Hell is the inevitable disaster of human ungodliness and rebellion facing divine perfection. God's "wrath," as the Bible calls it, is never anger likened to throwing a temper tantrum. It is unbearable holiness, met full force by an *unholy* and unredeemed creature.

When the wretched man in Luke 16 begged for drops of cold water on the tip of his tongue, he was told, "In your lifetime, you received your good things" (v. 25). Clearly, he reaped exactly what he sowed. Luxuriating for years in his mansion, he had enjoyed his earthly Disneyland—a fantasy existence. Jesus earlier said in Luke 6:24 to such negligent rich people: "Woe to you who are rich, for you have received your consolation." If you live entirely absorbed in worldly materialism, then this world will pay out all the heaven you can possibly hope to enjoy, and then it will disappear like a vapor.

## PRINCIPLES ABOUT HELL FROM JESUS

One foundational principle Jesus taught in the lesson of the rich man and Lazarus was that hell has no exit door. Father Abraham tells the writhing sufferer why his condition could not be remedied: "Between us and you a great chasm has been fixed, in order that those who would pass from here to you may not be able, and none may cross from there to us" (16:26). For almost forty years, the Berlin wall was a symbol of the Cold War that would never disappear or be breached, or so it seemed. In the 1960s for a short time the world watched some brave East Germans flee across the no-man's-land separating tyranny and freedom. A few actually made it; others died, their bodies hung up on barbed wire barricades. Remarkably, in 1989 the Berlin Wall was torn down, ending separation between free Germany and a Communist police state. However, the divide between eternal heaven and everlasting hell is made hard-and-fast by God's eternal decree. The word "fixed" in Luke 16:26 has about the same meaning as our phrase "cast in concrete."

C. S. Lewis wrote a clever book called *The Great Divorce*. Depicted in this extended short story was a bus trip departing from hell (called the "Gray Town"), fancifully permitting lost souls to make a short visit to heaven. These hell-dwellers find heaven a totally unpleasant place, since nothing about it was designed in accord with their remaining sinful lusts—which they still do not recognize. After the visitors briefly explore heaven's countryside, most are quite eager to reboard their transport back to the netherworld below, for in heaven's broad meadows they are transparent, ghostly personalities, while the heavenly residents are "solid people." Heaven's intense reality is not to their liking. A small taste of heaven made most of them more peevish and self-centered than they were on earth. Heaven was not a place where they were temperamentally suited to stay.[6] Lewis knew he was writing fiction and that his hell-to-heaven bus trip had no equivalent in Christian doctrine or any soul's experience. His title, *The Great Divorce*, had nothing to do with the breakup of a marriage; he wrote to illustrate the complete divergence between heaven and hell. A lost soul cannot rest easy in heaven; he prefers a place where his selfishness can still be indulged. Lewis concluded that hell has no true exit gate and heaven has no back door, because even if there were such, the unredeemed would not choose to go through them.

Luke 16 testifies that when an unbeliever becomes conscious of this tragic reality immediately after his own death, it is already too late to humble himself before the gospel of Christ and the cross, which he has spurned hundreds or thousands of times; it is too late to believe in Jesus as Lord; it is too late to beg for divine mercy. Scripture extends the opportunity of grace for every human being's full lifetime. We hear in 2 Peter 3:9 of the Lord's vast patience: ". . . not wishing that any should perish, but that all should reach repentance." Yet people *will* perish—once they have passed the doorway of death without knowing Christ.

Medieval theologians, who could not humanly endure the notion of a permanent separation of unbelievers from people of faith, plucked an idea from the apocryphal book of Second Maccabees. In 1439, the Roman Church Council of Florence formally authorized a dogma called *purgatory*, which theoretically provided a spiritual "halfway house" where souls might have opportunity for a vague second chance, to work out salvation and possibly to move on to better vistas. That this is based on a theology of salvation by meritorious works is enough to condemn the notion of purgatory. The concept has never been retracted by Rome to this day, despite there being no shred of substantiating Bible evidence—something Catholic scholars worth their salt will admit. Purgatory remains a fanciful philosopher's notion, invented by wishful religion to deceive the gullible. We need not devote any more ink to the issue. If Jesus is to be believed and trusted as our authority, hell is an eternally sealed chamber, and there is no halfway house.

Another principle Jesus taught in Luke 16:27–30 is that God's Word gives humanity sufficient warning about how to avoid hell. The rich man grasped it when the remedy could no longer personally help him. He experienced his first-ever altruistic impulse as he pleaded for a messenger to warn his family so they might avoid his plight. But he is told that testimonials from "Moses and the Prophets" are set before all living men (v. 29). God's revealed Word can tell mankind all we need to know about our sin and a Redeemer's grace. In Luke 11:28 Jesus declared, "Blessed rather are those who hear the word of God and keep it!" Do not miss a tremendous irony here. The rich man maintained that something *more* than God's Word is needed—perhaps a miraculous sign. He went so far as to predict the exact type of miracle that would communicate better than God's written Word: someone returning from the dead, to garner widespread public attention. What folly! Not long after teaching this gospel lesson, the same Jesus who narrated Luke 16 *arose* from the grave. And what resulted? A minority of people in the immediate precincts of Jerusalem embraced him as their living Lord. However, the majority scoffed and turned back to perusing their sports pages or looked to the stock market reports to discover what was new on that particular routine day. Unbelief determinedly shrugs off all historic proofs of Christ. The very One who was told that a family would surely respond to the supernatural wonder of a messenger from the grave *became* that miraculous messenger. And he is still being spurned.

If you rail against the biblical hell as though it were a cruel and unusual punishment, at least do not make the silly mistake of saying you had inadequate notice of its imminence. A just God cannot be accused of giving insufficient warnings about how to enter heaven. The very explicit communication he has made plain is refused daily by millions.

## ONE MAN ANONYMOUS . . . THE OTHER IMMORTAL

It is notable that the rich man does not get a name in Luke 16. As with most wealthy people, somewhere a granite marker probably was set up by his family, taller than its cemetery companions in the attempt to keep his name prominent after death. Yet if Jesus gave one character a name, signifying that the Lord God held him in close regard, while the other man remains Mr. No Name, we can assume this was deliberate. Lazarus clung to the hope embedded in his name that "God is my helper." Those who are not God's adopted children by grace through faith are nameless and eternally anonymous. Augustine commented, "God who lives in heaven kept quiet about the rich man's name, because he didn't find it written in heaven. But he spoke the poor man's name, because he found it written there. . . ."[7]

Suppose the Bible told us nothing about hell. Would that really make the Scriptures more "loving," or compassionate? Does concealing unpleasant truth demonstrate that you truly care more for others' destinies? What we find in Luke 16 is that the unique spokesman who most insistently announced a dreadful alternative to gracious divinely authored salvation is the same great Lord who died and rose to save us from hell.

Scripture is resolute: there is no means of escape *out of* hell. However, the gospel of God's love and mercy shows one way of escape *before* entering. Jesus told it in John 5:24: "Truly, truly, I say to you, whoever hears my word and believes him who sent me has eternal life. He does not come into judgment, but has passed from death to life." The NIV translates it, "He has crossed over from death to life." What a wonderful thing it is for a soul to "cross over"! Jesus firmly declared that you can only do so in this life, before entering an irreversible chamber of unspeakable woe. What you do with Christ right now counts forever.

Puritan writer Thomas Brooks's words are not fashionable in today's "lite" spiritual climate. But Brooks conformed to all we have explored in Luke 16 as he wrote, "Oh, but this word *eternity, eternity, eternity,* this word *everlasting, everlasting, everlasting,* will even break the hearts of the damned in ten thousand pieces! . . . only the impenitent sinner hath no hope in hell. He shall have end without end, death without death, night without day, mourning without mirth, sorrow without solace, and bondage without liberty. The damned shall live as long in hell as God himself shall live in heaven."[8]

For as the new heavens and the new earth that I make
shall remain before me, says the LORD,
    so shall your offspring and your name remain.
From new moon to new moon,
    and from Sabbath to Sabbath,
all flesh shall come to worship before me,
declares the LORD.

And they shall go out and look on the dead bodies of the men who have rebelled against me. For their worm shall not die, their fire shall not be quenched, and they shall be an abhorrence to all flesh.

ISAIAH 66:22-24


And the devil who had deceived them was thrown into the lake of fire and sulfur where the beast and the false prophet were, and they will be tormented day and night forever and ever.

Then I saw a great white throne and him who was seated on it. From his presence earth and sky fled away, and no place was found for them. And I saw the dead, great and small, standing before the throne, and books were opened. Then another book was opened, which is the book of life. And the dead were judged by what was written in the books, according to what they had done. And the sea gave up the dead who were in it, Death and Hades gave up the dead who were in them, and they were judged, each one of them, according to what they had done. Then Death and Hades were thrown into the lake of fire. This is the second death, the lake of fire. And if anyone's name was not found written in the book of life, he was thrown into the lake of fire.

REVELATION 20:10-15

*CHAPTER EIGHT*

# DOES HELL LAST FOREVER?

☼

*TUESDAY, SEPTEMBER 11, 2001. AMERICA'S* unforgettable date with terrorism happened to be this pastor's weekly day off. After a late breakfast at home, for an unknown reason I turned on CNN, something I rarely do at nine o'clock in the morning. What I saw made me immediately call my wife into the room. We stared speechless at a World Trade Center tower with black smoke pouring from it. We had not gotten our bearings on what we were seeing when, minutes later, we watched as a second passenger plane crashed into the other tower. I recall saying, "This is terrorism. And we just watched thousands of people die, before our eyes!" Later, my mind searched for any comparable moment in television news history—a real-time event of horror unfolding as cameras rolled. All I could think of was Lee Harvey Oswald's face contorted in pain as Jack Ruby shot him at point-blank range on Sunday morning November 24, 1963.

## THE INCONCEIVABLE HORROR

When I preached the core material of the previous three chapters and this one to my congregation on topics related to the Bible's view of hell, the same gut-wrenching horror I experienced in watching the World Trade Center on 9/11 gripped me for weeks. To prepare and deliver four messages on hell brought me into a dark room of spiritual oppression. I asked a few close friends who would take the request seriously to provide a shield of prayer. To speak about hell in serious tones is to enter a subject so overwhelming that neither speaker nor listener can be at ease. The topic holds no attraction for a sane mind; it is intolerable to dwell upon. Our cramped souls could not cope with a full-orbed revelation of hell any more than we could digest a more detailed revelation of heaven. Our capacity for either vision is too small.

One outspoken author who disavows the Bible's view of hell concluded that even the most conservative preachers now shrink from preaching on endless suffering in hell. He theorized that this silence constitutes proof that the classic doctrine itself is false: "Reticence [to preach on hell] is not so much due to lack of integrity in proclaiming the truth as to not having the stomach to preach a doctrine that amounts to sadism raised to new levels of finesse. . . . I take the silence of fundamentalist preachers to be testimony to their longing for a revised doctrine of the nature of hell."[1] The late Clark Pinnock was dead wrong about this (no pun intended). The version of hell found in Holy Scripture is simply so awesome that even those who accept it as from God tremble upon approaching it. We fear speaking too glibly about the great abyss of lost souls.

Hell certainly is declared by divine revelation in both Old Testament and New. Isaiah closed out his prophecy with God's vision of new heavens and a new earth as the eternal dwelling of righteous souls (66:22–23). But his final verse declares the parallel destiny for unbelief in a haunting image: "their worm shall not die" (66:24). Jesus Christ and all major authors of the New Testament expounded on the nature of hell's soul-consuming terror; it is the ultimate disaster for which salvation by the cross is interposed to spare believers in Christ.

Every time we mention hell, we realize that real people we interact with every day will experience it, just as hundreds of ordinary New Yorkers did while sipping morning coffee at their eighty-story-high Manhattan work stations. An astonishing fireball descended without warning, as an airliner loaded with jet fuel plowed into their World Trade Center offices. Personal souvenirs and framed family pictures on desks were obliterated. Human bodies were incinerated. Others who had some minutes to sort out their alternatives leaped to sure death in the street below rather than face unimaginable devastation inside a building which moments before was a man-made safe haven. Considering such things, if any preacher can speak about hell without tears in his eyes and his heart genuinely traumatized, you should worry about his mental state and simultaneously question the suitability of his ordination.

## 9/11 WAS TEMPORAL, NOT ETERNAL

Comparing hell to what happened in the Twin Towers is not really accurate, because amazingly that event of America's unbearable national pain is "too mild" to sustain the comparison! People who died on that day in 2001 were not being punished for their spiritual condition of unbelief, and many surely were received in the arms of their Lord and Savior. For all the terror that occurred on a fair September Tuesday, most 9/11 deaths happened swiftly; then it was over, as the great cloud of ash swirled in New York's streets. We must try to realize—though it is almost impossible to do it—that hell is not an issue of a few hours or one day. It has no terminus, not ever!

The Bible says hell is a place of great anguish, isolation, regret, and pain. Jesus declared it is the woeful destination for those who finally reject God's last overtures of grace. Hell is painted in vivid Bible metaphors, and too often we get lost in debating the specific figures of speech used—such as "fire" and the undying "worm"—without recognizing that the *reality* being portrayed by any metaphor must in fact be worse than any figure of speech depicting it. Mere words cannot carry the weightiness of this infinite depth. Hell is a place prepared for the Devil and his angels, but shared by some human beings. And hell is eternal. This would be intolerable if the great emphasis of Scripture did not herald that in Christ alone there is a sure way of escape.

We now engage the issue of the biblical *duration* of hell. Does hell have permanent occupants who continue an unresting existence and suffer unendingly? Or is it possible that lost souls are simply blotted out of existence after judgment, extinguished like a candle flame in the wind? This seems to be the hardest of all questions to ask about the biblical hell. Some do accept it as logical that irresolute unbelief should incur some just penalty from a holy God, but cannot bear the mental and emotional pressure involved with imagining unending suffering or woe for people we loved on the earth. That hell happens at all, therefore, becomes reason enough for some to declare themselves in favor of a doctrine known as annihilationism, which superficially seems more humane, though in fact it is not.

Mature Bible interpretation in this case requires us to take hold of our minds by the scruff of our theological necks, forcing ourselves to see that doctrines of Scripture must not be determined by what we happen to prefer, or what our human emotions are capable of tolerating. We must determine to stick to *who God is* and not construct an artificial universe with contours drawn by our own whims.

## DOES HELL MEAN EXTINCTION?

In early centuries a scattered few Christian thinkers held what is classically called the annihilationist position: the argument that declares that hell's judgment spells total extinction for lost souls. From the fourth century onward a minority of Christian scholars began to teach that after a historic general resurrection and God's day of judgment, the lost experience soul and body reunited, only to then be extinguished from any conscious state, as God's coup de grâce of condemnation. This idea was condemned as a heresy numerous times at church councils. Yet in the late twentieth century it emerged with renewed strength, advocated most often by some who did not appear to respect Scripture as God's Word, but surprisingly entertained by a few who do hold a high view of biblical authority.

Not all advocates of annihilationism should necessarily be dismissed as being apostate for asking tough questions along this line. The late John R. W. Stott was a Bible expositor of great wisdom and discernment. His commentaries are uniformly excellent, and as a Christlike evangelical leader, Stott had few peers. Late in his career he ventured tentatively into the annihilationist camp, and voices roundly condemned him as if this negated the entirety of his formidable gospel ministry. Stott wrote, "The ultimate annihilation of the wicked should at least be accepted as a legitimate, biblically founded alternative to their eternal conscious torment."[2] Without agreeing with him, we must say that John Stott was one opponent of the traditional view of hell who moved cautiously toward annihilationism, never lobbing blasphemous denials of God in the process. A helpful principle that guides me in matters of doctrine says we must distinguish between Bible truth, mistaken opinion, isolated error, systemic error, and heresy. According to that spectrum, I believe John Stott held to either an isolated or systemic error, as do other annihilationists. But there are others whose assaults against God and Scripture in this subject area do approach heresy.

Annihilationist arguments pivot mainly on Bible references to "destruction" and "perishing." The contention is that celestial "fire"—whatever that turns out to be—must burn up an object until it no longer exists. It is rightly pointed out that immortality is the essential property and possession only of God himself and those upon whom he bestows it (1 Tim. 6:16). Thus, annihilationist reasoning claims that *immortality* is Christ's unique gift bestowed to his redeemed; it is not man's proprietary possession to be continued in a nonglorified final state. (Their logic is sound up to this point.) Their train derails when they next insist that *extinction* of the lost is the only possible alternative to being an "immortal" bearer of Christ's resurrection life. You're either immortal, or as a reprobate you no longer exist. They say that since John 3:16 declares that those who have believed in Jesus will "not perish," apart from this faith, you will indeed perish—and "perish" has to mean all existence ceases.

To be fair, many texts do speak about hell in terms of "destruction." One is Matthew 10:28, where Jesus tells us to "fear [God] who can destroy both soul and body in hell." First Thessalonians 5:3 also says that at the Lord's great second coming, unbelievers will find that "sudden destruction will come upon them as labor pains come upon a pregnant woman, and they will not escape." Second Peter 3:7 speaks of the "destruction of the ungodly." So people naturally ask: "Don't words like 'destroy' or 'perish' mean the complete *end* of that human person?" We'll return to answer this in a moment.

A second argument made by annihilationism says that to imagine anyone suffering unending pain and woe for sins committed on this earth in historic time, when one's sin may have been launched perhaps by flawed thinking, a momentary weakness, being victimized by someone else, or self-deceit, seems a travesty of justice for a merciful God to tolerate. Dr. Clark Pinnock in later years of his life appeared to move beyond boundaries of classic evangelicalism, which he once championed. His comments against Scripture on this subject contain bitter invective. Pinnock asked, "What purpose of God would be served by the torture of the wicked except sheer vengeance and vindictiveness? . . . Unending torment would be the kind of utterly pointless and wasted suffering which would never lead to anything good beyond it. Furthermore, it would amount to inflicting infinite suffering upon those who had committed finite sins. . . . There would be a serious disproportion between sins committed in time and the suffering experienced forever."[3] He estimated that it is absurd to think of God meting out unlimited eternal penalties upon what Pinnock deemed to be only *limited* human offenses. In a word, to him the punishment simply did not fit the crime.

Third, annihilation advocates declare that a hell of endless suffering cannot coexist with God's *love*. This is similar to the previous contention, but it is distinct because it deals not with justice. Now the very heart of God's character is called into question. Hear Clark Pinnock once more: "How can Christians possibly project a deity of such cruelty and vindictiveness? Surely a God who would do this is more like Satan than like God."[4]

In perfect candor, we might all admit our own emotions to be sympathetically drawn toward annihilationism. Who wants to defend endless suffering? We're not sadistic monsters. Human impulse will definitely favor the annihilationist view because it seems the most compassionate by far. However, emotion alone is hardly the final arbiter in any matter of doctrine.

## THE BIBLE'S CASE FOR ETERNAL SUFFERING

As we respond to several main contentions raised by annihilationism, I will defend the position the mainstream of Christian orthodoxy has held for two thousand years. Despite tempting initial plausibility of annihilationism, close inquiry reveals too many weaknesses. Hard as it may be for anyone's sentiment to swallow, the Bible's greater evidence falls upon a doctrine of hell involving wrath meted out in justice, with woe, regret, and pain that is endless in duration.

First, let us consider New Testament words that speak of "destruction" and "perishing." The Greek words involved can have multiple meanings depending on their context. The *New Oxford American Dictionary* does give as the primary meaning for destroy as: "to put an end to the existence of something." However, the second given meaning is: "to ruin or spoil something; to ruin emotionally or spiritually." It is this secondary meaning the Bible often intends—the ruination of primary *function*, purpose, or usefulness, while the person or object continues to exist. Once I used a wood chisel and it hit a concrete surface, breaking off a large corner of the cutting blade. I could have said, in a biblical manner, "I just *destroyed* a chisel." I had ruined the steel cutting tool for its intended purpose, and it resides years later untouched in a drawer, of no value to me for fulfilling the tasks for which it was forged.

Can we understand similarly that *people* may suffer biblical "destruction" and yet still exist in their spiritually ruined state? In Matthew 9:17 the Greek word "destroy" describes a wineskin that has burst so it can no longer hold wine as it was made to do. When Jesus spoke about a "lost" coin or "lost" son in Luke 15, the word he used carried this meaning of being in effect ruined, though the things continued to exist. What human tragedy is worse than knowing that your God-created function to glorify God and enjoy him forever can no longer be fulfilled, while your soul continues existing as an empty shell of the divine image bearer you were created to be?

A second obstacle to annihilationism are other passages that speak of eternal suffering and eternal life as paired opposites, contrasted in the same verse, such as the separation of the sheep and the goats in Matthew 25:46. Jesus said, "And these will go away into eternal punishment, but the righteous into eternal life." The word *aionion* for "eternal" cannot mean two different things when used in the same sentence involving a direct comparison.[5] Gospel commentator Scot McKnight wrote: "'Eternal' modifies both punishment and life in Matthew 25:46. . . . However long the life extends is how long the punishment lasts, the durations are identical. It is grammatically unsuitable to drive a wedge between these."[6] Logic requires that if Christ spoke of eternal life in heaven and eternal destruction in hell in the same sentence, and we accept that the adjective for the heavenly destination is everlasting—without a terminus—the other must mean the same thing.

Revelation 14:11 speaks of lost people in a grim declaration: "And the smoke of their torment goes up forever and ever, and they have no rest, day or night, these worshipers of the beast and its image." It is hard to make that verse mean anything other than its plain statement. Robert Peterson wrote, "Despite attempts to prove otherwise, Revelation 14:9–11 unequivocally teaches that hell entails eternal conscious torment for the lost. In fact if we had only this passage, we would be obligated to teach the traditional doctrine of hell on the authority of the Word of God."[7] Peterson goes on to give a solemn warning to any who would avoid aspects of the Bible's teaching they dislike or feel offended by. Repentance and a submission of our wayward minds to God's truth is required from honest students of the Word.

I do not intend a full exegetical treatment of the text of Revelation 20. But I quoted it at the opening of this chapter because it is the final time hell is mentioned in the Bible. Telling of Satan's conclusive consignment to destruction, Revelation 20:10 says that in a "lake of fire" he will be "tormented day and night forever." Then 20:15 adds, "If anyone's name was not found written in the book of life, he was thrown into the lake of fire." How could humans once cast into this inferno be utterly obliterated in it unless Satan enjoyed the same relief? And we are clearly told that he does not.

## AGAINST WHOM DO WE SIN?

On the matter of God's supposed injustice in the face of eternal suffering, the reply of classic theology is that sin in any form is an assault upon the Holy God in all his perfections. David was right in his prayer confessing to murder and adultery when he told the Lord, "Against you, *you only*, have I sinned and done what is evil in your sight" (Ps. 51:4). Hell is without limitation of endurance because every offense punished there is a blow struck against *God* himself—the one Being who is all goodness, justice, and perfection. "The doctrine of hell confronts us with a God who is overwhelming in his anger [against sin], irresistible in his power, terrifying in his justice. A mighty Sovereign, who holds the earth between his fingers like a pinch of dust."[8]

This concept of God is certainly well-represented in Scripture, but almost never heard in contemporary feel-good churches, let alone by agnostic unbelievers. People simply do not want to have a God like that and will do whatever is necessary to subvert him. Nevertheless, this God is in total control of all things, and he is entirely just. "All the inhabitants of the earth are accounted as nothing, and he does according to his will among the host of heaven and among the inhabitants of the earth; and none can stay his hand or say to him, 'What have you done?'" (Dan. 4:35). Until people know the God of the Bible, they will not believe in hell. Intolerance of the God revealed in Scripture is the real problem.

We human beings tend to speak about "little sins" and "white lies" only because we have little concept of God's holy grandeur. James 2:10 declares, "For whoever keeps the whole law but fails in one point has become accountable for all of it." All sin is an *infinite* crime, because it screams to the infinite, eternal God, "I hate you and I defy you!" Clark Pinnock and others who cite that hell's punishment is "disproportionate" to the sin of a moment can make that claim only because no one sees the enormity of crimes against an infinitely holy God! "We are in no position to criticize the penalty because we have little understanding of the extent of the guilt involved," states Edward Donnelley. "Our concept of sin is utterly inadequate. Even the most sensitive conscience has little awareness of sin's true wickedness and we are simply not competent to assess how much punishment it deserves."[9]

Think of Isaiah the prophet, who found his knees turning to jelly in the presence of a grand vision in the temple. He saw God "high and lifted up," while seraphim called to one another, "Holy, holy, holy is the LORD of hosts; the whole earth is full of his glory!" (Isa. 6:1–3). The prophet wailed, "Woe is me! For I am lost; for I am a man of unclean lips" (6:5). Alec Motyer commented, "There is that in the nature of God which means ruination for sinners. Yet the actual sin Isaiah confessed [unclean speech] seems (to us) a comical anticlimax! We hardly recognize this as sin at all. . . . Isaiah, however, experienced a moment of truth. He saw sin as it appears in the awesome splendor and terror of the divine holiness . . . the flashing forth of the pure moral glory and passion of God against anything and everything that offends him."[10] This is the nub of the entire issue. No man or woman will accept the biblical doctrine of hell until they too, have had Isaiah's "moment of truth." Holiness eludes us until we fall on our faces before it. God's holiness can and will destroy the unconfessed sinner. Once we see this, all the objections of annihilationists and others to a biblical view of hell are so much fine dust.

As to annihilationism's alleged contradiction of the *love* of God, it was divine love that led Jesus Christ to his cross, where he met the awesome pain of hell and condemnation for us, and cried out, "My God, my God, why have you forsaken me?" (Matt. 27:46). Imagine this: God the Son abandoned by God the Father! The *cross* was everything hell is: a divine curse, a cup of pure wrath for sin that was not Jesus's own, abandonment of the Son by God the Father, physical torments, shame, and death. Jesus drained dry the foaming cup of God's wrath predicted in Jeremiah 25:15–29. Why was all this visited upon Jesus? Because God *loved* those he determined to save from before the foundation of this world. His love acted powerfully to prevent the ruinous condemnation of hell from resting upon his elect. If sin is trivial, would God ever have devised the tremendous plan of the cross with his Son as its hero and victim? Edward Donnelley said it well: "If we lose hell, we will eventually lose the cross, for if there is no hell, there ultimately is no point in the cross. The cross and hell stand or fall together. Hell is extreme, but that is because sin is extreme."[11]

The wrath of God is not about cruelty but perfect justice. The love of God is not defined by human sentimentality. Wrath and justice are the dark side of a fierce love like no other. At the cross "righteousness and peace kiss each other" (Ps. 85:10). Accept that the full sunshine of God's great love beams on his redeemed people in heaven, and you find that the logical corollary is the blast of his abhorrence for all sin, poured out in hell. Sinners demand a "loving God," but what they seek is meaningless mush. God displayed his love in the errand of his Son to bear the Father's wrath in our place, and they will have nothing to do with it. They trample on his cross and then protest: "Give me divine love!" They would have divine love make no demands upon those who willfully refuse its entreaty. What utter gall for anyone to say the doctrine of hell is "not loving." Christ the Son endured this hell on his cross so men might escape it. And they continue to spit in God's eye.

We could explore this matter in many more texts. My aim is not to be exhaustive but to sketch main arguments and counterarguments in large strokes. The Bible defends the hard concept of eternal suffering for the lost, not the relatively superficial answer of annihilationism. We may wish it otherwise, but the evidence is too clear.

## HELL'S (ALARM) BELLS

Does such a hard-edged doctrine teach us anything beneficial? For one thing, as we were instructed in kindergarten, it reminds us to color within the lines. If you would believe authentic biblical doctrine, you must firmly grasp the most prickly truths of Scripture just as willingly as you receive truths that delight you. We have to follow the Bible everywhere it leads, not reshape it to our own desires. Hell alarms us as nothing else can about the awful weight and penalty of sin. My own sinful nature is a loathsome, malignant cancer. Being capable of even one sin, I am equally capable of any monstrosity any man has ever committed.

Furthermore, we must reject naive assumptions that any human beings are naturally headed for heaven. This belief cannot be backed up in plain biblical teaching. As we saw in John 3:18, hell is our default destination from birth. Jesus refuted the idea that any person can ever deserve heaven as a man-centered delusion. Hell is our default destination. If we all deserve hell, no one in hell can possibly rail against God for unjustly sending him there. God really does not do this sending: people are in hell with no one to blame but themselves. Those who enter heaven do so only by God's sheer grace and mercy in Christ Jesus.

Contemplating hell even for a few minutes ought to quicken a true Christian toward fervent evangelistic prayer and thoughtful witness. Real people we all know and cherish are headed for this awful destination. You have no certain knowledge of the future destiny of your mailman, that helpful coworker in the next cubicle, or the person who cuts your hair. Would that God might use us to turn some of them to Christ!

In the 1960s, Dr. Francis Schaeffer taught college students about Christianity at his L'Abri center in the mountains of Switzerland. Once during a discussion at a meal, someone asked Dr. Schaeffer, "What will happen to those who have never heard of Christ?" Everyone was eager to hear what this noted theologian would say in response to that important question. No answer came. In a moment everyone realized Schaeffer had bowed his head and was weeping silently.[12] Can we handle this doctrine with any less profound compassion and sobriety?

## THROW A TRAFFIC CONE

British evangelist John Blanchard tells about a major highway accident that occurred in 1984 in dense fog near Surrey, south of London. Dozens of cars were wrecked in a chain reaction crash, and ten people were killed. As police arrived, they ran back from the accident scene toward oncoming traffic to warn drivers to stop. They waved their arms, shouted frantically, and finally resorted to throwing traffic cones at speeding vehicles, as most drivers heedlessly rushed right by, only to smash into the carnage ahead. One officer told of tears streaming down his face as car after car went past; he found he was mentally timing the moments until each one's screeching impact with the growing mass of wreckage.[13]

Perhaps you and I need to do some strenuous arm-waving to warn others, since we know what is immediately ahead after death if they do not hit the spiritual brakes and repent before God. (You might even consider your own version of throwing a traffic cone.)

It is not possible to be liked for preaching the Bible's doctrine of hell. But what if we are used by God's Spirit to save someone from it? Hear this word from Jonathan Edwards: "Some talk of it as an unreasonable thing to fright persons to heaven, but I think it is a reasonable thing to endeavor to fright persons away from hell. They stand upon its brink and are just ready to fall into it, and are senseless of their danger. Is it not a reasonable thing to fright a person out of a house on fire?"[14]

After considering this brief biblical case for the awesome nature of a hell of endless suffering, do you better comprehend the rescue mission of Jesus? Only the highest One of all was capable of plunging so low. Have you glimpsed in hell's howling wasteland, "the love of Christ that surpasses knowledge" (Eph. 3:19), lifting us from this fate forever? Do you now estimate the infinite worthiness of your Savior's death? Christ Jesus "descended into hell" upon his cross—enduring its holocaust so you would not have to. You must choose: either trust that the gospel is true when it says Jesus drank God's wrath down to the dregs in your place, or drink it yourself. Why would anyone do that?

# PART THREE

# ONE MINUTE AFTER A CHRISTIAN'S DEATH

You have come to Mount Zion and to the city of the living God . . . and to the assembly of the firstborn who are enrolled in heaven, and to God, the judge of all, and to the spirits of the righteous made perfect, and to Jesus, the mediator of a new covenant.

HEBREWS 12:22-24

For we know that if the tent that is our earthly home is destroyed, we have a building from God, a house not made with hands, eternal in the heavens. For in this tent we groan, longing to put on our heavenly dwelling, if indeed by putting it on we may not be found naked. For while we are still in this tent, we groan, being burdened—not that we would be unclothed, but that we would be further clothed, so that what is mortal may be swallowed up by life. He who has prepared us for this very thing is God, who has given us the Spirit as a guarantee.

So we are always of good courage. We know that while we are at home in the body we are away from the Lord, for we walk by faith, not by sight. Yes, we are of good courage, and we would rather be away from the body and at home with the Lord.

2 CORINTHIANS 5:1-8

Yet which I shall choose I cannot tell. I am hard pressed between the two. My desire is to depart and be with Christ, for that is far better.

PHILIPPIANS 1:22B-23

# CHAPTER NINE

# THE IMMEDIATE HEAVEN

☼

*A MAN ONCE SHARED WITH* me his supposition regarding the hardest task of a pastor's calling. He said, "When many are grief-stricken at a funeral, I wonder how you address all that raw emotion?" He was surprised when I told him that, as ministry opportunities go, it is often easier to connect with an audience at a funeral than it is at many weddings. I explained that frequently at weddings many attendees regard the pastor with polite but poorly disguised boredom. They have come for a happy celebration and wish that what they interpret to be dull religious preliminaries might end quickly so their plans for food, drink, dancing, and joyful frivolity can begin. But at funerals, even many non-church-goers are weighing somber matters about the end of life. They are hurting emotionally and asking silent questions they may not have seriously considered too often. I can confidently address them, because of Christ's resurrection and its transforming consequences for those who trust in him. Many will definitely listen to the message. Paradoxically, funerals are occasions when more folks tend to be all ears.

We now seek Scripture's reply to probably the most crucial inquiry in this book. The question, what happens to a Christian one minute after death? What does the Bible predict as the immediate reality every believer redeemed in Jesus Christ should expect when the physical body expires? We have covered the opposite fate for unbelievers in four previous chapters, and you should join me in great relief to have that material behind us. Now we speak only about what is ahead for Christian believers.

## DESIRING THIS WORLD TOO MUCH

Modern people harbor innate skepticism about eternal life primarily because it is so difficult to conceive of anything superior to our present life. Society surrounds most of us with such comforts and protections, we can scarcely imagine losing our positions in the La-Z-Boy recliner of the American good life. Sure, you might hate your job. Maybe you do not even have a job at the moment. You have financial struggles and family strife, and the evening news all too often is really disturbing. Yet when a circle of good old boys around a campfire on the TV beer commercial draws the conclusion "It just doesn't get any better than this," you need not be a beer aficionado for that general sentiment to strike a chord. Present-day life is grand in many particular ways.

If you hold an object as small as a quarter close enough to your eye, it blots out your view of the sun. Similarly, the relative goodness of material comforts discovered by being alive on earth can impede our sight of eternal things. This life for all its disappointments and struggles still affords many sweet moments. Who wants to depart from it for what is relatively unknown?

Scripture promises every Christian that it really does get much better than this, in fact, beyond the best we can imagine! Souls united to Christ by his redemptive grace do not "wait" for centuries in some ethereal holding pen until the second coming of Jesus before drinking deep of eternal glory. Moments after bodily death, believing souls shall behold the face of Christ their Lord. The Christian's next experience immediately upon death will be absolute security, dazzling sights, and thrilling experiences. The Westminster Shorter Catechism summarizes the New Testament view of this, as question 37 asks, "What benefits do believers receive from Christ immediately at death?" The answer stipulates, "The *souls* of believers at their death are made perfect in holiness and they do pass immediately into glory; and their bodies, being still united to Christ do rest in their graves until the resurrection." Let us examine some key texts to further open up this subject.

## THE SPIRITS OF RIGHTEOUS MEN

The author of Hebrews used a dramatic metaphor in chapter 12 of his letter, contrasting the radical difference between faith based only upon God's law and Mount Sinai where the presence of God was all burning fire, darkness, and gloom, versus the wonderful, welcoming prospect of "Mount Zion . . . the heavenly Jerusalem" (Heb. 12:22). Those who are in Christ today stand in spiritual solidarity with "innumerable angels in festal gathering." All these servants of God join us in singing the praise of

Christ our Lord. Hebrews 12:23 then explicitly names "*the spirits* of the righteous made perfect" as being among this heavenly assembly. Here is a clear description of believers who have departed earth and are with Christ today. They are not ghosts, but perfected souls. They are the "general assembly" and "the church of the firstborn." Their companions are angels and their Lord is Christ the Mediator and Judge of all. A similar reference to righteous persons in a post-death position is found when Revelation 6:9 speaks about "the *souls* of those who had been slain for the word of God and for the witness they had borne." This vision shows Christian martyrs of the past evidently existing as disembodied souls, already securely redeemed, but awaiting their final historic resurrection.

We conclude that after death and before the return of Christ, every believer continues to exist as a perfected soul, glorified in Jesus's righteousness. Evangelical theology shares the broad consensus that in biblical terms, "soul" (*psyche*) means the same thing as "spirit" (*pneuma*). The two terms stand for a single reality. When God created human beings in his divine image, giving mankind his breath (Gen. 2:7), he made us spirit/soul. Rational thought, abstract reasoning, willful choices, and spoken and written language all arise from this God-shaped bestowment. Jesus said true worship of God that communes with him happens "in spirit" (John 4:24). Thus, our finest intimacy with God is not conducted on the plane of mere physicality, nor in the rational mind, but in the dimension of the spiritual "me" that was made for eternity: my soul.

We still want to know what exactly a soul/spirit *is*. We cannot weigh or measure or draw a picture of a soul. Are souls ever visible? It has always helped me to understand that my soul is inseparable from the absolute essence of "me." I am able to lose my body and still exist, but I cannot lose my soul. If that happened, I would perish. A soul is not a spiritual possession, like a small cloud hovering inside me which could be taken away and "I" would still function without it. Men and women *are* souls! Right now, our souls are unified with a physical body giving us visibility and permitting language, sexual intimacy, friendship, and community relations with other humans. What becomes of souls after death when our bodies no longer function?

People worry whether in eternity they will be able to make love to a spouse, throw a Frisbee to their dog (or will there be a dog?), read books, or play eighteen holes of golf. By musing on such notions we show that our minds are more bound up in this material world than in the one to come. Our curiosity overreaches what God's Word intends to reveal. We must tread with considerable caution, in order to stick close to what has been made known in Scripture.

The dominant emphasis of Hebrews 12:23 is that at death, sanctification is completed for the "spirits/souls" of men and women in Christ who dwell in him today. They are "perfected." They lack no good gift of God except their promised final bodies of Christ-like glory. Being perfected means no longer committing sin and having no regrets; every struggle with temptation is banished, and there can be no more fractured, painful relationships. The judgment of divine justice does not await these souls of the "righteous," because that judgment wrath was spent on their behalf, upon Christ.

## DISEMBODIED SOULS

In 1 Corinthians 15 Paul famously predicted the second coming of Christ when believers will receive resurrection bodies, at history's final consummation. There Paul seems to assume he would personally be alive on earth when the second coming of Christ happened, since in 1 Corinthians 15:51 he said, "We shall not all sleep"—that is, some will live to witness the great return. In an early Pauline letter, 1 Thessalonians, the apostle twice included himself among "*we* who are alive" (4:15, 17) at the second coming of Jesus, as distinct from other believers who had previously died, whom Christ would "bring with him" (4:14).

Second Corinthians was written near the end of Paul's days, when there were clear reasons both personal and political for him to anticipate not living much longer. In 4:16–5:8 he had become pensive about a probability of his own physical death preceding the great day. He seemed to include himself as among those affected when saying, "If the tent that is our earthly home is destroyed . . ." (5:1). He qualified his own future, allowing for the possibility, if not probability, that he could die before Christ's return.

Second Corinthians 5:1–8 is viewed as one of only a few passages that crystallize what happens to the believer immediately after death. We must dissect this passage as a foundation for informed hope. We first note Paul's firm declaration in 5:1: "we *know*." The verb in the original language implies knowledge gained by intuition or revelation rather than by reasoning. The apostle is not speculating; the Spirit of God gave him certainty in this matter. Nothing less than God's sure promise of a new, more glorious resurrection body enabled Paul to consider dissolution of his own earthly frame with calm composure. We generally regard our earth-bodies as the epitome of human personhood. By comparison, whatever our eternal persona may be like after death seems like a puff of smoke. Yet our text turns that thinking inside out. This firm flesh I dwell in today is called a "tent," while the body guaranteed to me by the resurrection power of Jesus is a "building." The truly substantial existence is the one still to come!

As I write, thousands of impoverished Haitians still dwell in tent cities more than a year after a devastating earthquake shook their island. Even the best quality tent is a poor substitute dwelling for a building made of wood, brick, or stone. Tent stakes loosen and the roofline sags. Fabric seams eventually leak in the rain, while wind and cold penetrate the walls. Privacy is scarce in any tent. Tent housing is an option from which anyone would be impatient to escape. Can we allow our minds to be trained by Scripture to accept this new paradigm, which values our present bodies as no better than tents? May we join Paul in a conscious reversal of thinking concerning what constitutes truly solid shelter that is "eternal in the heavens"? Only those who are convinced that they lack any permanent dwelling on earth will begin to long for "a city that has foundations, whose designer and builder is God" (Heb. 11:10).

The "building" described in 2 Corinthians 5:1 in its ultimate sense is our resurrection body. Paul was fully mindful there was a logical and metaphysical "gap" between the moment of death and the time of receiving the resurrection body. Yet God did not speak through Paul to define what this experience would be like. Paul claimed no direct revelation about it. Yet he was not threatened by it as a disruption to his soul's security. God will securely shelter the believer's disembodied soul until our new resurrection body is delivered at last.

## WHAT DOES NAKEDNESS MEAN HERE?

Some find Paul's words in 2 Corinthians 5:2–4 confusing. What does "being found naked" mean? The simplest idea is that "naked" must mean a redeemed soul lacks a body to "wear." However, the full understanding goes deeper. In Scripture, "nakedness" commonly represents a state of exposure to shame—standing unprotected before God's righteous judgment. Think of Adam and Eve in Genesis 3:7 hunting for fig leaves, or Isaiah the prophet walking about naked as a living symbol of divine judgment coming upon negligent unbelief (Isa. 20:2–4). On various occasions Old Testament prophets depicted God's unfaithful covenant people as a prostitute with "your nakedness uncovered in your whorings with your lovers, and with all your abominable idols" (Ezek. 16:36). Unprotected exposure to God in the shame of our sins is the true nakedness.

In 2 Corinthians 5, ultimate protection from naked exposure to eternal condemnation requires a heavenly dwelling; a resurrection body will "house" us in the shelter of Jesus's righteousness. When Paul considers that he might die before the Lord returns to bestow the resurrection body, he naturally wonders how he will be protected *until* then. "His attention is now focused upon the intermediate period between sowing of the earthly body (in the grave) and the reaping of a heavenly body."[1]

The idea of a human being existing as a soul without a body was difficult for any Hebrew mind, since the Bible more commonly sees man as a body-and-soul unity. It was Plato who famously popularized the dualistic ideal that a soul was better off without encapsulation in a body of flesh. Although the thought progression in 2 Corinthians 5:1–8 is a bit complex to follow, the end result is not. Even if his soul—the essence of Paul's selfhood—was without its body immediately after death, Paul knew that no justified believer could be "found naked." The horrifying prospect of nakedness was the unthinkable fear of facing God without a Mediator and Redeemer. Since the believer has already "put on" Christ as a righteous covering against shame, the loss of a physical body cannot separate us from him (Rom. 8:39). "We are already incorporated into the heavenly body of Christ himself."[2] Paul knew his soul was "covered" by his unshakeable solidarity with the living Christ. He anticipated that his immediate after-death experience would include being "swallowed up by life" (2 Cor. 5:4)!

## GROANING FOR A GUARANTEE

Second Corinthians 5:2–4 speaks of Paul "groaning." Was this mortal *fear* of death expressing itself? Not necessarily. Spiritual "nakedness" was not something to fear. It is better to conclude that a "groan" from Paul evoked positive-spirited but impatient longing to grasp a wonderful promise. Second Corinthians 5:5 asserts that even if soul and body are to be separated for a span of time, it is *God* who made us for this very purpose. God will superintend the entire project of our redemption. Best of all, verse 5 reminds us God has "given us the Spirit as a guarantee." Every Christian has a substantial down payment against the final heavenly resurrection, assuring us that the remainder will be received in due time. When you make a 20 percent down payment on a house purchase, even though the bank owns 80 percent of the residence, you can at least tell yourself that, given diligence in making mortgage payments, you will one day realize full ownership. Similarly, a foretaste of my future consummation in Christ is already mine by the indwelling Spirit. The Holy Spirit testifies that heaven is our home and the resurrection body is our destiny. If you don't believe that God will finish a permanent home in heaven for you, then ask yourself: why would he have sent his architect and master builder—the Holy Spirit—to reside in you today, launching his spiritual renewal project? The Spirit's construction trailer is already parked in your heart.

Our present groaning for a new existence after death may be compared to a woman's groan in the pains of childbirth. The reality of a child's arrival presses upon the mother, and she is consumed by the sure prospect of this gift from God appearing soon. Romans 8:22 says that the natural created cosmos "has been groaning together in the pains of childbirth until now," awaiting final redemption by the Lord first for believers and then the natural order of creation. We groan from eager anticipation for what is just ahead. We have tasted heaven in Spirit-led knowledge of Christ. Our dim, fragmentary views of God's glory have us hungering for more. Those who have never tasted of heaven at all because they do not know Christ desire only the earth they know, and they fear everything else. But a believer's anticipation of what is ahead is not fear-based, but faith-hungry.

## SOULS GATHERED TO CHRIST

Second Corinthians 5:8 climaxes in the statement, "We would rather be away from the body and *at home* with the Lord." Here is the greatest depth of comfort to dying believers or their families. The word *home* is a powerful emotional anchor. A rather cynical definition I once heard said, "Home is that place where, no matter when you turn up or in what condition, they must take you in." We should prefer a more positive understanding. Home ought to be the dwelling place of people we love the best—a place of familiarity, reunion, fellowship, safety, and trust. As I get older, I cherish the simple pleasure of having at least a couple evenings each week free from ministry duties, just to be at home with my wife. As I look ahead in my weekly planner, I may write "Home" in bold letters over an evening when I believe I can be sure of being there. Writing it down as an actual appointment seems to certify for me a pleasure keenly anticipated. At home, I might build a fire in the fireplace, call family or friends on the phone, read a novel, or watch a movie. These welcome activities represent personal rest and delight.

We presently dwell under the fog of confusion that says *this* life is home. We need continual reminding that this is pure deception. The only true home for a Christian is where God our Father and Christ the Lord are found. The Bible defines heaven as that place where God himself dwells and sovereignly rules. Proximity to his holy Being is the core of that home, much as my wife's companionship transforms any locale into a home for me now. Revelation 21:3 has this resounding statement about heaven: "Behold, the *dwelling place* of God is with man. He will dwell with them, and they will be his people, and God himself will be with them as their God." That is the absolute consummation of God's covenant, begun in the Old Testament. Face-to-face union with our Savior is the anchor reality of our everlasting heavenly home. Samuel Rutherford said, "If heaven could be without Christ, what could we do there?"[3]

In 2 Corinthians 5:8, Paul expected no interruption from the moment of physical death to conscious awareness of our heavenly home—no intermediate stopover, no waiting room. Transition from this body to be home with the Lord will be instantaneous. We depart from the earthly reality and "the dawn of heaven breaks." We will not immediately gain a resurrection body—which was Paul's first preference. Yet conscious souls of the redeemed in Christ shall enjoy unbroken and greatly intensified communion with the Lord Jesus. Today we see him at best by secondary means, "in a mirror dimly, but then face to face. Now I know in part; then I shall know fully, even as I have been fully known" (1 Cor. 13:12).

## IS THIS THE "INTERMEDIATE STATE"?

You may be aware that many theologians and preachers use the term "intermediate state" for this 2 Corinthians 5 existence of our souls in Christ's presence after death, before a general resurrection. That term is an invention of convenience, found nowhere in the Bible. It is often employed by orthodox scholars to describe this biblical "interval." After years of consideration, I have chosen to abandon that terminology, while maintaining exactly the same doctrine as theologians who do use the term. I contend that calling our existence in Christ after death "intermediate" or "interim" is inadequate. The words imply incompleteness, like waiting for the other shoe to drop.

We've all had enough frustrating experiences with taking a number and waiting in line for an appointment. "Intermediate state" sounds too much like a doctor's waiting room; it tends to cloud the degree of joy to be expected in being "at home" with Christ. In name, at least, it calls to mind a long layover at O'Hare airport, squirming for hours on an uncomfortable plastic seat while awaiting a flight for Hawaii. Since Scripture never uses the term "intermediate," I propose using "immediate heaven" as a standard reference because it is accurate and hopeful. Departure from our physical bodies begins the sweet reality of *heaven* for the saints, so let us call it that.

## IMMEDIACY IS THE ISSUE

Numerous texts of Scripture give additional clues about the immediate heaven. In Matthew 10:28 Jesus said, "Do not fear those who kill the body but cannot kill the soul." He obviously meant that we as souls survive whatever happens to our body. Psalm 16:10–11 has David declaring that the Lord will not abandon his body to the grave. Quite otherwise: "In your presence there is fullness of joy; at your right hand are pleasures evermore." Psalm 73:24–26 tells of Asaph's ringing faith in the Lord: "You guide me with your counsel, and afterward you will receive me to glory. Whom have I in heaven but you? And there is nothing on earth I desire besides you. My flesh and my heart may fail, but God is the strength of my heart and my portion forever." Asaph knew God would be his full portion when his flesh was left behind. What these Old Testament saints anticipated was what Paul longed for in 2 Corinthians 5.

Many will also think of the bold reply of Jesus on his cross to the dying thief who said, "Jesus, remember me when you come into your kingdom" (Luke 23:42). Jesus responded: "Truly I say to you, *today* you will be with me in Paradise" (v. 43). That is breathtakingly simple. "Today" cannot mean centuries from now in a dim, unknown future. Jesus predicted an amazing truth to one miserable man to answer his mustard seed of sincere faith. If we might paraphrase him, the dying Lord said, "Friend, you and I shall physically die any moment. And as we depart from this terrible hour of blood and intense agony, we shall instantaneously meet again in the Paradise of God." Scripture labels the wonder of being gathered to our God immediately at death "present with the Lord" (2 Cor. 5:8, KJV). The term "paradise" that Jesus used on the cross meant in that time a walled garden; Jesus was talking about God's own sanctuary of repose and calm. Do we need to know more than this in advance, in order to desire it?

As seen in a previous chapter, if we are committed to the Bible alone as the exclusive sourcebook on life after death, the religious construct of purgatory as an intermediate position for souls departed has no place in this discussion. Purgatory is a wishful fiction, based on the unbiblical idea that our works after death can bring purification to a salvation which the gospel says is totally based on God's grace in the first place. At death, souls of believers are immediately with Christ. The nonbeliever is elsewhere. Those are the only options.

## FAR BETTER

Remember also that in Philippians 1:21 the apostle called his death a "gain." He said that to "depart and be with Christ . . . is *far better*" (v. 23). The apostle was honestly torn by desire to die today, versus continuing in his earthly ministry. However full and purposeful life may be today, the next stage for a Christian is superior in ways that cannot be grasped by an earthbound intellect. Our curiosity about details is left without satisfaction; yet the outcome stands assured. Presence with Christ is the shining sun. And the spiritual perfection of our souls promised in Hebrew 12:23 leaves no room for anxious fear. As daunting as bodily death seems, it ends the internal and external warfare of this life. The peace of Christ will be our all-consuming experience.

Deacon Stephen was martyred in the first-century Jerusalem church. Acts 7 tells the story of his tragic yet glorious death. Some may claim that Stephen was granted a special vision no other person could share, because he was a martyr. "Behold," he cried, "I see the heavens opened, and the Son of Man standing at the right hand of God" (Acts 7:56). I wonder if it is better to imagine that the unspeakable grandeur he described is the scene many believers already have witnessed in some measure as death closes in.

My paternal grandmother was a down-to-earth farmer's wife; I doubt if her practical but godly mind ever entertained a wisp of mysticism. In March 1961 she lay dying in a hospital bed on the morning of her sixty-fifth birthday. A duty nurse heard her call out repeatedly around three in the morning. Later this nurse told my grandfather that as she entered the room, my grandmother was sitting up, with a beautiful smile lighting her face. "Do you see the angels?" she asked the nurse. "Just look at them all!" The nurse settled her down for further sleep. But sleep was not appointed for Marguerite Rogers that morning. When her room was checked an hour later, my grandmother's soul had joined the angels who beckoned to her. Similar welcoming visions are told from the deathbeds of other believers.

That prospect is why Paul could say in 2 Corinthians 4:16, "So we do not lose heart." Everything God has done at the cross and is doing in every believer today by the Holy Spirit heads in one glorious direction. To be absent from this body brings the conscious Christian soul into the immediate presence of our God and King, for our true life is "hidden with Christ in God" (Col. 3:3). On the day you die, you will penetrate all the way into *life*!

Christian, is your perspective grounded in a strong hope of the immediacy of heaven awaiting you? Will you determine to deliberately fix your sights on these promises? Forceful redirection of our gaze is needed on a regular basis lest we falter in our hope. Calvin said, "A moment of time can seem long if we are only looking at things around us, but once we raise our minds to heaven, a thousand years can pass like a moment."[4]

Physical death remains a last enemy to be faced. Tears of loss at a Christian's graveside are painful indeed. But Stephen's soul-quickening epiphany awaits us! We can rest in joyful security. "'What no eye has seen, nor ear heard, nor the heart of man imagined, what God has prepared for those who love him'—these things God has revealed to us through the Spirit" (1 Cor. 2:9–10).

## NOT A FANTASY TALE

> Gandalf stood before him, robed in white, his beard now gleaming like pure snow in the twinkling of the leafy sunlight. "Well, Master Samwise, how do you feel?" he said. But Sam lay back, and stared with open mouth, and for a moment, between bewilderment and great joy he could not answer. At last he gasped: "Gandalf, I thought you were dead!

But then I thought I was dead myself. Is everything sad going to come untrue? What's happened to the world?"

"A great Shadow has departed," said Gandalf, and then he laughed, and the sound was like music, or like water in a parched land; and as he listened the thought came to Sam that he had not heard laughter, the pure sound of merriment, for days upon days without count. It fell upon his ears like the echo of all the joys he had ever known. But he himself burst into tears. Then, as a sweet rain will pass down a wind of spring and the sun will shine out the clearer, his tears ceased, and his laughter welled up."[5]

To the King of ages, immortal, invisible, the only God, be honor and glory forever and ever. Amen.

**I TIMOTHY 1:17**

He who is the blessed and only Sovereign, the King of kings and Lord of lords, who alone has immortality, who dwells in unapproachable light, whom no one has ever seen or can see. To him be honor and eternal dominion. Amen.

**I TIMOTHY 6:15–16**

[God] . . . saved us and called us to a holy calling, not because of our works but because of his own purpose and grace, which he gave us in Christ Jesus before the ages began, and which now has been manifested through the appearing of our Savior Christ Jesus, who abolished death and brought life and immortality to light through the gospel.

**2 TIMOTHY 1:9–10**

# CHAPTER TEN

# IMMORTALITY IS NOT ENOUGH

☼

*ANCIENT EGYPTIANS SHOWED INTENSE INTEREST* in life after death. Besides building colossal pyramid tombs for their pharaohs, the Egyptians specialized in preserving cadavers of important personages, then interring with them practical implements of daily life in order to assure comfort and fulfillment in the afterworld. Hinduism promotes reincarnation, also known as the transmigration of souls, supposedly reborn into other living forms. Your ancestor could return to earth as another human being or an animal, or theoretically he may even be present in the insect you just swatted. Buddhism has no formal concept of a soul entering another existence, nor of a great God in control of everything. Instead, the Buddhist is always in the process of turning over on the "great wheel of becoming," with no definite objective in sight other than a blissful extinction.

The intriguing subject of the immortality of human souls has produced scores of imaginative concepts like these from the creativity of man-made religions. With the notable exception of Buddhism, most religions contrived by man appear to have some idea that human souls inevitably survive into an afterlife. What people call "immortality" is usually considered to be part and parcel of our humanity, implicit within us. Human beings are deemed to have "everlastingness" in their DNA. Chances are, you grew up assuming that because you were alive you already were an immortal soul. Many Christians join the general American population in holding this idea. But your thinking needs an adjustment if you intend to have Holy Scripture as your authority.

## TRADITIONAL IMMORTALITY IS NOT BIBLICAL

For the first time in these pages we pay full attention to immortality. The word does appear in the Bible in a limited way—but with a meaning different than many understand. The concept of immortality believed by most Americans is not derived from Christianity but is inherited from eighteenth-century Deism. Primary issues for classical Deism were the existence of God, the importance of human virtue, and the immortality of the soul. However, the last of these is not supported by the Bible in the sense most people assume.[1] Still, most untutored Christians will talk about "my immortal soul."

The full phrase "immortality of the soul" is nowhere in the Bible. (Read that last sentence again, because you probably do not believe me.) Dutch Reformed theologian Herman Bavinck stated, "The Scriptures never mention it [immortality of the soul] in so many words; they never proclaim this concept as a divine revelation and nowhere place it in the foreground."[2] According to an English Bible concordance, the word *immortal* occurs just three times in Old and New Testaments: Romans 1:23; 1 Timothy 1:17; and 1 Timothy 6:16. And the word *immortality* is not much more frequent, found just five times in all of Scripture (Prov. 12:18; Rom. 2:7; 1 Cor. 15:53–54; 2 Tim. 1:10). Thus, we build whatever understanding we can have about this subject upon a relatively small base of Bible truth. However, some definite principles can be established from these eight citations. Second Timothy 1:10 declares, "Our Savior, Christ Jesus, has destroyed death and has brought life and immortality to light through the gospel." This suggests that only the cross and resurrection of Jesus bring any human being into possession of immortality. In God's word, immortality is God's own unique possession. It is also a *gift* he sovereignly bestows on the redeemed in Christ—never a right held by human birth. Herman Bavinck asserted: "God alone is life itself; he alone is immortal (1 Tim. 6:16). If the soul continues to exist, this can only occur in virtue of God's omnipresent and omnipotent power."[3] True life, or immortality, is found only in restored fellowship with God. Since only God himself can put this right again, we have no immortal soul until we are *endowed* with one by the immortal God.

## WHERE WRONG NOTIONS CAME FROM

The brand of immortality some people subscribe to is partially based on wish-fulfillment. That is to say, because we are self-conscious, thinking personalities (souls), it is humanly difficult to accept the idea that upon my death the rational computer known as "me" could simply be extinguished. Will my internal hard-drive crash and all the accumulated data from my unique existence just be dumped? Our view of immortality derives partly from what we *want* to believe must be true. "I" must continue existing, because I earnestly wish to, and I can hardly conceive otherwise. I cannot abide the notion of my own nonexistence! So I tell myself it cannot happen. Some others might argue from a moral basis. They are sure there must be soul-survival for all because of all the rank injustice existing in this world. They claim we need another phase of existence beyond this life as a divine-justice clearinghouse where all the cruelty and suffering of this life will somehow be sorted out and put right again. Otherwise it seems that the moral order of the universe is left hopelessly askew. And that appears to defeat the whole idea of a just God.

A seedbed for thinking about the classic notion of the immortality of the soul came quite early in Western civilization from Greek philosophy, from Plato in particular. Plato (427–347 BC) theorized in his book *Phaedo* about a radical separation at death of the human soul, which he posited was rational and pure. He said the soul preexists in the heavens before our birth, and the material body is full of evil lusts and acts as a prison to entomb the "good" soul. For Plato, death should be welcomed as the liberation of the soul, which blissfully escapes its bodily prison-house. The Greek master philosopher theorized that since your soul enjoyed a preexistence, it will enter its post-existence once freed from the inferior flesh. Early Christian theology was unhappily influenced too much by Platonic thinking for centuries, at the expense of Scripture. Greek philosophy led many Christians to assume that our flesh is naturally bad, but the spirit is always good. This false dichotomy belongs more to Gnosticism than to real Christianity, and it influenced twisted views of sexuality in early Christianity. Quite contrary to Plato and Christian Gnosticism, Scripture views us as whole persons—body and soul. God's aim in redemption is to restore both in our final resurrection state.

## IMMORTALITY BELONGS TO GOD

First Timothy 1:17 makes a grand statement which Jonathan Edwards credited as the verse that sparked his conversion: "To the King of the ages, immortal, invisible, the only God, be honor and glory forever and ever." Edwards wrote in his *Personal Narrative* about the singular impact that text had upon his decisive conversion to Christ in his late teens: "As I read the words there came into my soul and diffused all through it a sense of the glory of the divine Being; a new sense quite different from anything I had experienced before. Never any words of Scripture seemed to me as those words did. I thought to myself, how excellent a Being God is and how happy I would be if I might enjoy that God and be swallowed up in Him forever!"[4] Edwards was captivated by the sheer "otherness" of God. Qualities assigned to God in 1 Timothy 1:17 are: (1) He is eternal, with no beginning or end; (2) He is immortal, unable to suffer decay or death; (3) He is invisible, yet entirely real. No other being can have those inherent characteristics.

First Timothy 6:15–16 echoes the citation from the first chapter of the epistle: "He who is the blessed and only Sovereign, the King of kings and Lord of lords, who *alone has immortality*, who dwells in unapproachable light, whom no one has ever seen or can see . . ." Paul marveled that divine holiness defines Jehovah God, making him singular from all that we are.

The key definition of the Greek word for immortal is "incorruptible." Laws of physics tell us that the entire cosmos is in gradual decline, running down. After the age of fifty we all become acutely aware that our bodies are failing in any number of ways. Philip Ryken comments, "Unlike the milk in your refrigerator, God does not have a 'use by' expiration date."[5] Only God is not subject to decay or decline. He is not cooling off or growing old. Decay and death do not apply to him in any sense. He is just as holy, powerful, loving, and wise today as he has ever been. Being immortal also means that God is the intrinsic source of *life*. In Psalm 36:9 David told the Lord, "With you is the fountain of life." If immortality is a God-like trait, God holds the original patent and operates the exclusive franchise.

## WAS ADAM IMMORTAL?

We might wonder: Were Adam and Eve created to live forever in harmonious fellowship with God? Were they "immortal" from the beginning, before the fall? Since human death was not present in the prefall world, we have to believe the correct answer is yes. Their grievous rebellion introduced the judgment of bodily and spiritual death into Eden and shattered the man and woman's access to immortality. We were created to live, not die; to fellowship with God, not to be cut off from him. John Calvin taught that Adam's soul was initially immortal.[6] Deathless immortality was lost as one of the great calamities of the fall into sin.

Yet the Bible also claims that what was lost will be restored to some, but not all. Immortality is a gift God now grants human beings as his crowning bestowment of eternal life, to all those who believe in the Risen Son as Lord. John 3:36 says, "Whoever believes in the Son has eternal life; whoever does not obey the Son shall not see life, but the wrath of God remains on him." The "everlasting life" well known to us in John 3:16 is a synonym for restoration of our lost-in-Eden immortality. By raising Jesus from the dead, God opened a way to give immortality to some mortals— those who belong to Christ. When Paul spoke of final resurrection of our bodies at Christ's return, he said, "this mortal body must put on immortality" (1 Cor. 15:53). In a real sense, that resurrection moment is our irrevocable return to Eden! In Christ we gain back what Adam so recklessly lost.

## NO IMMORTALS IN HELL

Just as immortality is never applied to mere naturally born human beings before redemption in Christ, it also is not even once spoken of to describe any soul outside of heaven. No soul in hell is correctly called "immortal" just because it continues to exist. The unbeliever's soul survives death to begin experiencing woe, regret, and pain. He enters the domain of something disastrously worse than he ever knew upon the earth. Immortality implies a qualitative vigor and bliss these condemned souls never taste. The afterlife of the unbeliever cannot possibly be immortal, since immortality implies the breathtaking joy of sharing in God's own endless life; souls in hell have none of this. More than a mere semantic difference is at stake when we divide souls who have been granted immortality by God's act of redemptive grace in Jesus Christ and souls merely surviving in hell-bound alienation from their Creator.

Souls in hell are destined to be raised in the general resurrection, and they are given bodies, yet they do not "live" the life of immortality! We must label an unbeliever's existence beyond the grave as entirely opposite from a Christ-endowed immortality. It is more accurately a *living death.* In fact, the Bible calls it "second death."

## CHRIST OR PLATO?

Are you learning about future hope from Christ or from Plato? Christian hope respects the majesty of the material creation and our wonderful bodies. Your body is not inherently evil, nor is it a prison house for your perfect soul. On the contrary, the Bible urges you to respect your physical body as a "temple of the Holy Spirit" (1 Cor. 6:19). Our final glorification will not be consummated until the redeemed soul is reunited with a glorified body and planet earth is renewed. Then will believers inherit recognizable and deathless bodies that are like Christ's own, as immortality's crown. The *resurrection* is our password to obtain immortality from Christ.

Practically speaking, a biblical view of immortality overrules superstitious and silly ideas like reincarnation or spiritualism. It is a disgrace resulting from poor Bible teaching in churches that surveys consistently claim that a startling minority of professing American Christians hold to some vapid notions of reincarnation. Resurrection and reincarnation are oil and water to each other—entirely incompatible. Reincarnation consigns your soul to travel a confused, aimless path through a Godless afterlife. Homeless souls do not wander in this world to rap signals on the bedroom walls at night or rattle chains in the attic. Leave séances and Ouija boards strictly alone. At best they are amusements run by charlatans to entrap weak minds; at worst, they may be the tools of demons.

## OUR PROSPECTS BETTER THAN ADAM'S

If biblical immortality is correctly understood as that which Adam and Eve originally and briefly possessed when God's shining image was factory-new and his incomparable smile beamed upon them—then no less bliss will be *ours* as God's gift in eternity. In fact, we should expect something far *better* than Adam ever had. Why? Because of Christ's victory! Adam and Eve in their original immortality had the fateful temptation of Satan and the terrible fall into sin in their immediate future. The Christian's enjoyment of immortality allows for no similar undoing ahead of us. Our battle with sin and death will have been decided, completely resolved. It can never be brought up or even whispered to us again.

Human-based immortality is insufficient for real hope. The Bible does not teach the inherent indestructibility of the human soul. The gospel of a believer's resurrection and glorification in Jesus Christ offers infinitely more than a Greek philosopher's abstraction. Cling to Christ alone, so you may "have *life* and have it abundantly" (John 10:10). The immortality given to the Christian involves undying personhood, soul and body together in resurrection glory with our incorruptible Lord.

The barren philosophical idea of immortality for naturally-born human souls is a cheap bill of goods. If you trust in nothing better than that, you've been sold downriver.

# PART FOUR

# HISTORY'S CONSUMMATION

But we do not want you to be uninformed, brothers, about those who are asleep, that you may not grieve as others do who have no hope. For since we believe that Jesus died and rose again, even so, through Jesus, God will bring with him those who have fallen asleep. For this we declare to you by a word from the Lord, that we who are alive, who are left until the coming of the Lord, will not precede those who have fallen asleep. For the Lord himself will descend from heaven with a cry of command, with the voice of an archangel, and with the sound of the trumpet of God. And the dead in Christ will rise first. Then we who are alive, who are left, will be caught up together with them in the clouds to meet the Lord in the air, and so we will always be with the Lord. Therefore encourage one another with these words.

**I THESSALONIANS 4:13–18**

"I wonder whether people who ask God to interfere openly and directly in our world quite realize what it will be like when he does. When it happens, it is the end of the world. When the Author walks on the stage, the play is over. God is going to invade, all right: but what is the good of saying you are on his side then, when you see the whole natural universe melting away like a dream and something else—something it never entered your mind to conceive—comes crashing in; something so beautiful to some of us and so terrible to others that none of us will have any choice left? For this time it will be God without disguise; something so overwhelming that it will strike either irresistible love or irresistible horror in every creature. It will be too late then to choose your side. . . . That will not be the time for choosing; it will be the time when we discover which side we really have chosen, whether we realized it or not."[1]

**C. S. LEWIS**

# CHAPTER ELEVEN

# THE FINAL HEAVEN INAUGURATED

☼

*IN CHAPTER 9 WE EXAMINED 2 CORINTHIANS* 5 regarding the grand spiritual reality every Christian can expect to enter immediately at death. The redeemed in Christ are instantly present with him as souls perfected in righteousness; absence from this body equals immediate presence with the Lord. We do not receive resurrection bodies right away, yet we shall be at home and entirely secure in the presence of God our Savior. I stated a strong preference for the name "immediate heaven" to label that first level of Christian bliss after death. Now is the time to speak of a "final heaven," which we will explore in this and subsequent chapters.

A sequence of awe-inspiring events is set in motion by the historic second coming of Jesus Christ to history. His promised return is the stage curtain rising on the last phase of eternity. Jesus's bodily resurrection the third day after his death was the decisive point at which the age to come burst into this age. When Jesus appears on the clouds as Lord and Judge, his summons will call for a great resurrection of all the dead—believing and rebellious—and his undeniable judgment will be visited upon unbelief, followed by an amazing re-creation of heaven and earth.

## THE MOMENTOUS EVENT

In Mark 14:62 Jesus predicted, "You will see the Son of Man seated at the right hand of Power, and coming with the clouds of heaven." We now look to 1 Thessalonians 4, because it fully describes Christ's visible appearing. Some consult this passage to satisfy curiosity about how the great event fits on a prophecy timeline. It is often called the "rapture," and it is fine to use that term, though the word does not appear anywhere in the Bible. Speculations about "end-times events" arranged in elaborate schemes are not our interest here. You will need to refer to other resources to compare the various millennial charts and debates. But keep in mind that there is no sound scriptural evidence for theories of Jesus coming multiple times. There is one grand finale event.

Our concern is the personal aspect of the event as individuals will face it, summarized in Colossians 3:4: "When Christ who is your life appears, then you also will appear with him in glory." We look to Jesus being revealed from heaven not as a historic curiosity, nor the solving of a prophecy puzzle, but as God's consummation of all things in heaven and earth.

Recently I heard something referred to as "the most watched event in all of history." Turns out it was merely an upcoming Super Bowl game. That is pitiful, since the second advent of Christ will be unrivalled as the most watched event of history. No eye on earth will miss this! All the splendor, honor, and authority presently belonging to Jesus as Lord will be supernaturally visible to the entire world. Christ will not display *more* glory than he already has, but finally all mankind will *see* what is true about him as he now is. Every eye will see him and every knee will bow to him. Commentator Greg Beale wrote: "When Christ appears, he will not descend from the sky over Boston or London or New York City or Hong Kong or any other localized area. When he appears, the present dimension will be ripped away, and Christ will be manifest to all eyes throughout the earth (see Matt. 24:27). Just as one can see a map of the whole world and see it all with one glance, so Christ will appear and be able to behold humanity at one glance, and they him."[2]

Tragically for many, that recognition of Jesus's lordship will come too late. They will recognize him as Lord without adoring him by faith. But for those who greet him with settled faith, this hour means a transformation of everything. God's great saving work will be concluded in us and all around us. Enemies of Christ will be banished entirely from his presence, and his loving subjects will step forward to be invested as knights and ladies of his eternal court, enfolded into the brightness of his kingly splendor.

Jesus will be revealed in power and majesty, in what he once told the Father was "the glory that I had with you before the world existed" (John 17:5). First Thessalonians 4:16 declares this to be the supreme *public* event of all time. The sometimes popular notion of a "secret rapture," in which Christians are removed from earth while others remain for a time, not knowing what happened to their neighbors, is mistaken speculation tied to complex extrapolations out of the book of Daniel. Secrecy has no part in the clearest display of Jesus's return found in the New Testament from 1 Thessalonians 4. There is nothing hidden about the "loud voice of the archangel and the trumpet call of God." The noise level Paul describes at the second advent will finally accomplish something my mother frequently predicted of the racket being made by my friends and me at play: it will conclusively "wake the dead"!

Notice the purpose for which Paul wrote this passage: to allay fears of Thessalonian believers who thought that fellow Christians who had already died would miss participation in, or benefits derived from, this tremendous day. These early Christians expected the Lord's return within their lifetimes. Understandably, some supposed that already deceased Christians were at a terrible disadvantage, since they would not be on-hand to welcome the Lord. Were they all right? Was there a realistic hope of seeing them again? Pastor Paul banished needless fears.

Christians grieve for believers who precede us in death, but we do so quite differently than the secular world weeps for those with no certifiable hope. Paul decried pagan sorrow as the polar opposite of Christian hope. Ephesians 2:12 speaks of those "having no hope and without God in the world." We who are in Christ have no common ground with secular sad sacks. On behalf of departed believers, we cry only tears of anticipation for a sure reunion—no wails of despair for us.

## FALLEN ASLEEP?

Several times Paul labeled believing dead as "those who have fallen *asleep*" (1 Thess. 4:14–15). Both the Old Testament and a handful of New Testament sources use this terminology for death (see Gen. 47:30; Deut. 31:16; 2 Sam. 7:12; Matt. 27:52; John 11:11–13). The crass literalism of *souls* truly sleeping is never taught by the Scriptures. In John 11:14 Jesus took the trouble to correct disciples who misunderstood his meaning when he had said, "Lazarus is sleeping." He spelled it out bluntly that Lazarus's body was dead.

Various groups in Christian history have advocated a literal sleep of the soul after death, in the intermediate state, because they doubted there could be any conscious state of existence before the return of Christ. One of John Calvin's earliest Reformation tracts was written under the

Latin title *Psychopannychia* (1534), on "soul-sleep," opposing that error held among some Anabaptists of the time.[3] Soul-sleep advocates argue that unity of body and soul is essential to normal human experience, so if the two are separated, there cannot be real consciousness. However, both Hebrews 12:23 and Revelation 6:9–11 refute this by depicting believers who have died—who as yet have no bodies—but are in real fellowship with the Lord. In 1 Thessalonians 5:10 Paul said, "Whether we are awake or asleep we might live with [Christ]." This declares the dead in Christ to be "living" now.

Don't we all tend to dress up death with softer terms? We speak of someone who has "passed away" or just "passed." Saying that persons have "fallen asleep" in Christ is also a euphemism; it is not intended to be understood literally. Parents must be cautious about using such euphemisms when speaking to a young child who could perceive a literal meaning. It is probably a bad idea to tell a child that "Grandpa fell asleep." Children are better realists in handling fairly straight talk about death than many people give them credit for.

Pagan cultures sometimes spoke of death as sleep for all souls. But in the Bible's usage, "falling asleep" is applied only to believers who die, never to unbelievers.[4] More specifically, the expression applies only to Christian *bodies*, not their souls.[5] When a body is asleep, the condition is temporary. That body will awaken; its residence in the grave is not permanent. Sleep also implies rest, and believers do rest in their trustworthy Savior. Although the idea of soul-sleep is still promoted by some present-day cults, it is not taught in mainstream Christian orthodoxy. We ought to simply read the term in the symbolic way God's Word intended it to be understood.

## TWO STREAMS OF SAINTS

Our Thessalonian text declares "the dead in Christ will rise first. Then we who are alive, who are left, will be caught up together with them in the clouds to meet the Lord in the air" (1 Thess. 4:16–17). Paul says much the same in 1 Corinthians 15:51–52, "Behold! I tell you a mystery. We shall not all sleep, but we shall all be changed, in a moment, in the twinkling of an eye, at the last trumpet." Verse 53 adds, "For this perishable body must put on the imperishable, and this mortal body must put on immortality." We picture massive crowds, since hundreds of millions of Christians will be rising to meet the Lord from graves, from the sea, or as living persons from earth. It sounds like history's colossal traffic jam, so many resurrections processing at once! However, we need not think of resurrection investiture in new bodies taking a long time, nor imagine that millions of us will wait in ten-mile long queues for our turn. Paul states it will occur *instantaneously.*

I once saw a comedy farce in a theater, with a main character who made a very rapid costume change just off stage. He continued talking loudly from his position in the wings to a lady who was on stage. He was supposedly in his bedroom for about thirty seconds looking for something to wear to a concert the two were to attend. He expressed frantic doubts as to whether he could find anything dressy enough for the occasion, as he noisily ransacked his unseen closet and his rejected suits were flung unto the stage. Then he cried, "Eureka, I found it!" and immediately as he said those words, leaped back on stage outfitted in a tuxedo with tails and top hat, replacing the casual clothing he'd worn only moments before. The audience applauded with delight at this transformation accomplished in half a minute. (I learned afterward from a critic's review that this trick required several dressers and that the actor's costumes were fastened by Velcro to make his transformation so quick.)

Think of the long process of shopping, selection, and fittings that brides-to-be undergo so they can appear at their wedding in the splendid white gown of their dreams. When Jesus the Lord comes to unite redeemed souls with made-to-order bodies of resurrection, we who are his bride, his living church, shall be "clothed" instantly in bodily forms that will present us in our best appearance ever. My wife keeps fastened on her mirror in our bedroom a yearbook photo of me taken in college when I was twenty. It is almost the only picture of myself I have ever liked, and it sometimes makes me wonder if she is pining for the man who once looked that good! And will the Lord in his resurrection research understand that I'd be glad for a restoration to something like that long-ago image?

Philippians 3:21 declares that Christ "will transform our lowly body to be like his glorious body, by the power that enables him even to subject all things to himself." With the risen Christ as the prototype, I do have strong hopes of looking much better than any snapshot from college days. No extensive shopping, no fittings with a tailor or seamstress, and no waiting for delivery will be required for us to enjoy this great gift. After all, it is not what we will wear but what we simply will *be*. The great One whom we will mirror will constitute our true glory in that final day. We will marvel at how God's miraculous power reassembles "me" and "you" into recognizable bodies once more. It will not matter if fire, explosion, or centuries of decay might have desiccated the molecules of our earthly flesh and bones. We shall gain a new-world body for a new-world order, having continuity with and similar configuration to our earthly body—sufficient to be recognized by those in the heavenly fellowship who knew us before.

In the monthly real estate magazine produced in my local area one woman appears to be the reigning queen of the high-end home listings. She often has two pages of elite homes and estates for sale. At the center of her exclusive pictorial listings is this agent's personal image, in what I call a "glamour" photo. She probably paid a lot to have her hair perfectly styled and makeup professionally over-applied. The finished photograph has been airbrushed until her countenance simply glows, as she awaits my phone call to purchase a palatial home I could never afford. However, if this lady is a daughter of Christ by God's grace, I can imagine that her resurrection appearance will be exquisite to a measure so far beyond this magazine pose, that in the light of eternity her contrived real estate glamour photo will be like a crayon drawing her four-year-old might make today of "my mommy."

Your unique image—your own personality—will be miraculously renewed in a spiritual body of resurrection by the God who first created all things out of nothing. This will not be mere resuscitation, nor renovation; it will be transformation. More will be said on this subject in the next chapter.

## ASSURANCES OF THE FINAL HEAVEN

Bear in mind two distinct reassurances touching on these wonders to come. First, we must trust God's Almighty power to bring this grand event to completion. The most ardent believer has minor questions or even nagging doubts about the final appearance of Christ in history. When an event has been awaited this many centuries, it seems much of the time that it may never come. The result is that even ardent Christians can admit that the return of Jesus seems like an impossible science-fiction drama.

The second advent of Christ is predicted to be such an all-embracing disruption of life as usual, that by comparison Pearl Harbor or a presidential assassination will seem like back-page, one-paragraph news stories nestled among the want ads. How can such a convulsion of all that we know take place in the setting of everyday experiences of family, house-cleaning, shopping, work, and Christmas? Oh, we do say we believe that someday it will occur—but moments later we whisper to ourselves, "Just not too likely within *my* lifetime!"

When Christians quietly question the second coming of Christ, we need reminding that if the one true God in his sovereignty could create a universe by speaking it into existence; if he could send his preexistent Son to dwell as a man conceived in a virgin's womb; if he could raise that Son from death in mighty power—then the second coming hardly poses too great a challenge for him. It will not overtax our God's miracle-working capacity, which he has already demonstrated in world history.

Second, when we think about the Lord's power to perform all this, we ought to consider the "shout" of God mentioned in our text as the voice of an imperial commander who cannot be disobeyed. This shout "denotes an authoritative utterance," wrote Leon Morris. "It is the cry made by a ship's captain to his rowers or by a military officer to his soldiers or by a hunter to his hounds or by a charioteer to his horses. . . . It is a battle cry."[6] God's executive order enacted in Christ's grand return is absolutely decisive, just as Scripture reports that at the very beginning, he said, "'Let there be light' and there was light" (Gen.1:3). His command will bring it to pass; his gospel plan for all of us will be inexorably completed by his mere spoken word.

## THE CHURCH TOGETHER AT LAST

Notice how 1 Thessalonians 4 emphasizes unity of the entire church of Jesus Christ from across history. In this tremendous scene of bodily resurrection, Adam, Moses, and Mary will precede you and me, as will Martin Luther, Augustine, and your Christian grandparents. We will be gathered as one body from across the ages to answer the summons from Christ to receive our final inheritance, "caught up together with them in the clouds" (4:17). In the Greek, to be "caught up" means literally to be seized or carried off by force.

Entirely too much of our concept of Christianity is wrapped around the small nucleus of "my" individual salvation. Here is a place where the corporate nature of God's great covenant of grace first promised through

Abraham comes into its full fruition. "And [the Lord] brought him outside and said, 'Look toward heaven, and number the stars, if you are able to number them.' Then he said to him, 'So shall your offspring be'" (Gen. 15:5). On the final day of Christ, this covenant fulfillment will be wonderfully evident.

At Pittsburgh, Pennsylvania, two separate rivers, the Allegheny and the Monongahela, flow south and west until they merge in the broad Ohio River. When Christ comes, not only will the division of soul and body end for every individual believer in the unity of soul/body again, but the painful social separation we have endured from all those we have loved in Christ who left us behind at their deaths will be cancelled. All believers will join in one heavenly confluence. Neither the Christian dead nor living believers will have an advantage over the other. We will be "caught up" together into a solidarity death itself cannot hold back (Rom. 8:35–39).

We should be mindful of this anticipated union even today. Christian friends and families who have preceded us to the immediate heaven are now experiencing intimate fellowship with Christ Jesus. As we worship corporately on a given Lord's Day, we might picture a four-dimensional reality. Gathered around us invisibly yet in true fellowship, crowding into those empty sanctuary seats, are not only a myriad of angels, but according to Hebrews 12:22–23, also present in our midst is "the assembly of the firstborn who are enrolled in heaven." Not ghosts, but perfected souls are true companions of our corporate worship! Since we believe the reigning Christ himself meets us by his Spirit at the table of the Lord's Supper, is it not also biblical to picture departed saints of the Lord seated in our midst as we worship at the Lord's Table? What else is "the communion of the saints" we declare in the Apostles' Creed? Our separation from all of them is only temporary. We are united to the church triumphant by bonds of God's Spirit that cannot be broken. Hebrews 12:1 reminds us of "a great cloud of witnesses" who spur us on to faith and good works in Christ, and Hebrews 11:40 promises, "Apart from us they should not be made perfect."

Everlasting union with Christ and unity with all his people in perfected bodies is the fulfillment of the final heaven. Jesus pledged in Matthew 11:43, "Then the righteous will shine like the sun in the kingdom of their Father."

Thank God, none of this is based on Paul's guesses or speculations, which might prove to be no better than the latest prophecy guru who sets a date for the "end of the world" and becomes a public mockery when his calculation is proved false. Paul said in 1 Thessalonians 4:15, "This we declare to you by a word from the Lord." He reinforced his claim to distinct revelation from God. This either is God's truth, or the apostle joins the lowest level of liars.

Further implications will be discovered beyond 1 Thessalonians 4 that are not told in this one centerpiece passage. "We have no liberty . . . to stretch the text [of 1 Thessalonians 4] beyond what the apostle intended to say," wrote John Stott. "To be sure, it is tantalizing that Paul says nothing here about the nature of the resurrection body, the resurrection of unbelievers, the judgment day, the new heaven and the new earth, hell, or the final reign of God."[7] We must keep building a composite picture that includes those interlocking realities, woven together from additional Bible sources.

This momentous event is a reason for every Christian to walk through life with uplifted head. We can be encouraged! All human beings and all coming world events are in God's sovereign hands; men and time and nations all flow toward this appointed event of all events. Be comforted about the dead in Christ. Their end is secure together with us. Raise your drooping heads. This amazing final day is closer to us now than ever before.

The old Puritans knew how to pray in anticipation of Jesus's coming. Here is how one of them did so: "O Lord, I live here as a fish in a vessel of water, only enough to keep me alive, but in heaven I shall swim in the ocean. Here I have a little air to keep me breathing, but there I shall have sweet and fresh gales. . . . Quicken my hunger and thirst for the realm above. Here I can have the world; there I shall have thee in Christ. Give me to know that heaven is all joy. . . . And lead me to it soon. Amen"[8]

But someone will ask, "How are the dead raised? With what kind of body do they come?" You foolish person! What you sow does not come to life unless it dies. And what you sow is not the body that is to be, but a bare kernel. . . .

What is sown is perishable; what is raised is imperishable. It is sown in dishonor; it is raised in glory. It is sown in weakness; it is raised in power. It is sown a natural body; it is raised a spiritual body. . . . Just as we have borne the image of the man of dust, we shall also bear the image of the man of heaven. . . .

Behold! I tell you a mystery. We shall not all sleep, but we shall all be changed, in a moment, in the twinkling of an eye, at the last trumpet. For the trumpet will sound, and the dead will be raised imperishable, and we shall be changed. . . . When the perishable puts on the imperishable, and the mortal puts on immortality, then shall come to pass the saying that is written:

> "Death has been swallowed up in victory."
> "O death, where is your victory?
>    O death where is your sting?"

**I CORINTHIANS 15:35–55**

# CHAPTER TWELVE

# WE SHALL ALL BE CHANGED

☀

*JONI EARECKSON TADA IS WIDELY* known as an author, conference speaker, and advocate for the physically disabled. In the summer of 1967 a teenage diving accident left her a quadriplegic. For decades since, Joni has been paralyzed from the shoulders down and is entirely dependent on others to do simple daily tasks for her. This woman also has a well-grounded biblical viewpoint, demonstrated in her book *Heaven, Your Real Home.* Because her earthly body functions only with huge limitations, Joni thinks about her resurrection body more than most of us ever do. She wrote, "Somewhere within my broken, paralyzed body is the seed of what I shall become. Paralysis makes what I am to be all the more grand when you contrast atrophied, useless legs against splendorous, resurrected legs. . . . A gigantic oak tree bears no resemblance to a tiny acorn. . . . Right now I am just an 'acorn' when it comes to understanding heaven. But I can tell you whatever my acorn shape becomes in all its power and honor, I am ready for it."[1]

Within every Christian created new by God's life-giving Spirit in Jesus Christ is the dormant prototype of a thrilling resurrection upgrade. No matter what your present ailments and despite all disappointments you may have with your physical body, the final new heaven and earth will see you personally remade in vigorous bodily splendor. C. S. Lewis once mused about how we daily rub shoulders with people who ultimately will be like either Christ in grandeur or demons in revulsion. Lewis marveled, "It is a serious thing to live in the society of possible gods and goddesses, to remember that the dullest and most uninteresting person you talk to may one day be a creature which, if you saw it now, you would be strongly tempted to worship, or else a horror and a corruption such as you now meet, if at all, only in a nightmare."[2]

## OUR COSMIC MAKEOVER

In the sequence of cosmic events following Christ's return there will be a general resurrection of all the dead—unredeemed sinners as well as saints. Unbelievers are not raised to glory, but raised they are, nonetheless. You probably noticed this resurrection of the lost was not described in 1 Thessalonians 4, presumably because it was not germane to Paul's purpose there. The apostle's emphasis was on the unity of believers, so the unbeliever was temporarily left in the shadows. Actually nowhere in Scripture is much fuss made over the resurrection of the nonelect. But a handful of passages do matter-of-factly predict a general resurrection for all who have lived. A broad, general resurrection will be timed congruently to the resurrection of believers. Daniel 12:2 speaks of a general resurrection: "And many of those who sleep in the dust of the earth shall awake, some to everlasting life, and some to shame and everlasting contempt." Another key text is John 5:28–29 where Jesus said, "An hour is coming when all who are in the tombs will hear his voice and come out, those who have done good to the resurrection of life, and those who have done evil to the resurrection of judgment." Acts 24:15 also mentions "a resurrection of both the just and the unjust." And do not miss Revelation 20:12, as the gathering at the final judgment of the great white throne is described: "And I saw the dead, great and small, standing before the throne, and the books were opened."

The resurrection bodies of unbelievers could not bear the sheer weight of Jesus's reflected glory, any more than a mouse can carry away a concrete block to his mouse hole. Remember from our previous study that unrighteous souls are not called "immortals"; the word is never applied to them. These nonimmortal, once-but-no-longer humans are vessels fit only for dishonor, judgment, and banishment from the presence of the Lord. God will make no silk purses from a sow's ear when he raises those who are bound for hell by their own determined choices. Beyond the bare fact that a general resurrection event is promised in the passages mentioned above, the Bible elaborates nothing specific about the bodily status of lost persons. They evidently have souls united to bodies as vehicles in which to suffer. Beyond that, Scripture leaves an ominous silence brooding over the resurrection of the unredeemed.

C. S. Lewis helps with the imaginative side of these biblical truths.

Speaking about fanciful visitors from hell who take a brief tour of heaven in *The Great Divorce*, Lewis wrote, "Now that they were in the light, they were transparent. . . . They were in fact ghosts: man-shaped stains on the brightness of that air. One could attend to them or ignore them at will, as you do with the dirt on the window pane. I noticed that the grass did not bend under their feet: even the dew drops were not disturbed."[3] In this way Lewis dismissed the resurrection bodies of reprobate men. They have a type of existence, but it is not immortality; their personhood is no longer of consequence. Perhaps J. R. R. Tolkien had the correct notion with his frightful "ringwraiths."

Believers in Christ will spend eternity in bodies wonderfully formed to recapture the perfection of God's image, once disastrously damaged by the fall. C. S. Lewis continued his creative portrait of heaven by describing a sight of resurrected saints whom he called *solid* people: "I saw them when they were still very distant and at first I did not know they were people at all. . . . The earth shook under their tread as their strong feet sank into the wet turf. . . . Some were naked, some robed. But the naked ones did not seem less adorned, and the robes did not disguise in those who wore them the massive grandeur of muscle and the radiant smoothness of flesh."[4] Compared to resurrected wraiths of the condemned, these risen saints made the earth tremble underfoot!

Genesis 2 teaches that God uniquely joined the dust of our physical nature to his Spirit, so humans alone possess the image of God. Evolutionists love to crow that chimpanzee DNA is 98 percent identical to that of humans. For that matter, I believe earthworms share nearly the same chromosomal makeup as ourselves. However, we need to look hard at the wonder residing in that 2 percent—for there dwells a universe of divine distinctiveness. No worm will ever write a calculus textbook, perform heart surgery, compose a sonata, or preach a sermon. Neither worm nor ape can possibly bridge the Grand Canyon of separation dividing them from mankind, because God stands squarely in that gap.

God cannot stop with halfway redemption: he saves our souls by the atonement for sin at the cross, then, as a crowning gift for those who are in Christ, he renews the fearful beauty he first designed human bodies to display as mirrors of his image. Arthritis, diabetes, cancer, dementia, and cataracts will afflict us no longer. Better still, we shall be renovated within so all our secret sin devices and lusts—the spiritual toxins of a fallen nature—will be gone from our natures. We alone are Eden's bearers of the divine image, and in the end of time this spectacular gift will shine forth from every perfected saint. We are destined to be the "solid people."

As I recite the Apostles' Creed with God's worshipers on most Sundays, I hear the congregation say, "I believe in the resurrection of the body." I sometimes wonder how many dwell upon what we have just affirmed. Do people realize that we have announced that in the new earth, every hospital, medical clinic, police station, prison, and morgue will be out of business, due to our ultimate bodily resurrection with Christ?

## CHANGED IN A MOMENT

Most elements of salvation in Christ that we experience before death involve a long and sometimes arduous process of development. Our sanctification takes time, and its changes can seem to move by imperceptible millimeters. So much so, we often assume no work of the Spirit or growth in personal holiness is really underway in us, when it actually is. Other people may glimpse God's molding results in us better than we will ourselves—just as a grandmother living at a distance exclaims over how tall her grandson has grown during a six-month absence from the sight of him. But in the final hour of history, something will happen to change us very quickly: "We shall all be changed, in a moment, in the twinkling of an eye, at the last trumpet. For the trumpet will sound, and the dead will be raised imperishable, and we shall be changed" (1 Cor. 15:51–52). This "twinkling of an eye" event will make us over before we comprehend it has happened. We position this promise alongside Philippians 3:20–21, where Paul wrote, "But our citizenship is in heaven, and from it we await a Savior, the Lord Jesus Christ, who will transform our lowly body to be *like* his glorious body, by the power that enables him even to subject all things to himself."

Threads predicting this resurrection event began in the Old Testament. The reality was foreseen, but the prophetic vision was dim. We noted in chapter 1 a few breakthrough insights, like Job's amazing declaration in Job 19:25–26: "I know that my Redeemer lives, and at the last he will stand upon the earth. And after my skin has been thus destroyed, yet in my flesh I shall see God." In John 14:19 Jesus gave this promise: "Because I live, you also will live." The same body in which the Lord suffered and was crucified is now raised and glorified. "There is a genuine continuity between Jesus' pre-resurrection and post-resurrection body (not bodies)."[5]

Christ's resurrection in a real body was no one-time flash-in-the-pan event. Easter Day brought the return of a breathing, fish-eating, Aramaic-speaking Jesus as God's working model for a great miracle he intends to reproduce for millions at the last day. God's greatest miracle in history is transferable. Our final glorification brings us into conformity to the image of the master pattern, Jesus Christ. "For those whom he foreknew he also predestined to be conformed to the image of his Son, in order that he might be the *firstborn* among many brothers" (Rom. 8:29). Matthew Poole commented on Romans 8:29: "Though there be a likeness in us unto Christ, yet there is not an equality; he still retaineth the dignity of the firstborn, and hath a double, yea, a far greater portion. He is the Head and Ruler of all the family in heaven and on earth."[6] We will not be Christ's equals, but we will be "like" him in ways that remain partly mysterious, but very grand.

## RECOGNIZABLY THE SAME

Now we look to 1 Corinthians 15:35 and following. Paul's subject was the "how" aspect of a Christian's resurrection. Corinthian people were also curious about the manner in which this marvel would affect them. What will I look like or be like after the resurrection? In the attempt to summarize a complex passage, let us keep in sight the overall conclusion Paul develops: that in our resurrection state, we will be recognizably the same, yet also profoundly different.

There will be a large degree of sameness about our risen bodies—enough so our unique personalities will survive. Others will know me by a definite continuity about "me-ness." Whether this will be most evident from my face, hair, inflection of speech, dimple in the chin, or what, we cannot exactly say—it will most likely be an amalgamation. Who would argue that if God has power to raise us in the first place, he certainly will not lose track of a myriad of details that identify each one's subtle unique-ness? The prime example supporting this is in the way the risen Jesus was recognized by others after their first shock of meeting him on Easter day. The human body Jesus inhabited on resurrection morning and until the ascension was the very body in which he died on the cross; it was not a different body. In John 21:7, John recognized a man speaking from shore to those in the fishing boat. He told Peter, "It *is* the Lord!" And Peter threw himself into the surf, to come to Jesus. The sheer thrill of recognizing the humanity of the Jesus whom the disciples had known so well leaps off the page. Luke 24:39–40 underscores the nature of Jesus's risen body as being a continuation of the one he'd inhabited for thirty-three years. The risen Christ presented himself to frightened, doubtful disciples and said, "See my hands and my feet, that it is *I myself*. Touch me, and see. For a spirit does not have flesh and bones as you see that I have" (Luke 24:39). This is a remarkable statement. Phantoms do not invite physical contact. Jesus expected the disciples to identify the firm stuff of his flesh. They could shake his hand and embrace him, and it is further implied that his nail wounds were visibly intact (John 20:27).

In John 20:16 Mary Magdalene at first did not recognize Jesus. But as soon as he spoke her name, she was suddenly overcome by the familiar voice. Mary was told by Jesus somewhat enigmatically, "Do not cling to me, for I have not yet ascended to the Father" (20:17). The best way to interpret those words is not that there was impropriety in touching Jesus's resurrection body—since in Luke 24:39 and John 20:27 disciples were freely invited to do so. But John 20:17 was the beginning of instruction for Mary and other disciples that they should no longer expect to cling to Jesus as a mere earthly man. Although he inhabited the body they knew well, he was soon to become more than they imagined, when in forty days he would ascend to the right hand of his Father. Mary and the others needed to discover that the focus for trusting and worshiping Jesus would shift to his soon-to-be ascended position of universal Lord and Christ.

Philippians 3:21 promises that our resurrection bodies will be *"like* [Christ's] glorious body." Resurrected saints shall not become unrecognizable aliens any more than Jesus did. The process of resurrection will render a similar "likeness" to our earthly selves as the risen Jesus had to his pre-Calvary body.

Have you ever, after months of absence, met a friend who had lost thirty pounds? You told that radically transformed person, "You look fantastic!" and you meant it. Multiply that experience many times over and intensify it, then you may begin to imagine those we once knew and loved on earth, visibly perfected in body and spirit. We will remain independent beings, yet our King will fill us with so much of himself that our new bodies and souls will be "filled, flooded and drenched with God!"[7]

The fact that a resurrection body will be recognizably the same tells us that no one today can be regarded as God's physiological mistake. Our present bodies are not inherently evil. Nor should they ever be judged as ruined beyond redemption, no matter what defects we were born with or how badly we might have abused or degraded our flesh by our sins. The psalmist said that we are all "fearfully and wonderfully made" (Ps. 139:14). God is our designer and maker. He is not going to scrap us and start all over again. Like a Rembrandt painting which at some point in its existence was painted over by an amateur's cheap portrait, we are all masterpieces worthy of restoration because God's original work—his fingerprints and brushstrokes—are evident upon us. Christian, despite your physical shortcomings now, God will preserve your personality not because you are so great, but because you have always been his handiwork.

## PROFOUNDLY DIFFERENT

First Corinthians 15 also takes pains to illustrate how the resurrection body will also be profoundly different. In what way do tiny tomato seeds resemble those tall plants they produce, bearing heavy fruit? Paul pressed his argument with analogies to nature, reminding us that we cannot evaluate the final body God will remake based on our present raw material. In verses 42–44 in particular, he draws four distinctions. Your body now is perishable, dishonorable, weak, and natural. Then he gave four parallel contrasts. The new body will be imperishable, glorious, powerful, and spiritual. Let us consider each.

First of all, "imperishable" means impervious to death. If you drink no water for seven days, or if you go without food for more than about six weeks, you will die. Bodily decline and decay keep doctors and hospitals in business. From our early twenties onward, we are on a downward physical slide. Disease or old age overtakes every one of us. I am dying as I write and you are dying as you read. There may be a rare Jack LaLanne with rippling biceps maintained into his nineties, but Mr. LaLanne, the supreme fitness exemplar, has died. By contrast, our resurrection bodies will not be susceptible to decline or expiration, under any circumstances.

Second, the word "glorious" is not so simple. The Bible word for glory implies "weight" and "heaviness." One of the best English words we have for this is "gravitas," to describe the dignity of a statesman—that intangible bearing Abraham Lincoln and Winston Churchill possessed as leaders of men. It is one of those qualities you cannot describe readily, but you definitely know it when you see it. This glory will be seen visibly in us. In Matthew 13:43 Jesus said, "The righteous will shine like the sun in the kingdom of their Father."

Women (and men) spend much earthly time trying to enhance their own beauty, hoping to turn heads as they pass through a crowd. The righteous saints in Christ will "shine" in a manner that does not come from makeup, hairdos, or primping at the mirror. Sinless perfection will radically change us from within; holiness will reach its zenith of expression. The feeblest and filthiest of us will unselfconsciously reflect back to God his own holy beauty, joy, and love.

The third contrast found in 1 Corinthians 15:43, "power," is a bit easier to understand. Human bodies on earth grow weaker every year. I am regularly surprised at how basic strength and stamina I once took for granted is receding; more than three flights of stairs leave me breathing hard. Fragility and vulnerability of this present body will be replaced by the indestructible power of the resurrection body. Bear in mind how Paul contrasted our present "tent" with a "building" from God" (2 Cor. 5:1). Possibly Isaiah 40:31 can be understood to prophetically foreshadow our promised resurrection stamina, when Isaiah predicts, "They shall mount up with wings like eagles; they shall run and not be weary; they shall walk and not faint."

The fourth contrast of 1 Corinthians 15:44 may confuse us the most, as it is said that we will have a "spiritual" body, not a "natural" one. The word spiritual used here does not mean nonmaterial or nonphysical. Matthew Poole clarifies: "Spiritual not as to the substance of it, for in that sense a spiritual body is a contradiction."[8] Christ's postresurrection body was certainly physical. Jesus said he had "flesh and bones"; he ate food and spoke with travelers to Emmaus who thought him to be a common stranger, a man in every way like themselves.

The intended meaning of "spiritual body" does not deny physicality of definite bodily form or substance.[9] Nor is it about substance versus ghostliness. The correct understanding of *spiritual* in 1 Corinthians 15:44 is that our new and substantial resurrection bodies shall be dominated and animated entirely by the Holy Spirit. In the new age, the Spirit will rule over joyful responses from perfected saints who are passionate about compliance to God. Instead of resisting his Spirit-control as sinful lusts and temptations war against us and frequently defeat us, our new, risen bodies will be obedient servants of all God's desires and commands. "Spiritual" is contrasted to that person of today who is guided only by natural, base instincts. Then we will be directed by the Spirit's least touch or suggestion, instead of being rebellious mules balking at God's word and brought under control only by a hard hand upon our reins.

We never in our lives have beheld another person with this combination of body and soul characteristics, so it is impossible for our present "flesh and blood" minds to absorb what this will be like. The best theologian in this case becomes like a deaf mute trying to deliver the Gettysburg Address. Perhaps by charade-type gestures, some of the substance of Lincoln's great speech could get across, but never the nuances, the intonation of voice that would reproduce the substance of the speech in its full glory. There must be a radical change that only God's miracle power can work in us before we will grasp this reality. He has promised to do this instantaneously when Christ returns.

## WHO WILL RESCUE ME?

You could be reading this and wondering, will this dazzling prospect of a future resurrection body actually include *me*? Maybe you feel uncertain because you have messed up badly in your stewardship of the body God made, and you wonder if yours will ever be made new again to be like Christ's. You might be like Paul in Romans 7:24, wailing, "Wretched man that I am! Who will deliver me from this body of death?"

God's Word speaks to your anxiety. You can be sure God will complete your bodily resurrection on the final day of the Lord, if he has made any *beginning* in you of spiritual transformation. Once his salvation is begun in our justification, God "will bring it to completion at the day of Jesus Christ" (Phil 1:6). Paul knew the answer to his rhetorical Romans 7:24 question even as he asked it. He responded to his own query immediately by declaring, "Thanks be to God through Jesus Christ our Lord!" (Rom. 7:25). And just a bit further on he wrote, "If the Spirit of him who raised Jesus from the dead dwells in you, he who raised Christ Jesus from the dead will also give life to your mortal bodies through his Spirit who dwells in you" (8:11).

The resurrection body of every Christian believer is the capstone of God's salvation that begins in our new birth of trusting Jesus as Lord.

Justification makes us positionally perfect today in God's kingdom and family. Being perfected bodily through and through still awaits us. For you, a new body is the last crowning reward in an inevitable chain of God's redeeming work. For every Christian, 1 John 3:2 affirms, "We shall be like him, because we shall see him as he is."

Has God begun to change you today in mind and spirit? I pray that he has. Paul described our present condition: "Though our outer self is wasting away, our inner self is being renewed day by day. For this light momentary affliction is preparing for us an eternal weight of glory beyond all comparison" (2 Cor. 4:16–17). May he encourage you from this day forward in a growing sense of secure hope about his glory that one day will be perfectly revealed in your new, immortal body.

I hope you might reverently pray this doxology uttered by the apostle Peter, as we conclude this subject for the moment: "Blessed be the God and Father of our Lord Jesus Christ! According to his great mercy, he has caused us to be born again to a living hope through the resurrection of Jesus Christ from the dead, to an inheritance that is imperishable, undefiled, and unfading, kept in heaven for you, who by God's power are being guarded through faith for a salvation ready to be revealed in the last time" (1 Pet. 1:3–5). Amen.

Now concerning the times and the seasons, brothers, you have no need to have anything written to you. For you yourselves are fully aware that the day of the Lord will come like a thief in the night. While people are saying, "There is peace and security," then sudden destruction will come upon them as labor pains come upon a pregnant woman, and they will not escape. But you are not in darkness, brothers, for that day to surprise you like a thief. For you are all children of light, children of the day. We are not of the night or of the darkness. So then let us not sleep, as others do, but let us keep awake and be sober.

I THESSALONIANS 5:1-6

For we must all appear before the judgment seat of Christ, so that each one may receive what is due for what he has done in the body, whether good or evil.

2 CORINTHIANS 5:10

When the Son of Man comes in his glory, and all the angels with him, then will he sit on his glorious throne. Before him will be gathered all the nations, and he will separate people one from another as a shepherd separates the sheep from the goats. And he will place the sheep on his right, but the goats on his left. Then the King will say to those on his right, "Come, you who are blessed by my Father, inherit the kingdom prepared for you from the foundation of the world." . . .

Then he will say to those on his left, "Depart from me, you cursed, into the eternal fire prepared for the devil and his angels." . . . And these will go away into eternal punishment, but the righteous into eternal life.

MATTHEW 25:31-46

# CHAPTER THIRTEEN

# THE DAY OF THE LORD

☼

*AT MORE THAN ONE POINT,* Christianity is offensive to people who do not bow to Christ. An often-cited affront is the Bible's allegedly narrow-minded assertion that salvation is granted no other way but by trusting in Christ as the exclusive way, truth, and life (John 14:6). Another hated offense for unbelievers is hearing the merest suggestion that God would judge any and consign them to eternal condemnation, while others enter heaven's bliss. This of course is labeled "unfair."

When affirming the Apostles' Creed, we say that the risen Christ shall return from heaven "to judge the quick and the dead." (I trust you know that "quick" means living—not being able to run fast.) Adding to the so-called certainties of death and taxes, a third sure thing awaits us immediately after the return of Christ and the general resurrection: divine judgment from which none are exempt. No one will flee fast enough to escape it. James 5:9 warns us that "the Judge is standing at the door," prepared for his decisive entrance.

From an elementary school spelling test to a teenage driver's licensing exam or a police-administered lie detector test, no form of earthly judgment is comfortable or unconditionally welcomed by those subjected to it. My wife majored in music at college with organ as her primary instrument. Before she was eighteen she played pipe organs in churches with skill that greatly blessed people and brought glory to God. In college she faced periodic "juries" at which she had to perform assigned pieces before a panel of several music faculty members with red pens in hand. Despite her talent, and a reasonable expectation that she would do well, mere anticipation of those events unnerved her for days.

## JUDGMENT BY THE SAME GOD OF LONGSUFFERING GRACE

To be judged is to be put on the defensive, called to account. While any examination might end in an exoneration of charges, joyful advancement toward needed credentials, or even honors being bestowed, we are all keenly aware that the result could also expose our weaknesses and bring us failure or shame. It is easy to understand why next to the rejection displayed toward the doctrine of hell, the very idea of God's perfect judgment assessing condemnation for human sin is a much reviled subject among the masses.

More than 270 years after it was first preached in New England, a sermon by the Rev. Jonathan Edwards titled *Sinners in the Hands of an Angry God* qualifies in many minds as the most notorious of all pulpit messages ever heard in America. The sermon is printed in high school literature anthologies, and I have learned vicariously through English students in my home that it draws unbridled ridicule from secular teachers who totally misunderstand Edwards's biblical thesis. The master preacher of Northampton spoke of sinners walking across rotting floors about to give way underfoot, or being upheld by a mere spider's web above the burning wrath of God. Dismissive sneers of secular teachers assume this illustrates "hell fire and brimstone" from an age of ignorance when religion simply was not in touch with warmer, more cuddly versions of God. Rarely is it understood that Edwards emphasized the miracle of God's *grace* as the only spiritual support upholding millions of negligent people who deserved destruction. The preacher declared that unredeemed humanity's natural fate by all rights was to fall right through that rotting floor. Yet God persists in upholding us in the present hour by unmerited mercy alone.

Readers of the famous sermon generally just don't get it: Edwards sought to communicate *grace*, not damnation. Condemnation he took for granted, but it was the offer of grace in Christ he earnestly proclaimed! Many original hearers comprehended the distinction, but our contemporaries—gripped by the notion that man, not God, is supreme—cannot detect the obvious thrust of divine grace in the famous sermon. Our culture heaps scorn on the God who even dares hold human beings accountable to him as their Judge. It has been said that today the message could be titled, "God in the hands of angry sinners."

## CHRIST'S RETURN IS THE DAY OF THE LORD

We now look to 1 Thessalonians 5, where Paul first raised a question about *when* the Lord will make this return and quickly moved to the fact that after the resurrection of our bodies, judgment is due all mankind without exception. In 1 Thessalonians 5:1–2, Paul said he intended no timetable for the second coming. Jesus elsewhere addressed this when he said, "Concerning that day and hour no one knows, not even the angels of heaven, nor the Son, but the Father only" (Matt. 24:36). One thing is certain: no human prognosticator will have the date nailed down by advance predictions. Harold Camping and his kind will never guess it, for all their foolish Bible algorithms. Paul told the Thessalonians, regarding the final appearing of Christ, that they ought not to anxiously clutch a timetable, but know that our Lord's appearing sets in motion a sequence of events marking the long-promised end of the ages. The nature of the Lord's final revealing will be sudden and inescapable.

First Thessalonians 5:3 announces to those who are outside of faith in Christ that judgment day follows the general resurrection of all dead, bringing "sudden destruction" for unbelief. God's judgment is the infinite penalty for the infinite crime committed against an infinite Person: the Lord God Almighty. Ligon Duncan declared, "The doctrine of judgment is not a peripheral, harsh addendum that can easily be expunged from the Christian Scriptures, instead, it is at the very heart of everything that God is doing, because it is God's purpose to see evil totally expunged from the moral universe."[1]

If there would be no judgment day at all, we could never convincingly claim God is good or ultimately just. All of history cries out for judgment to occur. Christ himself, the Alpha and Omega, says on the Bible's last page, "Behold, I am coming soon, bringing my recompense with me, to repay each one for what he has done" (Rev. 22:12). Even non-Christians are drawn by compelling logic to hope that deep evil in the present-day world demands some final accounting. Yet they prefer that this reckoning might apply only for the alleged "exceptional" evil produced by Hitler or El-Qaeda terrorists, not to their own sin.

Believers in Christ will have a very different fate in this judgment and will have nothing to fear from what will be described in this present chapter, which applies to unbelievers who face God without a covering of Jesus's righteousness. First Thessalonians 4 says the initial act of Jesus's return bestows resurrection bodies for all believers who are gathered up to him (vv. 6–7). Events introducing the final heaven move forward for the redeemed saints, with no possible threat or danger to them, despite the fact that cataclysmic events happen almost simultaneously to the unbeliever and the entire created order. Chapter 14 will speak more about the believer's judgment and potential rewards.

By speaking of a "day," the Bible does not mean a whole sequence of events necessarily is completed within twelve or twenty-four hours. Note that 1 Thessalonians 5:2 calls the return of Christ the *day of the Lord.* The term is no novelty; it appears many times in Old Testament Prophets. Some dispensationalists will argue that Christ's return and the day of the Lord are different events. However, 2 Thessalonians 2:2 is another place where Christ's return and the day of the Lord are referred to as one reality. (I choose to stay on topic here and not be drawn into a debate on the obscure subject of the dispensational concept of end times, as it is sufficiently answered by other sources that the reader can access. The whole interpretive scheme undergirding dispensationalism unfortunately is not sound.[2])

The fundamental basis of divine judgment is to produce an irrevocable separation between saved and lost. "The justice of God certainly is not about the malevolent anger of a despot with a grudge; it is judgment according to truth; awesome, but also liberating and comforting."[3] The Old Testament contains scores of predictions about this day of the Lord, with Joel 1:15 as but one example, "Alas for the day! For the day of the LORD is near, and as destruction from the Almighty it comes." It will be a climactic terminus when God reveals himself, and alongside every believer's vindication and glorification, judgment on unbelief will rain down in perfect divine justice. It is charted to be earth's final hour. The whole creation anticipates this climax: "For the creation waits with eager longing for the revealing of the sons of God. . . . The creation itself will be set free from its bondage to corruption and obtain the freedom of the glory of the children of God" (Rom. 8:19, 21). Mountains, oceans, fields, and streams have carried a burden of victimization by humanity's vandalism. The verdant planet God once made longs to shed itself of oil spills, strip mining, and polar ice cap meltdowns. And it will.

However, no unbelievers will desire this day to come if they have any concept of what it holds for them. Isaiah 2:10–11 predicts, "Enter into the rocks and hide in the dust from before the terror of the Lord, and from the splendor of his majesty. The haughty looks of man shall be brought low, and the lofty pride of men shall be humbled, and the Lord alone will be exalted in that day." The last chapter of the Old Testament anticipates this all-conclusive day of the Lord in Malachi 4:1 this way: "For behold, the day is coming, burning like an oven, when all the arrogant and all evildoers will be stubble. The day that is coming shall set them ablaze, says the LORD of hosts, so that it will leave them neither root nor branch." However, Malachi clarifies that this judgment day will not bring doom for those who trust in the Lord: "But for you who fear my name, the sun of righteousness shall rise with healing in its wings. You shall go out leaping like calves from the stall. And you shall tread down the wicked, for they will be ashes under the soles of your feet, on the day when I act, says the LORD of hosts" (vv. 2–3). I love Malachi's calf metaphor, since I live near a Lancaster County, Pennsylvania, Amish farm, where I frequently see young calves and heifers chasing each other around a pasture, gamboling in pure animal joy. Knowing that believers will greet their Lord that way, I shall be on the lookout for some of my more starchy Presbyterian friends to kick up their heels! The day of the Lord will be a display of concurrent judgment on unbelief and delightful mercy to the righteous people of God.

"Day of the Lord" terminology also is found in 2 Peter 3:10, where we read, "But the day of the Lord will come like a thief, and then the heavens will pass away with a roar, and the heavenly bodies will be burned up and dissolved, and the earth and the works that are done on it will be exposed." First Corinthians 3:13 calls this event by a shorthand name, as Paul wrote, "Each one's work will become manifest, for *the Day* will disclose it, because it will be revealed by fire, and the fire will test what sort of work each one has done." This will be the "Day" to end all previous days, the epicenter of God's display of himself in his holiness.

The Westminster Confession of Faith summarizes the goal God will achieve in all of this: "The *end* of God's appointing this day is for the manifestation of the glory of his mercy in the eternal salvation of the elect, and of his justice in the damnation of the reprobate, who are wicked and disobedient. For then shall the righteous go into everlasting life and receive that fullness of joy and refreshing which shall come from the presence of the Lord; but the wicked, who know not God, and obey not the gospel of Jesus Christ, shall be cast into eternal torments, and be punished with everlasting destruction from the presence of the Lord, and from the glory of his power" (33.2).

## DAY OF DREAD

Step back for a moment to ponder the Bible's promise that this day arrives with the suddenness of a thief's entry in the night. My wife and I were victims of a burglar early in our marriage. We dwelt in an apartment building with flimsy locks on all the doors. The unseen caller showed us no consideration: he came in the afternoon when we were out; he sent no notification informing us he might be dropping by to clean out loose cash or valuables. Of course, surprise is a thief's stock-in-trade. Likewise, believer and unbeliever alike will be utterly stunned by Christ's appearing.

All persons who have ever lived will be judged. John's apocalyptic vision included this scene: "And I saw the dead, great and small, standing before the throne, and books were opened. Then another book was opened, which is the book of life. And the dead were judged by what was written in the books, according to what they had done" (Rev. 20:12). From that first instant of shock, emotions proceed in two very opposite trajectories. The believer will behold Christ with amazed joy and wonderment; an electric thrill of delight will animate us, and we will have shouts of praise because "there is therefore now no condemnation for those who are in Christ Jesus" (Rom. 8:1). The unbeliever will see the same sight of Christ and be entirely undone in mind and spirit. If he makes any sound, it may be a scream. No nightmare he has ever experienced could bring him more horror.

I have not been a formal student for decades, but I occasionally relive a dream in which I discover there is to be a test announced in a class that I've not prepared for. I awaken in a cold sweat, surprised at how an adolescent fear can still unnerve my subconscious mind. Imagine facing that discovery when the surprise examination confronting you is God's own review of your life—knowing instinctively that you can only flunk—and that unalterable consequences indelibly written on your record will abide not for one semester's report card, but for eternity.

## CHRIST IS THE JUDGE

The last judgment will be administered by Jesus Christ, who has been appointed by his Father as the Lord over all. John 5:22–23 declares, "The Father judges no one, but has given all judgment to the Son, that all may honor the Son, just as they honor the Father." Acts 17:31 confirms, "[God] has fixed a day on which he will judge the world in righteousness by a man whom he has appointed; and of this he has given assurance to all by raising him from the dead." How completely appropriate is this delegation of judgment from Father to Son. After all, Christ is the one who became incarnate, died, and rose again for the salvation of his people. Jesus Christ bore divine judgment (Matt. 27:46). He was made a curse (Gal. 3:13). He was made to be sin for us (2 Cor. 5:21). Divine judgment was integral to understanding what he did on his cross. "Since those who believe in him are saved through him, how fitting it is that he should be their judge . . . this work will be Christ's final exaltation and greatest triumph."[4]

The last judgment exercised by Jesus will not resemble an earthly courtroom trial where *investigative* procedures aim to discover and establish facts unknown. Jesus Christ as God certainly knows every fact about us that can possibly be known. Jesus the Good Shepherd said in John 10:14, "I know my own and my own know me." We need to keep reiterating that Christians may know in advance that they are safe through this judgment. The blood of Jesus is our safe conduct! "We must say it again—in all this searching inquiry, the salvation of the individual Christian is not for a single moment in the slightest doubt. . . . The dying thief is the exemplar of all the redeemed, as he proceeds from the death of sin directly to the bliss of paradise by simple faith in Christ" (Luke 23:43).[5]

The flip side of Christ's all-comprehending knowledge of his elect is that his recognition applies equally to those who never have belonged to him. They are destined to hear, "I never knew you; depart from me, you workers of lawlessness" (Matt. 7:23). Until this final hour comes, some men and women are able to pose as Christians and deceive even leaders of the church, since elders and pastors lack the flawless discernment of Jesus. Paul Helm wrote, "No human judge has all the facts. No jury is completely unbiased, even though every effort may be made to reduce bias. Re-trials, appeals against sentence, perversions of justice, mistaken identity—these features of human judicial systems testify to the fact that human (court) arrangements are fallible."[6] On a few occasions as a pastor, I have dealt with individuals who had nearly mastered the Christian masquerade. These people quote Scripture often and with fluency beyond the level of many authentic believers. Only over a long span of time does the behavior of these people, or maybe a lack of holy behavior, prove them to be entirely self-serving and deeply hypocritical. Fruit of the Holy Spirit is invisible in their actions and their treatment of others.

However, when a church session makes a prayerful, long-considered judgment that such people should be excommunicated and judged not to be believers for their unrepentant offenses, some Christians, who are still being taken in by the slick charade of the apostates, will protest. In the very end—standing before Christ—these people will find no place to hide from the all-knowing gaze of Christ the King on this judgment throne. "God judges the *secrets* of men by Christ Jesus" (Rom. 2:16). The fictional X-ray vision of Superman is nothing compared to Christ's gaze upon every thought and intention. As sovereign Ruler over all mankind, Jesus will wield absolute authority for holy discrimination based on what his all-knowing eye beholds. He will judge human beings based on what we have done with his cross and his lordship before that fateful hour comes.

## THE STANDARD OF DIVINE JUDGMENT

Sentences administered by human courts do have some aim of punishment in view, but especially in the last century there has been the hope of rehabilitation, restoring the offender to the status of being a law-abiding citizen once more. We must realize that Christ exercises total justice that in no sense is remedial or rehabilitative in its intent; it does not expect to produce better behavior the next time around. This justice is directed against the intrinsic moral character of sin, as defiance toward the God of righteousness. Paul Helm stated, "Sin is in its essence rebellion against God. . . . By disobeying God the sinner attempts to rob God of his glory, to de-throne him. Happily, it is a rebellion that never succeeds. . . . So instead of thinking, 'Sin is not so bad, how extreme it is of God to punish it in hell,' we must think, 'What must sin be like, if it results in sinners justly going to hell?'"[7]

Divine judgment is nothing less than the outworking of God's perfections. Some people hear of God's wrath for sin, and they think this means their shallow notion of a normally calm and polite God suddenly goes berserk with uncharacteristic anger. Heaven's mild-mannered Dr. Jekyll changes into the monstrous Mr. Hyde. But God is no chameleon. He need not transform his character to execute judgment upon evil and sin. He only needs to be himself.

Judgment, in fact, dwells at the very core of God's holy perfection. Habakkuk had it spot on when the prophet addressed the Lord saying,

"You who are of purer eyes than to see evil" (1:13). The prophet understood a holy intolerance is intrinsic to the divine nature. In Genesis 18:25 Abraham expressed confidence that God would correctly discern between evil and righteousness. He said, "Shall not the Judge of all the earth do what is just?" This eradicates any possibility of God's final accounting against sinful humanity resembling a divine temper tantrum. At the heart of everything the Lord does in history, he aims for evil to be finally wiped off from his creation and for his justice to be triumphant.

We must stop trying to domesticate God. People are puzzled upon hearing Hebrews 10:31 declare: "It is a fearful thing to fall into the hands of the living God." The fear of God primarily indicates that he is not to be trifled with. Biblical words like "wrath," "fury," "vindication," or "indignation" do not describe God suddenly breaking away from the moorings of his former character. His wrath is a completely appropriate and necessary response of the Holy One toward evil and sin—after he has shown longsuffering mercy for centuries. Sin is intrinsically a moral violation of God's very essence and it must be judged, or else God denies what he is. This means that the "abnormal" situation is not an hour when judgment finally does fall, but rather the centuries of merciful withholding of perfectly measured strokes of just wrath. *Mercy* is abnormal! We have become so used to the abnormality of prolonged mercy that the normalcy of visible justice startles us.

God is therefore glorified by all his acts of judgment because at long last, justice shines forth. The praise of his justice, mercy, and grace are splendidly displayed whenever evil is indicted and finally deposed. Judgment covers God with magnificent credit. His fame for righteousness will beam forth, when he visibly acts in complete conformity to his nature.

There is no proper sense in which you should ever picture God's justice and his love engaged in a tug of war where one must "win" against the other. The love of God never acts at the expense of any other divine attribute. Paul said God's grace "reign[s] through righteousness" (Rom. 5:21). Only because Christ Jesus perfectly kept the just and righteous demands of the law could he become the perfect fulfillment of God's love for us at the cross. Only by the Son following divine justice perfectly in his active obedience to the Father are the love and grace of God offered to us in Christ. There will be no contradiction in the final disposition of God against unbelief: he must be righteous in his wrath and loving in his justice!

## SAME JUSTICE FOR ALL?

Cornelis Venema comments that God's justice "will be the same for everyone: whatever has been revealed to them concerning God's will."[8] Differing levels of revelation are given to various men and nations. Jesus made it clear on many occasions that whoever receives the most privileged knowledge of God's Word will have the highest accountability required. In Matthew 11:20–22 he verbally blasted the towns of Chorazin and Bethsaida, since they beheld very full and direct revelation of him, but nonetheless rejected him. Romans 1:19 teaches that all mankind is fundamentally culpable to judgment, because "what can be known about God is plain to them, because God has shown it to them." There are indeed people living in gospel darkness who lack the full revelation of Christ. Despite this, all are responsible to God for acting upon whatever light they do have.

Contrary to our ideas of fairness, the Bible says that even natural revelation, which remote nations and tribes all have, is sufficient to test whether they will turn to God or against him. "Although they knew God, they did not honor him as God or give thanks to him, but they became futile in their thinking, and their foolish hearts were darkened" (Rom. 1:21). *All* will bear the full weight of responsibility at the last day for what they have done with divine revelation they rejected. Although some have had less detailed knowledge, they still are not excused for throwing aside what they did possess. No one can be excused on the basis of ignorance. However, there is some suggestion of differing levels of punishment in hell based on privileges rejected. See Luke 12:45–48, where unfaithful servants are said to get varied punishments from their master. But since this subject is not well developed in Scripture, we have no license to speculate about it.

## GIVE US PEACE AND SECURITY

First Thessalonians 5:3 states, "While people are saying 'there is peace and security,' then sudden destruction will come upon them . . ." Do you realize that peace and security is a dominant theme of modern life? Dr. Francis Schaeffer famously indicted American Christians in the 1970s when he predicted that we would allow government to roll over us with increasing threats to our liberty and morality as long as we could cling to our "personal peace and affluence." He was right. What is it most Americans want our local and federal governments to provide? Above all else, a guarantee that my little domestic cocoon can remain intact, unmolested by economic or international threats.

Has this yen for peace and material security anaesthetized us against a fervent biblical expectation of the ultimate body/soul disaster? Let me state the question in a very down-to-earth way. What if I knew by some prophetic revelation of God (and I do not admit to ever having such revelations) that on Sunday next, your house would blow up at three o'clock due to a natural gas explosion. If I absolutely knew that this would occur, do you think I would shake hands at the church door and tell you with a smile, "Have a peaceful Sunday afternoon. Enjoy your day at home with your family." No! I would say, "Be sure to get your family and valuables out of that house before 2:45 p.m." Then, if I came to your house early that afternoon and realized you were not heeding my dire warning, I'd bang on the front door, pleading with you to get out. I'd urge you not to stop to fill a suitcase or rescue the antiques—just get *out*! And if you still would not heed me, I might grab your children and run with them, hoping that would lure you to follow. This was all Jonathan Edwards was doing when he preached *Sinners in the Hands of an Angry God*. But it seems people prefer to blow up, inside their unsafe dwellings.

The response of unbelieving humanity to God's historic warnings of an imminent day of the Lord matches the prediction of Jesus in Matthew 24:37. He said, "As were the days of Noah, so will be the coming of the Son of Man. For as in those days before the flood, they were eating and drinking, marrying and giving in marriage, until the day when Noah entered the ark." Can you dispute this, from observing the common habits of society today? Second Peter 3:4 so ably describes people who boldly declare, "Where is this promise of his coming? For ever since the fathers fell asleep, all things are continuing as they were from the beginning of creation." People discredit the Bible's predictions of a final cataclysmic accounting for sin by wiping their memories clear of the fact that God once judged all mankind by means of a great flood. It is one thing to be disingenuously ignorant, but people prove they are *willfully* ignorant. They deliberately reject or suppress the knowledge of God available to them.

"Peace and security" people tend to watch the stock market reports intently. They ask how their baseball team is doing in advancing toward the playoffs, and they pay rapt attention to the evening news when that day's lottery numbers are announced. While doing these things, they privately spit in the face of Christ, the coming Lord and Judge. Pursuits of this earth have become their all-consuming goals. They have no mind at all for eternity looming at their doorway. The unbeliever has no capacity to consider a crashing end to his idyllic daydream world.

## SUDDEN DESTRUCTION

First Thessalonians 4 predicts that the action of Christ toward the believer will mean blessed deliverance: He gathers his own and gives them resurrection bodies. We read in chapter 5 about those who are likewise stuck in unbelief. "Sudden destruction will come upon them as labor pains come upon a pregnant woman, and they will not escape" (5:3). *Destruction* is a terrible word. Paul later calls this "eternal destruction, away from the presence of the Lord and from the glory of his might, when he comes on that day to be glorified in his saints, and to be marveled at among all who have believed" (2 Thess. 1:9–10).

I dearly wish that "eternal destruction" could mean simple extinction or obliteration. I desire it. But to tell you so would be to perjure myself as a teacher of God's Word. Eternal destruction at its bare minimum means banishment from the blessing and protection of the living God. I ruefully must declare that those who *want* to be separated from the right knowledge of God and his Son today will finally get their wish. God will most assuredly rule over the hell they occupy, but never will his smile of goodness or his mercy mitigate the disaster experienced there.

All this comes with the suddenness of a bolt of lightning. It will *seize* the unbeliever, as a woman's labor pains of birth begin. She has no choice in that hour to say, "Oh wait—I cannot give birth today. I have a hairdresser's appointment, and it just is not convenient for my plans." She is swept into an event in which her body overrules all other choices. The thief-in-the-night image used by both Paul and Jesus emphasizes total surprise. A "birth pains" metaphor underscores that there is no escape for unbelief in the day of the Lord. Those who oppose and disregard the gospel of Christ crucified and risen are not simply discovered in some minor error that can be easily put right in the hereafter. In one stroke of history's clock, they will be irreparably undone.

You will tell me this chapter is heavy with gloom. Some have discarded this book in disgust by now. People did the same with Edwards's famous sermon. I now hold out to you the same grace of God that my eighteenth-century brother from Massachusetts preached so passionately. *Today* is the day of God's infinite grace. Jonathan Edwards was absolutely right about a rotten wooden floor that could give way any moment and plunge you into wrath. However, you have not yet broken through, and you need not do so! Right now is the time to consider your eternal predicament and respond to the God of mercy who has protected you from disaster so far.

In mid-April 1912, several ships brought survivors of the RMS *Titanic* disaster into New York Harbor. Officials of the White Star Line compiled two lists. They had taken down each name of the 706 passengers they'd rescued alive. Then they compared this list to the ship's original passenger manifest and thus learned the names of the 1,517 out of 2,223 on board who did not survive. All were stone dead in twenty-eight–degree North Atlantic water, where the opportunity for survival was about fifteen minutes, maximum. Only two types of people were on board the Titanic—the saved and the lost.

Paul concluded in 1 Thessalonians 5:4–6, "But you are not in darkness, brothers, for that day to surprise you like a thief. For you are all children of light, children of the day. We are not of the night or of the darkness. So then let us not sleep as others do, but let us keep awake and be sober." Jesus bore his Father's judgment. The divine Son's cry of dereliction, "My God, my God, why have you forsaken me?" (Matt. 27:46) proved that the full chastisement of our sins crashed down upon him. And now we await this same Jesus who will come as the only qualified Judge of humanity.

Run to Christ the Judge today, and grasp the hem of his fearful yet splendid judicial robe with all your might.

> Great and amazing are your deeds,
>     O Lord God the Almighty!
> Just and true are your ways,
>     O King of the nations!
> Who will not fear you, O Lord,
>     and glorify your name?
> For you alone are holy.
>     All nations will come
>     and worship you,
> for your righteous acts have been revealed. (Rev. 15:3–4).

Then Peter said in reply, "See, we have left everything and followed you. What then will we have?" Jesus said to them, "Truly, I say to you, in the new world, when the Son of Man will sit on his glorious throne, you who have followed me will also sit on twelve thrones, judging the twelve tribes of Israel. And everyone who has left houses or brothers or sisters or father or mother or children or lands, for my name's sake, will receive a hundredfold and will inherit eternal life. But many who are first will be last, and the last first."

**MATTHEW 19:27–30**

Now if anyone builds on the foundation with gold, silver, precious stones, wood, hay, straw—each one's work will become manifest, for the Day will disclose it, because it will be revealed by fire, and the fire will test what sort of work each one has done. If the work that anyone has built on the foundation survives, he will receive a reward. If anyone's work is burned up, he will suffer loss, though he himself will be saved, but only as by fire.

**I CORINTHIANS 3:12–15**

# CHAPTER FOURTEEN

# ARE CHRISTIANS JUDGED FOR REWARDS?

☼

*IF THERE IS A YOUNG* music student in your family, you as a parent, grandparent, aunt, or uncle might be invited to a children's recital. Attending the event you will hear some fairly credible music performed by older players; you will also hear some stumbling melodies and awkward rhythms from the youngest players. However, it is certain that *all* musicians who perform will be applauded enthusiastically. Every parent will beam with pride, regardless of the degree of talent shown by their young musician. No prizes are awarded to differentiate winners or losers in such a program—the salutation for effort is democratic. Similarly, in recent years it has become common with children's sports teams for every child participating to receive a small trophy—all of identical size. Self-esteem psychology of today dictates that we do not want anyone to feel unappreciated, regardless of athletic ability.

Do those examples resemble what we Christian believers should anticipate when the Lord Jesus welcomes us to heaven's final home with his warmly spoken, "Well done, good and faithful servant" (Matt. 25:21)? What does the Bible teach us to anticipate about any possible degrees of differentiation in our kingdom reward?

Christians have always wondered about a recompense for being Christ's disciple. Peter asked, in so many words, "What will I *get* for my sacrificial discipleship?" We have been asking that—at least silently—ever since his time. Should trophies be awarded for obeying God's law over the course of a lifetime? For influencing many souls to trust in Christ, as Billy Graham has done? The missionary who forsook a career in medicine to serve in a third world country at very modest salary must think about this once in a while. I have pastor friends who are very poorly paid and have been mistreated by congregations, yet they are talented men who might have made a mark in other career fields. What is the reward for their perseverance in a calling to gospel ministry? Is this an unworthy question to be entertained?

The psalmist Asaph once cast too many side-glances at fat-cat materialists of his time—folks who seemed to prosper without Godward faith. After doing this for a while, he moaned, "All in vain have I kept my heart clean and washed my hands in innocence" (Ps. 73:13). It seemed to Asaph as if all the world's goodies rolled into the laps of those who ignored God, while believers got nothing for moral living and godliness. Haven't you thought this yourself—at least sometimes?

There are definite places where Scripture appears to recognize individual rewards for Christian discipleship, humility, and faithfulness on earth. However, whatever recognition comes our way is only an expression of God's gracious dealing, not meritorious distinction—only abounding gifts from God's grace, layered upon the foundation of a gracious salvation. For believers, the final judgment simply reveals to plain sight what is already true. We read in Romans 2:16, "God judges the secrets of men." Jesus also said, "On the day of judgment people will give account for every careless word they speak" (Matt. 12:36). And Paul said that Christ will "bring to light the things now hidden in darkness and will disclose the purposes of the heart. Then each one will receive his commendation from God" (1 Cor. 4:5). Having innermost thoughts and idle words exposed seems primarily threatening. Yet God's purpose is not to ruin us in this shameful exposure. This unmasking of secrets and tearing away of our best maintained privacy curtain might seem like the unveiling of the phony Wizard of Oz in his hidden control booth, but it cannot condemn any who are already Christ's possessions.

First Corinthians 4:5 says that "commendation" not "condemnation" will follow this deep probing of the believer—for among our "secrets" will be quiet deeds of service and compassion done for Jesus's sake, sacrificial giving, devoted worship, long labors in prayer—all unseen until that hour. The great white throne will be our place of vindication. Even viewing a formerly secret mound of my sins heaped up like a warehouse-sized manure pile will bring greater glory to my Savior, since he covered them once-for-all in his righteousness. In the light of that clear day, my every sin will be a forgiven sin! Thus Jesus the Judge says, "Come, you who are blessed by my Father, inherit the kingdom prepared for you from the foundation of the world" (Matt. 25:34).

## ONE CROWN OF LIFE

We must consider the background of Matthew 19:27–29. Peter had previously heard Jesus say that the rich young ruler who claimed to have scrupulously kept God's law was *not* qualified for eternity based upon good works (19:23–26). Chewing on that, Peter impulsively cried, "See, we have left everything and followed you. What then will we have?" (v. 27). A further indicator that questions about status and rewards were very much alive among the disciples of Jesus came just after this, in Matthew 20:20–21. The stage mother of James and John apparently had no shy bone in her body when it came to promoting her two sons to sit on eternal thrones flanking Jesus's right and left sides. Other disciples also had thought about this pecking order among them. Even as they came to the upper room for the Last Supper with Jesus, disciples murmured over which one of them ranked above the others (Luke 22:24). They were not blind to realize that there was an inner circle composed of Peter, James, and John who were accorded certain privileged experiences with Jesus. The mother of James and John was simply the boldest to speak out about this.

If you don't think a consciousness of kingdom status is around today, you would find it enlightening to listen in upon any gathering of pastors who come together as strangers at a seminar or conference. Within a relatively short time after introductions, many will find some way to learn the membership size of congregations served by other pastors around them, and the men will be mentally sorted and categorized accordingly. These are games pastors play!

We all possess a baseline commercial attitude for estimating the good that we imagine our lives contribute to the world. Since we pay cash for goods and services, and since we consume and are paid by the hour or week to labor for an employer, it comes naturally to our mercenary minds that good deeds, acts of kindness, charitable giving, spiritual faithfulness, or even having more sheep in your congregation's corral should somehow be paid back in spiritual economics.

If my neighbor uses his snowblower to open the drifts across the mouth of my driveway, should I ask my wife to bake him a pie as a gift— or is it enough for me to verbally thank him and leave it at that? If I am the one using the snowblower for the same kindly deed, do I quietly watch to see if there will be recompense forthcoming from my neighbor, yet act surprised when it is given? We are truly devious creatures as we keep score in these matters.

Jesus told Peter that all who sacrifice any tangible benefit in this life for his sake, whether wife, family, or real estate will receive "a hundred-fold" back, and inherit eternal life as well (Matt. 19:29). This is an indication of definite future rewards. While the Lord's terms go beyond mere replacement value, the exact form the future reward might take is unspecific. The tone of such a text cautions us from applying a crass mathematical formula to precisely calculate heavenly wealth—lest we miss the whole point. Jesus seemed to say that the privilege of being with him in eternity is in itself a blessing beyond calculation. Once we enter that reward, the notion of comparing it to some miniscule loss we sustained for him will make us laugh at the idea that these eternal things could ever be calculated on an earthly economic scale. Disciples "judging the twelve tribes of Israel" is a metaphor, but a powerful one nevertheless. It tells us that Jesus saw his spiritual kingdom in the church as the fulfillment of Israel's national destiny.

Immediately after Peter's inquiry about rewards, Matthew 20:1–16 presents the parable of workers in the vineyard. There Jesus taught about workers hired at different times for day-labor in the fields, with all being paid the same wage at sundown. Those who worked all day had at first agreed to the wage, so it was fair for them. For those who worked only the last two hours of the afternoon, the same wage was superfair. No one was cheated. This employer's action obviously demonstrated God's abundant grace: one and the same salvation is experienced in equal measure by a first-century apostle of Jesus like Peter and by the lowliest believer in the twenty-first century; there is fundamental equality at the base of our salvation. "For by grace you have been saved through faith. And this is not your own doing; it is the gift of God, not a result of works, so that no one may boast," declares Ephesians 2:8–9.

No human being who enters God's final dwelling in the new heaven and new earth will dare say, "Thank goodness I was found worthy." Perish the idea! All who are redeemed in Jesus Christ are equally redeemed. In terms of salvation, all believers receive one identical crown of grace as God's free gift.

If you must think of salvation in terms of rewards, consider it as a portion of the prize God the Father gave Jesus the Son for his perfect obedience unto death. Isaiah 53 predicted that the will of the Lord will prosper in Jesus's death and resurrection. God predicted of his Son, "Therefore I will divide *him* [Christ] a portion with the many, and he shall divide the spoil with the strong, because he poured out his soul to death and was numbered with the transgressors" (v. 12). The kingdom of heaven is God's reward given to Jesus. He shares it by sheer grace with all who believe on his name. He is the general after a great victory, parceling out spoils from the vanquished army among his loyal troops.

## JUDGMENT BASED ON WORKS?

Based on what has just been said, people who know the New Testament gospel may be confused by what Jesus said in Matthew 25 about separating "sheep and goats." The confusion comes because it appears the basis of eternal separation between the two groups is evidence of *works* men do—did they visit the needy, clothe them, or bring them food? (Matt. 25:35–40). At a superficial level we could wonder if Matthew 25 is telling us that salvation is based on social outreach programs to feed the poor. However, there is no contradiction.

Gospel salvation still is only by God's grace through faith in Christ and never merited by our works. Yet Christ the Judge infallibly identifies his people by the outworking of his salvation in deeds of mercy or obedience. Matthew 25 absolutely does not teach that works save anyone. It says that the all-seeing judgment of Christ measures visible works of righteousness as trace evidences of redeeming grace in lives of true disciples—like indicting fingerprints at a crime scene. James 2:26 and other texts teach that "faith apart from works is dead." God's final evaluation of who is truly in Christ will not reward empty professions of faith. John Calvin's classic statement is, "It is faith alone that justifies, yet the faith which justifies is not alone."[1] Works always accompany this faith. The Savior expects visible fruit to grow on the tree of our profession. By this fruit you will be vindicated. "There is a vital distinction to be drawn between a judgment that is according to works and judgment that is *for* works. . . . No one is justified *for* works, nor *for* faith. We are justified by faith and according to works."[2]

## A DIFFERENCE IN FINAL STANDING

Now we examine some passages that say there will be certain differentiations among God's saints in heaven. A prime example is 1 Corinthians

3:10–15. Paul was aware of differing ways ministers of the gospel might carry out preaching and disciple-making ministries. Evidently it was (and is) possible for some to be saved men, although as gospel servants they were either lazy or guilty of poor workmanship. Perhaps they mixed truth with error, or were superficial in applying God's truth to needy souls. Like characters in the nursery rhyme *The Three Little Pigs*, these servants of the Lord built with "wood, hay, straw." Their cheap materials and shoddy workmanship will not endure. First Corinthians 3:13 says, "The Day will disclose it, because [the work] will be revealed by fire, and the fire will test what sort of work each one has done. If the work that anyone has built on the foundation survives, he will receive a reward. If anyone's work is burned up, he will suffer loss, though he himself will be saved, but only as by fire."

These people, escaping condemnation "as through flames"—with their clothing figuratively singed and earthly accomplishments dissolved—are contrasted to gospel witnesses who taught the depths of God's truth. They worked humbly and gave people the pure bread of life to eat. These witnesses built with "gold, silver, precious stones" and thus, their ministry works endure for God's glory. Only these faithful servants are said to have a "reward" (3:14.) So it appears that even Christian leaders may have different standing in heaven based on faithfulness while on earth. Yet once again, we are given no specific measurements of how God calculates this, or descriptions of what their reward will look like. That is left entirely for Christ to determine.

Other similar texts can be cited. Matthew 5:12 says those who are persecuted for Christ on earth have a great reward in heaven—a reward most Americans will never receive, for we do not taste painful rejection because of the gospel that thousands of our brethren do in Islamic or atheistic countries. Matthew 10:41 also mentions a "prophet's reward." Exactly what that amounts to is left deliberately vague. The ego of every "prophet," ancient or modern, has to be better off by letting that obscurity remain.

Second Corinthians 5:10 has a key word on this subject: "We must all appear before the judgment seat of Christ, so that each one may receive what is *due* for what he has done in the body, whether good or evil." Again, Paul is not suddenly preaching salvation by works, and the Christian's salvation is not in jeopardy within the scrutiny of this judgment. Quiet moral character, integrity in our words, endurance of suffering by faith, winning souls to the gospel, faithful stewardship, hidden prayer, hospitality to God's people, dying for Christ, and much else will figure into this wondrous evaluation of Christ, completed in an instant.

## NO MERIT BADGES IN GRACE

Let us bring these ideas together in a synthesis: (1) There is one crown of life by grace through faith in Christ which is the same for all. (2) Believers can do some actions that God will recognize as worthy of commendation or undefined rewards. (3) We do not know the exact nature of the rewards. Obviously, we are not dealing with the *Boy Scout Handbook*, where a scout consults the manual to learn exact requirements to earn the auto mechanics or the astronomy or the cooking merit badges. I once attended a ceremony in which a young man from my congregation received his Eagle Scout award. He wore a sash across his shoulder to display what seemed to me like thirty or more merit badges. No uniformed scout in the room had nearly as many. I was duly impressed. I knew he must have followed many patient steps to finish designated projects to earn those badges. The Bible never prescribes any similar systematic process for singling out Eagle Scout disciples. Instead it gives us the revealed will of God for a life shaped by the way of the cross. We are called to trust in Christ, counting the cost of submission to him. We are to serve others, pray, witness, and sacrifice; to put pride to death; to humble our hearts and be thankful. The earthly outcome could be that I die with Auca Indian spears piercing my body, or I get fired from my pulpit because influential folks in the congregation don't like my peculiarities of character. It could mean alienation from your son who chooses a homosexual partner over godly parents. Christians who look for proportionate rewards in this lifetime are misguided. At the end of the day, Luke 17:10 speaks best for the right attitude shown by a disciple of Jesus: "When you have done all that you were commanded, [you should] say, 'We are unworthy servants; we have only done what was our *duty*.'"

Beware of the same grasping mindset that snared Judas. Although more than one motive likely propelled him to betray Jesus, it seems clear that a main thrust was his private calculation that he somehow had more coming to him than he had received. The word "mercenary" means anyone who serves primarily for the reward or pay he expects to get. Judas was a mercenary disciple—and therefore no Christian at all. Never allow a notion of building merit for yourself to motivate Christian service. "Rather than serving the Lord out of gratitude for his grace in Christ, the Christian life would degenerate into a selfish pursuit of personal advantage and gain."[3] Our self-seeking pride could thereby smash the very reward it prizes most.

## UNEQUAL VESSELS, EQUALLY FILLED

Jonathan Edwards most helpfully said, "The saints in heaven are like so many vessels of different sizes, all cast into a sea of happiness in Christ, where every vessel no matter what its size is full to the brim." I find that image very helpful. Edwards continued, "Everyone will be completely satisfied and full of happiness, having as much as he is capable of enjoying or desiring. . . . God's will [shall] become so much their own, the fulfilling of his will, let it be what it may, fills them with inconceivable satisfaction."[4] Different gifts and capacities apparently will still be evident in our resurrection lives. God's kingdom is egalitarian in terms of the foundation of grace in eternal life. Whether you are a one-quart vessel or a gallon vessel, you will nevertheless be just as full to overflowing with the glory of Jesus Christ!

An illustration from church history demonstrates how to wear our merits lightly in this world. It comes from the relationship of two godly eighteenth-century men, the Rev. George Whitefield and the Rev. John Wesley. Whitefield was a Calvinist who emphasized grace and divine sovereignty in salvation, and his preaching was God's instrument to launch Great Awakening fires of revival in Britain and America. Wesley was the Arminian who more ardently defended human free will. Early in life they were close friends. Then Whitefield, the younger man, rose to prominence first, and he chose John Wesley to take his place as an open-air preacher in England when he visited America. Wesley's ministry then flourished with God's blessing largely because Whitefield launched him as his replacement on that occasion.

However, in what many at the time judged to be a bizarre act of ingratitude, John Wesley, with no provocation, later attacked Whitefield's doctrinal views on election and predestination with a sharply worded printed tract. This caused a public breach between the two men and their followers which lasted for years before it was eventually reconciled. Whitefield's friends wanted him to fight back and publish a counterattack on Wesley. He repeatedly refused. (When he did finally write a reply, it was a model of gracious theological discourse.) Whitefield continued to speak well of John Wesley to his followers, causing them consternation. One of them asked Whitefield if he expected to see John Wesley in heaven. Whitefield famously replied, "I fear not . . . for he will be so near to the eternal throne and we at such a distance, we shall hardly get a sight of him."[5]

Can we persevere with Christ in daily faithfulness, while being humble, gracious, and unselfconscious of good in ourselves, as George Whitefield was? Any eternal rewards we may receive from our Lord will only be more grace piled on, just as we did not merit the first stroke.

In light of my own tremendous demerits, it is utterly amazing to think that my Lord might tell me, "Well done, good and faithful servant" (Matt. 25:21). I can produce no evidence for why he should say, "Come, you who are blessed of my Father, inherit the kingdom prepared for you from the foundation of the world" (Matt. 25:34). Hearing that, Christian friends, we will be overwhelmed by everlasting joy! Therefore, let us live obediently before Christ, with our minds well marinated in humble gratitude for his extraordinary promises of grace upon grace reserved for us.

*Amen!*

# PART FIVE

# THE FINAL HEAVEN

But the day of the Lord will come like a thief, and then the heavens will pass away with a roar, and the heavenly bodies will be burned up and dissolved, and the earth and the works that are done on it will be exposed. . . . But according to his promise we are waiting for new heavens and a new earth in which righteousness dwells.

**2 PETER 3:10, 13**

Then I saw a new heaven and a new earth, for the first heaven and the first earth had passed away, and the sea was no more. And I saw the holy city, new Jerusalem, coming down out of heaven from God, prepared as a bride adorned for her husband. And I heard a loud voice from the throne saying, "Behold, the dwelling place of God is with man. He will dwell with them, and they will be his people, and God himself will be with them as their God. He will wipe away every tear from their eyes, and death shall be no more, neither shall there be mourning, nor crying, nor pain anymore, for the former things have passed away."

And he who was seated on the throne said, "Behold, I am making all things new."

**REVELATION 21:1–5**

# CHAPTER FIFTEEN

# NEW HEAVENS AND A NEW EARTH

☼

*AN OLD GOSPEL SONG SAYS,* "This world is not my home, I'm just a-passing through; my treasures are laid up somewhere beyond the blue. The angels beckon me from heaven's open door, and I can't feel at home in this world anymore." The song correctly emphasizes lasting detachment from things of the present world because we are only pilgrims on earth. However, the notion that our heavenly destination is "somewhere beyond the blue" is utterly wrong—if it leads you to picture the final heaven of God located in the dim ether of outer space, on cloudland. Life in the heaven of popular imagination is so spiritualized as to be barren and sterile.[1] Everyone dressed in identical white robes, carrying a harp to choir practice is not only unappealing, it is totally unbiblical. The Bible teaches that our final dwelling for eternity shall in fact be a renewed version of planet *earth*.

This material world, after a tremendous makeover, will become the permanent dwelling place for the saints of God in Christ. It is amazing how many Christians who should know better are completely surprised by this concept. Randy Alcorn wrote, "We are pilgrims in this life, not because our home will never be on earth, but because our eternal home is not currently on earth. It was [in Eden] and it will be, but it's not now."[2]

## WHAT NO EYE HAS SEEN

We are generally comfortable and contented in our present lives. Even to Christians, the idea of heavenly life is moderately disturbing. Who wants to go through a radical change of all things familiar? Moving only upsets people—we'd rather stay put! With our definition of hard reality fixated in the present world, Christians in their own quiet ways may end up joining materialists in dismissing the Bible's view of heaven as "pie-in-the-sky, bye-and-bye."

First Corinthians 2:9–10 declares, "'What no eye has seen, nor ear heard, nor the heart of man imagined, what God has prepared for those who love him'—these things God has revealed to us through the Spirit. For the Spirit searches everything, even the depths of God." What a paradoxical statement. No man has seen the final heaven, yet God's Spirit has given us enough prophetic and symbolic foretastes to be able to long for it. How would the Spirit make glimpses of heaven known, except on the pages of Scripture? The Bible contains enough clear glimpses, apocalyptic visions, and heavy hints about the final heaven, that we are not entirely clueless.

Symbolic pictures in the Bible cause us problems because we are always forgetting they are figures of speech, not the reality itself. The jeweled symbolism of the new earth that includes streets of gold, gates of pearl, and names written on foreheads is chockablock with poetic metaphor, meant to emphasize dazzling splendor and the incalculable value of heaven. If we literalize such descriptions, the images depict a place that is cold, hard, and unnatural.[3] Scripture images of our eternal dwelling were not given us to be the equivalent of travel brochures illustrating Norway's fjords or Alaska's mountains, meant to tantalize me as I plan a vacation. In films or television travelogues, we are able to see exactly where we might visit in Paris and to know the specific sights of Rome before we arrive. However a "wall built of solid jasper" (Rev. 21:18) or a "tree of life with its twelve kinds of fruit" (Rev. 22:2) are not photographic images. God did not intend that literalism. We always need to ask what a symbol represents—what is it meant to *teach*?

We are infected by too many purely imaginative ideas of heaven that have no root in Scripture at all. Worst of all is the downright foolish notion of cartoonists that we become angels after death. If there is one declaration we may make with complete certainty it is that no human being will ever become an angel, not under any circumstances—and we will not walk upon clouds.

Paul Helm illustrated the matter this way: "It might be said that a valid ticket to York is the pledge of my arrival in York. Yet possession of the ticket gives me no idea at all of what York will be like; its history, its atmosphere, the architectural wonder of Yorkminster Cathedral, and so on."[4] God has not left us clueless—yet heavenly wonders awaiting us are multidimensional. Now we know only by suggestion or inference what will be fully revealed. "For now we see in a mirror dimly, but then face to face. Now I know in part; but then I shall know fully, even as I have been fully known" (1 Cor. 13:12).

## PARADISE LOST AND REGAINED

Now we consider a further stunning aspect that Scripture unfolds from the complex event called the day of the Lord. Having already considered the believer's resurrection body, we turn to the resurrection of our *planet*. Heaven in a true sense was separated from the earth by Adam's sin. Eden fled from precincts of earth, and no archeologist has located any geographical remains of the garden of Eden in some corner of Iraq—nor will that site ever be identified on a Middle East map.

A few miles from me in Lancaster County, Pennsylvania, is a little crossroads village. Sometimes I drive through it, noting a sign that says "Eden," and I think to myself: "Oh—if only it were! But it cannot be, not yet." The splendor of Eden will be brought back into this present dimension of existence. Earth's paradise lost will become paradise regained. The work of Christ was not only intended to save individual souls; the entire cosmos awaits rescue from the blight of human sin. The final heaven will be a made-over version of the earth and skies we have today. We may expect this reconstituted final heaven-on-earth to bring us beauty, sensory delights, and experiences bursting with ongoing joyful discoveries.

## THE RENEWAL OF ALL THINGS

Beginning with the venerable television program *This Old House*, I have always enjoyed home makeover shows—especially when the house being remodeled is a historic home from the eighteenth or nineteenth centuries, with good architectural bones that display authentic features from its period. It is a joy to see 1950s pink linoleum peeled away or a walled-up stone fireplace revealed or original Chestnut ceiling joists exposed to sight. Likewise, a correct understanding of the new heavens and new earth does not require *de novo* creation out of nothing, as God performed the first time in Genesis 1–2. It is more about renovation to "put things back" to original glory, before the cosmos suffered from the rack and ruin of human sin. In both 2 Peter 3:13 and Revelation 21:1, the Greek word for the newness of the earth is not *neos* but *kainos*. The first means new in time or point of origin; the second means new in its nature or quality, which is formed in continuity with a present planetary existence.[5]

It must be significant that nearly all of Jesus's miracles done on earth, with a few exceptions, were acts of *restoration*. For the most part, Jesus did not create brand new things. Instead, blind eyes saw again; demons were cast out; deaf ears heard; dead bodies rose—original creaturely wholeness was reinstated. So in the day of the Lord, God's natural creation returns to the Creator's prototype. Gone will be smog and polluted rivers. Sperm whales will no longer be hunted. Broad hints from the Prophets say that the animal kingdom will no longer tremble at man's approach. In Genesis 1 the Lord called all that he made "very good." We can imagine Christ saying this once more, in our hearing. The original creation mandate to the first man and woman was, "And God blessed them. And God said to them, 'Be fruitful and multiply and fill the earth and subdue it and have dominion.' . . . And God saw everything that he had made, and behold, it was very good" (Gen. 1:28, 31). Since we together with our first ancestors lost that blessed place and so much of the superb quality of life as destined for us there, all of Adam's descendants have been "homesick" for Eden. Our first ancestors delighted in direct fellowship with the Lord, and we ache to have that back—or more accurately speaking—we long to taste it for the first time.

The biblical story began from nothing and ends with a new beginning built upon the creation damage we have done. Eugene Peterson wrote, "The sin-ruined creation of Genesis is restored in the sacrifice-renewed creation of Revelation."[6] Did you ever think about how the last two chapters of the Bible, Revelation 21 and 22, mirror Genesis 1 and 2? Rivers, mountains, and trees reappear in the garden of God in Revelation, as matching bookends to the Bible's beginning. You can frame the big picture of Bible history by thinking of man's existence in just three epochs: First is original mankind before the fall, as told in Genesis 1 and 2; the location is Eden. Second comes the long episode of fallen mankind, narrated from Genesis 3 to Revelation 20; this saga occurs all over the sin-cursed earth. Third, we have redeemed humanity in Revelation 21 and 22, where the setting is earth made new again. So we have two shining chapters at the very beginning. Sandwiched into the middle is an arduous struggle to regain this lost estate, made possible only by Christ's victory. Then we have two chapters at the end to restore redeemed humanity back where we first began. That is a simple but quite accurate timeline of Bible history.

Jesus spoke in Matthew 19:28 about "the new world, when the Son of Man will sit on his glorious throne." The NIV interprets that phrase as "at the renewal of all things." Other texts predict that our final destination is a return to Eden, redeemed by God, with its curse gone forever. Isaiah spoke of a day when "the wolf shall dwell with the lamb, and the leopard shall lie down with the young goat. . . . They shall not hurt or destroy in all my holy mountain; for the earth shall be full of the knowledge of the LORD as the waters cover the sea" (11:6, 9). Although that is a figurative picture, the language promises a final paradise on the earth. Second Peter 3:13 echoes Old Testament predictions: "According to his promise we are waiting for new heavens and a new earth, in which righteousness dwells." Ephesians 1:10 paints God's big-picture plan for history, calling it "a plan for the fullness of time, to unite all things in [Christ], things in heaven and things on earth."

Put to death mythology and fantasies you have collected about the "cloudland" version of heaven, and replace them with the concept that we will walk barefoot on Gulf of Mexico sands, camp out in the Maine woods, and climb Pike's Peak—all in God's new earth. "This world is to be our home. We were made to live here. It has been devastated by sin, but God's plan is to put that right. Hence, we look forward with joy to newly restored bodies and living in a newly restored heaven and earth. We can love this world because it is God's, and it will be healed, becoming at last what God intended from the beginning."[7]

## HEAVEN AND EARTH BECOME ONE

Heaven is presently God's dwelling place in another dimension of space and time. Right now the church triumphant is gathered with Christ. "You have come to Mount Zion and to the city of the living God, the heavenly Jerusalem, and to innumerable angels in festal gathering, and to the assembly of the firstborn who are enrolled in heaven, and to God, the judge of all, and to the spirits of the righteous made perfect, and to Jesus, the mediator of a new covenant" (Heb. 12:22–24). Jesus was incarnated as a man of earth in order to effect the great reuniting of earth and heaven. In the end there will be no wall of division between the spiritual and physical realms. God's dwelling will descend to earth, and thereafter there will be only one entity, bright with God's glory.

## EARTH SHAKEN ONCE MORE

Naturally we are curious about *how* this cosmic restoration will happen. The Bible is reticent on most particulars, with a singular exception in 2 Peter 3:10 and following. When superficially read, this text seems to describe international terror: "Then the heavens will pass away with a roar, and the heavenly bodies will be burned up and dissolved, and the earth and the works that are done on it will be exposed." Chronologically, we assume this occurs after the white throne judgment of Christ. Satan and all unbelievers will have already been banished, while Christ the Judge holds his flock of resurrected saints close to his side.

We could easily wonder how God's people will endure a worldwide firestorm. Without knowing how, we can confidently say that God's preserving us whole through all of this is guaranteed. The universal upheaval will be real, yet I need not worry about my safety. Christ my King will deflect or absorb whatever heat is generated. The Lord is able to carry out his tremendous purge of the earth in an instant while simultaneously protecting us. Do you think he would complete all that our redemption required, only to let us finally slip through his fingers during a planetary purge? Not a chance. Remember: the grand objective is not "burning up" for the sake of wholesale planetary destruction, but a cleansing bonfire of refinement. God's "fire" mentioned in 2 Peter 3 is for purification, not destruction. Who can analyze the chemistry or physics of this?

Moses saw a bush that burned without being consumed. Nuclear holocaust has been suggested as a way 2 Peter 3 might be realized, but that is almost surely the wrong idea, since it would waste and devastate the earth, not cleanse it. The better comparison is to a metallurgist's furnace in which silver or gold is heated to burn away impurities, leaving only the purest metal for working into an object of cherished beauty. Careful attention to 2 Peter 3:10 shows that while some English translations say the "earth and all that is in it will be burned up," the ESV says the end result will be that "the works *that are done* on it will be *exposed*." The NIV text says "laid bare." This implies that mankind's fallen works are what is done away with, not the natural world itself. We can hope for this cleansing fire to leave redeemed human beings and wildflowers and whales unscathed.

God's intention is to take things back to their originally created beauty and purity by removing all accretions of human vandalism.

Possibly Psalm 102:26 offers an explanation in its poetic images: "The heavens are the work of your hands. They will perish, but you will remain; they will all wear out like a garment. You will change them like a robe, and they will pass away." Instead of leaving behind a burned cinder, when God has finished with this renovation, our planet will be clothed anew, teeming with fertile life, and our eyes will drink deep of its splendors. Chemical dumps, smoke-belching factories, and slums will be gone. A sparkling Eden will span the entire earth in a manner we have never beheld. Decontamination and renewal are God's aims—much as he accomplished when he purged the earth in the flood of Noah's day. Rather than destroying it, he obliterated the disaster of human sin and gave Noah an old/new earth on which to begin life again.

Edward Thurneyson concluded, "The world into which we will enter in the parousia of Christ is therefore not another world, it is this world, this heaven, this earth; both however passed away and renewed. It is these forests; these fields; these streets; these people that will be the scene of redemption. At present they are battlefields, full of the strife and sorrow of the not yet accomplished consummation; then, they will be fields of victory, fields of harvest where out of seed that was sown with tears the everlasting sheaves will be reaped and brought home."[8]

We are dwellers in the material order today, and this natural array will not end. Eugene Peterson concluded, "Our existence is framed in matter. Nothing in the gospel is presented apart from the physical, nor can it be understood or received apart from the physical. . . . The gospel does not begin with matter and then gradually get refined into spirit. . . . Creation, heaven and earth, is God's workplace."[9]

## NATURE WAITS FOR US

A grand climax of planetary cleansing will not be concluded apart from redemption of God's people. Romans 8:21 says, "The creation itself will be set free from its bondage to corruption and obtain the freedom of the glory of the children of God." J. B. Phillips's scintillating paraphrase of this verse was, "The whole creation is on *tiptoe* to see the wonderful sight of the sons of God coming into their own." Creation was "subjected to futility" (v. 20) because of the fall of man. Gazelles and wild horses,

Amazon rainforests, and never-seen creatures in Atlantic depths await the finalization of God's covenant work of perfecting every believer he has foreordained to be included in his forever-family. Herman Bavinck declared, "The rebirth of humanity is completed in the rebirth of creation. The kingdom of God is fully realized only when it is visibly extended over the earth as well."[10] The gospel of Jesus isn't only good news for repentant sinners; it is a gospel for a diminished polar bear population, blighted apple trees, and dying star systems.

The total work of Christ includes the divine ambition to redeem God's creation from every cursed sin effect. The errand of Jesus Christ included rebirth for the created universe. Colossians 1:19–20 declares it: "For in him all the fullness of God was pleased to dwell, and through him to reconcile to himself all things, whether on earth or in heaven, making peace by the blood of his cross." Ephesians 1:9–10 adds, "[God] set forth in Christ as a plan for the fullness of time, to unite all things in him, things in heaven and things on earth."

## THE HOME OF RIGHTEOUSNESS

Revelation 21 paints the future entirely in symbols. A symbolic city called New Jerusalem (v. 2) should not be visualized as a cube-shaped urban sprawl of city walls, castle ramparts, and gates. Instead, it is throngs of saved *people*, said to be "prepared as a bride for her husband." It is a bride-city composed of a vast crowd of redeemed saints. The Holy of Holies inner room in Solomon's temple was a symmetrical cube, and now God's glorified people represent perfect proportions. The unusual visual image seems to tell us that all parts of the church are proportionate to everything else. Balance, harmony, and proportion prevail; everything fits. The place where God dwells and the true home of his saints are merged at last. Our many Sunday worship repetitions of "thy kingdom come, thy will be done in earth, as it is in heaven" will be totally fulfilled (Matt. 6:10 KJV). Second Peter 3:13 says the renewed earth will be "the home of righteousness" (NIV).

How many temporary dwellings on earth have provided a residence for you in your lifetime? Quite rare these days are seniors who have spent all their earthly years living in the same house. My own personal tally of lifetime addresses due to transiency in young adult years extends to about eighteen dwellings. The four walls and roof within which I write these words seem more a home to me than most other houses, primarily because my wife and I designed the place and had it built a decade ago. Recently an earthquake tremor emanating from northern Virginia made our eastern Pennsylvania floors tremble. When that happens within weeks of a hurricane reaching inland to hammer Vermont and New Jersey, and you witness on television the deadliest year for tornadoes in the American heartland in decades—suddenly your own domicile seems less permanent. When I hear that God will shake all things, I realize that my present home is no more than an address at which I receive mail for a few blinks of earth time. Someday it will be gone. But my Jesus promised, "In my Father's house are many rooms. If it were not so, would I have told you that I go to prepare a place for you? And if I go and prepare a place for you, I will come again and will take you to myself, that where I am you may be also" (John 14:2–3).

Eugene Peterson spoke vividly about what we can expect, "There is not so much as a hint of escapism in St. John's heaven. This is not a long eternal weekend away from the responsibilities of employment and citizenship, but the intensification and healing of them. Heaven is formed out of dirty streets and murderous alleys, adulterous bedrooms and corrupt courts, hypocritical synagogues and commercialized churches, thieving tax-collectors and traitorous disciples: a city, but now a holy city."[11]

Several refugee families worship in my congregation, one group from Burma and another from Nepal. It is very hard for me to comprehend the language and cultural walls they must deal with, as displaced persons from their native lands. Yet they left those places willingly for freedom and economic opportunity in America. Today we all are refugees, separated from our true home. Our citizenship is in the final heaven, not here. In Christ, we are pilgrims moving ever closer to this destination. Can we possibly prefer this present-day, temporary internment camp, where we merely await final resettlement?

The final home of people sealed in Christ—after God's extreme makeover is done, and with earth and heaven merged into one breathtaking new reality—will be just as Revelation 21:3 announces: "Behold, the *dwelling of God* is with man." God will be in our midst and overwhelm us with himself. How we should long to see this! When new heavens and a new earth merge into our eternal home with God, the prophecy of Habakkuk 2:14 will at last come true: "The earth will be filled with the knowledge of the glory of the LORD as the waters cover the sea."

For if Joshua had given them rest, God would not have spoken of another day later on. So then, there remains a Sabbath rest for the people of God, for whoever has entered God's rest has also rested from his works as God did from his.

Let us therefore strive to enter that rest, so that no one may fall by the same sort of disobedience.

**HEBREWS 4:8-11**


And I heard a voice from heaven saying, "Write this: Blessed are the dead who die in the Lord from now on." "Blessed indeed," says the Spirit, "that they may rest from their labors, for their deeds follow them!"

**REVELATION 14:13**

*CHAPTER SIXTEEN*

# A SABBATH REST FOR GOD'S PEOPLE

☀

ON MAY 10, 1863, IN the Chandler farmhouse near Fredericksburg, Virginia, one of the most skillful military tacticians this country ever produced lay dying from friendly-fire wounds received at the battle of Chancellorsville. In his final hours, General Thomas J. Jackson lapsed in and out of consciousness. His wife Mary asked him, "Do you not feel willing to acquiesce in God's allotment, if he wills you to go to heaven today?" In a firm voice Jackson said, "I prefer it." Told that he would almost surely die before the day closed, Stonewall Jackson, the devout Christian, answered, "Yes, I prefer that. It will be my infinite gain to be translated to glory." Later he said, "It is the Lord's day. I have always desired to die on Sunday." He spent further time in a comatose state, but then the General rallied enough to say distinctly, "Let us cross over the river and rest . . . under the shade of the trees." With that desire voiced, Tom Jackson went home.[1]

Stonewall's often repeated dying words no doubt arose from a subconscious memory of a military command. But his words beautifully testified to a Christian's immediate prospect of enjoyment in Christ. The biblical word *rest* holds strong associations for a disciple entering the final heaven.

## FUTILE PURSUIT OF REST

Consider the moment when you put your head on your pillow after a rough day, as your whole body aches for sleep and at last you can blissfully close your eyes. Or, remember how your ten-year-old legs ran homeward from the school bus after the final day of fourth grade, as you savored a seemingly endless summer of unrestricted playtime stretched out before you. We all have an innate desire for release from toil, suffering, conflict, pressing duties, and physical strain. We yearn for true relaxation of mind, body, and soul. This desire is not only physical in nature. In our strife-torn, confrontational, too-busy society it includes escape to some place where tensions of daily coping can be released. This rest always proves elusive.

The psalmist wrote a theme song for millions of twenty-first-century leisure seekers when he wrote, "Oh, that I had wings like a dove! I would fly away and be at rest; yes, I would wander far away; I would lodge in the wilderness; I would hurry to find a shelter from the raging wind and tempest" (Ps. 55:6–8). Americans invest billions of dollars in glass-fronted beach homes in the Outer Banks of North Carolina, rustic hunting cabins, time-shares in Florida, and gated golf communities. These are payments against the often futile pursuit of the biblical ideal of authentic "rest." The respite we seek is spiritual; its cry arises from the deepest part of us. Do you realize we are longing for Eden to be restored?

I was startled by an on-line interview with an NFL quarterback, one of the very best in the game. This man is an automatic all-pro nearly every season, and he has three Super Bowl rings from his five appearances in that big game. His wife is a gorgeous former model. He could buy anything his heart desired. Despite phenomenal success that any young male might consider the pinnacle of life, Tom Brady mused to the interviewer, "Why do I have three Super Bowl rings and still think there is something greater out there for me? I mean, maybe a lot of people would say, 'Hey man, this is what it is. I reached my goal, my dream, my life.' Me, I think, '——, it's got to be more than this.' I mean this isn't, this can't be all that it is cracked up to be." The interviewer asked the Patriots' quarterback, "What's the answer?" Brady replied, "I wish I knew. I wish I knew. I love playing football and I love being quarterback for this team. But at the same time, I think there are a lot of other parts about me that I'm trying to find."[2] Without Christ, this yearning for inward fulfillment and peaceful repose will never find resolution.

The rest we crave cannot be obtained from a bottle of alcohol or Valium. It will not be found in extramarital sex, vigorous exercise at the health club, or travel to exotic new places. The reprieve we long for gnaws at us in the core of our being. We begin to know its resolution in a restored relationship with God our Savior at the cross; and it will be enjoyed unendingly in the new heaven and earth Christ prepares for his believing family.

## A PROSPECT OF SABBATH REST

Genesis 2:2–3 lays a foundation for this subject, speaking of God the Creator resting on the seventh day of creation: "On the seventh day God finished his work that he had done, and he rested on the seventh day from all his work that he had done. So God blessed the seventh day and made it holy." The seventh day of creation is a continuing day; it is not concluded by the phrase "there was evening, and there was morning," which marks a definite end to each of the first six creation days. The Lord God is not a man who needs labor union regulations to limit him to a forty-hour work-week. Genesis features God's continuing rest as a pattern for humanity's blessing through the ages. After six days of hard work, all men and women need a respite for worship and bodily refreshment with the worship of the Lord as the keynote. Scripture calls this institution "Sabbath." Those who ignore the God-ordained pattern become slaves to their own commercial materialism. They never learn that "man shall not live by bread alone, but by every word that comes from the mouth of God" (Matt. 4:4).

Later in biblical history Israel was promised rest, as they left Egyptian slavery. Chattel slavery was the worst existence imaginable, antithetical to all notions of rest. Bodies were treated as machines, and minds were dominated by tyranny. Moses led the Israelites toward their Promised Land as an earthly home, which Deuteronomy 12:9 called their "resting place" (NIV). Exodus 20:8–11 tells how, along the way, the concept of Sabbath rest transitioned from being an ordinance born in creation to the fourth commandment Moses brought from Mount Sinai. Yet because the Israelites doubted both Moses and the word of the Lord, they endured forty more years of aimless wandering. Spiritual rebels always miss God's rest. Later still, kings David and Solomon built Israel up materially and politically until it could be said they "rested" from warfare with their enemies for extended periods. It may have briefly seemed that rest was achieved by wealth and political power. Then in years after Solomon, the kingdom divided and collapsed under strife against one another and God.

The biblical Sabbath was never meant to be a joyless day hedged about with thorny rules. God intended it to be a visit to heaven each week! On the Sabbath day the Lord's good things were served up; milk and honey could be had without price. It was never meant to be a day for passive dormancy. Nor was it God's aim that a man keep the Sabbath best by attaining the greatest state of physical inertia, as Pharisees seemed to claim.[3]

Through the prophet Isaiah, the Lord signaled how a weekly Sabbath day ought to provide a foretaste of divine rest in the fullest, heavenly sense: "If you . . . call the Sabbath a *delight* and the holy day of the LORD honorable . . . then you shall take delight in the LORD, and I will make you ride upon the heights of the earth" (Isa. 58:13–14). Jesus corrected Sabbath negativism in his declaration taught in all the Gospels: "The Sabbath was made for man, not man for the Sabbath" (Mark 2:27). One day in seven was set apart for our good, foreshadowing eternity's rest. However, to all who have rebellious, unbelieving hearts toward him, the Lord made his classic declaration in Psalm 95:11: "They *shall not* enter my rest."

These broad strokes of biblical development regarding Sabbath rest bring us to Hebrews 4, where the author reminds Christians that Joshua did *not* lead God's people to experience politically or physically God's final rest, which they so long had sought. The fault was not in the leadership of Joshua, nor Moses before him. The breakdown came from deficient faith in Jehovah by the people of Israel. They lost what was promised by not looking for the Lord to be the apex of faith's fulfillment.

Today the prospect of enjoying this Sabbath rest of God is offered to all persons who embrace the cross and resurrection of Jesus. Only as the community of faith in Christ comes one final day before God's eternal throne will we enter the full blessing of God's Sabbath rest, mirroring God's own repose of satisfaction and delight in his works. Hebrews declares, "So then, there *remains* a Sabbath rest for the people of God, for whoever has entered God's rest has also rested from his works as God did from his. Let us therefore strive to enter that rest, so that no one may fall by the same sort of disobedience" (4:9–11).

## REST FOR YOUR SOULS

Jesus spoke with the weight of Old and New Testament doctrine behind him in Matthew 11:28, issuing his classic invitation: "Come to me, all who labor and are heavy laden, and I will give you rest." One day when I was almost eight years old, I sat in the front seat of my grandfather's car, waiting for him to return from a brief errand to purchase something in a store. He was delayed, and I was bored. I opened the glove compartment of his Chrysler New Yorker to see if there might be anything there to read.

I found a Christian tract with its message built around Matthew 11:28. Mind you—I was a young boy in the midst of a secure, carefree childhood and under no peculiar stress. I surely had not been a Hebrew slave, nor had I experienced any unusual pressures of a broken home, abuse, severe illness, or suffering to weigh down my spirit. Nevertheless, I vividly recall how Jesus's words in the tract, promising he would give me "rest," made a piercing appeal. A sweet yearning was born, and I know today that the Holy Spirit was beginning to woo me to the Savior. Not long afterward I consciously gave my heart to Christ. My enduring rest in him began in 1957, the year America as a nation discovered a new source of angst, when the Soviet Union sent the Sputnik satellite into orbit and we as a people collectively felt the pressure of another superpower beating us in the race for space conquest and possible world dominance. Perhaps our prosperous and free American way of life was not the total panacea we thought it was?

Jesus added in Matthew 11:29–30: "Take my yoke upon you, and learn from me, for I am gentle and lowly in heart, and you will find rest for your souls. For my yoke is easy, and my burden is light." The burden he promised to take away is described by the same Greek word used for the unloading of a ship's large cargo. Christ promised us the exchange of our crushing weight of sin, shame, and the empty pursuit of something unnamed (which we cannot find apart from him), for his light yoke of disciple-faith.

Have you begun to taste God's Sabbath rest, as you trust fully in Christ? He can bestow a gyroscope of peace that remains steady in the midst of turmoil in this world. It consists of certainty about your place in God's eternal plans. Forgiveness of sin in Christ is the foretaste of every heavenly enjoyment. Either you already know something about this, or you remain caught up in the worrisome, angry spiral of contemporary life. If you doubt that most people are bereft of the rest of God in Christ, try sitting on a bench at a busy shopping mall for an hour. Study the faces in the crowds that pass by. How many would you say appear to be at peace within, or are even conversing happily with a companion beside them?

## PRACTICAL IMPLICATIONS OF HEAVENLY REST

Whenever a member of our congregation dies, I announce it the following Sunday morning. After mentioning the member's name and the funeral service arrangements, my people hear from me the solemn yet wonderfully comforting words of Revelation 14:13: "Blessed are the dead who die in the Lord from now on . . . . They may rest from their labors, for their deeds follow them!" What John was told about rest is a reality now for the dead in Christ. And that text further exhorts us that a legacy is left behind by each one who has faithfully walked the path of a disciple of Jesus. Let's think about a few of many things this can mean.

Puritan author Richard Baxter wrote a nearly seven-hundred–page book about heaven called *The Saint's Everlasting Rest*. Baxter said that at last we will enter a life of total satisfaction and pure enjoyment. When we are with Christ face-to-face, no waves of unrest can toss us about. We will not struggle against sin, because there will be no sin. We will be beyond Satan's reach and influence, for he will have been destroyed. Our new bodies will not suffer our present weaknesses of temptation.

Today when we see something beautiful in this world, it very soon becomes new bait to our lust. We can scarcely open our eyes without seeing new dangers for our covetousness to feed on. Paul said, "I do not do what I want, but I do the very thing I hate" (Rom. 7:15). We all identify with that, daily striving against our own flesh. But at last, vulnerability to sinful weakness will be gone from all of us. In heavenly rest, our mental understanding will not be vexed with unresolved questions. There will no longer be such a thing as "unanswered" prayer. Nor will we blame God for misfortunes we experience, or question his mysterious providence. In heaven the weakest Christian will comprehend more theology than the most spiritual scholar of God's Word knows today. Our present ignorance will give way to light, and we will be satisfied with all the ways of God. Think of the relief to us when human pride is extinguished. All the saints will see themselves as equals before God's grace; human relations will be free from rivalry, strife, racism, competition, misunderstandings, and rudeness. Richard Baxter spoke of life as a person "in motion." Then he offered this definition: "Rest is the end and perfection of our motion. The saint's rest . . . is the most happy estate of a Christian, having obtained the end of his course. Or, it is the perfect, endless fruition of God by the perfected saints, according to the measure of their capacity, to which their souls arrive at death, in both soul and body most fully after the resurrection and final judgment."[4]

The rest we seek is not a motionless yoga pose. It will be rest from the opposition, strain, and stress arising from powers that aim to destroy the joy of God in our souls. We shall rest from all varieties of suffering. Today, we know what fragile vessels are these bodies in which we dwell. We are "frail children of dust, and feeble as frail," as one hymn writer phrased it.[5] Resurrection bodies will be free from disease, injury, and disability. Heaven will abolish every form of persecution; no antagonist will malign God's loved ones. And what about tragic divisions with other Christians that too often fracture us into so many denominational boxes? Just think of this: no Presbyterians, Lutherans, Methodists, or Baptists will be registered as such in heaven's final home. Every secondary issue of doctrine that is not germane to the gospel of grace will fall away, and our worship will be consumed with Christ alone. That is true rest!

## ALL ANXIETY GONE

When Revelation 14:13 says your "deeds follow [you]" into heavenly rest, this underscores our present influence as Christians. Many who have lived in quiet service to others will be surprised, even amazed, to find other souls present in glory who were somehow influenced to trust in Jesus by our example, prayers, and testimonies. Today, a serious-minded Christian ought to be burdened to pray for those he knows who do not walk with Christ. We strive to witness and pray for people we care about, pleading with God that they might trust in Jesus as Lord. Bearing this evangelistic burden, we have no complete ease regarding the desolate souls of certain family or friends who remain apart from the Savior. There is a strain of gospel concern for them. But this too, will be lifted at last. Eternal destinies will be resolved before the final heaven dawns, according to the mystery of God's sovereign will. There can be no person we might anticipate ever being won to Christ who by then is not present and accounted for.

One problem is often discussed as if it represents a dark blemish on our bliss of heaven, namely, how can heaven be glorious when we are conscious of loved ones who are not there? Scripture does not directly address the matter in so many words. However, the Bible does suggest that "so clear will be our vision of the holiness of God and the sinfulness of man, and so full our deliverance from the presence of sin in our own hearts, that we will be able unhesitatingly to recognize God's absolute righteousness in his acts of judgment."[6] Revelation 19:1–2 depicts "a great multitude in heaven, crying out, 'Hallelujah! Salvation and honor and power belong to our God for his judgments are true and just.'" We will be among them.

We will see that God has acted according to perfect justice and praise him accordingly. Today's anxiety over anyone who is lost will dissolve. Incredibly, our relationship with persons not in heaven will have ended, and so we will neither miss them nor sorrow for them.[7]

This sounds harsh for us to accept now, because we are still bound so close in earthly relationships of family love, friendship, or general compassion. You will be released from those bonds, by the firm separation that will exist between hell and the final heaven. Jonathan Edwards preached a sermon boldly titled *The Torments of the Wicked in Hell—No Occasion of Grief to the Saints in Heaven*. He declared according to biblical logic, "Then there will be no more remaining difficulties about the justice of God, about the absolute decrees of God, or anything pertaining to the dispensations of God toward men. . . . The heavenly inhabitants will then be perfectly conformed to God in their wills and affections. They will love as God loves and that only."[8] Edwards's answer to how we could ever be at complete rest about this perplexing issue is that *only* human relationships sealed by commonality of belonging to Christ will endure beyond this life. We simply will have no occasion to remember others. Isaiah 65:17 speaks from the Lord: "For behold, I create new heavens and a new earth, and the former things shall not be remembered or come to mind." Difficult as it may be to accept, all memories of people separated from Christ will be swept away in the sea of God's perfect justice. The unrest we feel over them today cannot finally endure.

## THE MARRIAGE SUPPER OF THE LAMB

Just try to take all this in. Who of us right now can claim that even one day in every year is 100 percent free from all strain, worry, conflict, or pain? How can we imagine an estate of perfected life when we shall never again spend a moment in such concerns?

Revelation 19:7–9 depicts the signal event of our entry into heaven's rest as the marriage of the Lamb to his bride, the church: "Blessed are those who are invited to the marriage supper of the Lamb" (v. 9). In almost every world culture, a bride-to-be and her parents plan with exquisite care all the details of a wedding reception. Most people expect to look back on this occasion as the pinnacle social event of their lives. The guest list, food, table settings, music—all are designed to highlight a day of joy that signals a new phase of life begun. Using that imagery, which we can confirm from our own experience, the King of heaven intends to spread his table for each of us, and Christ Jesus will be delighted in his guests. Isaiah also pictures that wonderful day: "And the ransomed of the LORD shall return and come to Zion with singing; everlasting joy shall be upon their heads; they shall obtain gladness and joy, and sorrow and sighing shall flee away" (35:10). Randy Alcorn exhorts us accordingly: "We need to stop acting as if heaven were a myth, an impossible dream, a relentlessly dull meeting or an unimportant distraction from real life. We need to see heaven for what it is: the realm we're made for. If we do, we'll embrace it with contagious joy, excitement and anticipation."[9]

The homing instinct of Eden silently beckons me. Any peace I enjoy today has meaning only as a dim copy of my splendid, final rest in Christ. The sure prospect of being at home with him keeps me moving forward in this life to a goal that is nearer and sweeter all the time.

And I heard a loud voice from the throne saying, "Behold, the dwelling place of God is with man. He will dwell with them, and they will be his people, and God himself will be with them as their God. He will wipe every tear from their eyes and death shall be no more, neither shall there be mourning, nor crying, nor pain anymore, for the former things have passed away."

And he who was seated on the throne said, "Behold, I am making all things new." . . .

And I saw no temple in the city, for its temple is the Lord God the Almighty and the Lamb. And the city has no need of sun or moon to shine on it, for the glory of God gives it light, and its lamp is the Lamb.

**REVELATION 21:3–5, 22–23**

They will see his face, and his name will be on their foreheads. And night will be no more. They will need no light of lamp or sun, for the Lord God will be their light, and they will reign forever and ever.

**REVELATION 22:4–5**

For from him and through him and to him are all things. To him be glory forever. Amen.

**ROMANS 11:36**

*CHAPTER SEVENTEEN*

# IN EMMANUEL'S LAND

☼

*IN A 1733 SERMON TITLED* "The Christian Pilgrim," Jonathan Edwards declared, "God is the highest good of the reasonable creature, and the enjoyment of Him is the only happiness with which our souls can be satisfied. To go to heaven fully to enjoy God is infinitely better than the most pleasant accommodations here. Beside him, fathers and mothers, husbands, wives, or children or the company of earthly friends are but shadows; but the enjoyment of God is the substance. These are but scattered beams, but God is the sun. These are streams, but God is the fountain. These are but drops, but God is the ocean. . . . Why should we labor for, or set our hearts on, anything else but that which is our proper end and true happiness?"[1] Edwards was nearly intoxicated by contemplation of the incomparable glory of God. Some have categorized him as an odd mystic. However, it seems better to ask, why are more of us not like him?

Samuel Rutherford, a Scottish Puritan minister born a century earlier than Edwards, was equally besotted with delight as he dwelt upon the excellence of knowing Christ in heaven. In a letter of June 10, 1637, Rutherford wrote his friend John Laurie: "Oh that I could have leave to look in through the hole of the door, to see [Christ's] face and sing his praises! Or if I could break one of his chamber windows, to look in upon his delighting beauty; 'til my Lord send more, any little communion with him, one of his little looks should be my heaven begun. . . . I think I see more of Christ than I ever saw; and yet I see but a little of what may be seen. Oh what price can be given for him? Angels cannot weigh him. Oh his weight, his worth, his sweetness, his overpassing beauty! If ten thousand worlds of angels were created, they might all tire themselves in wondering at his beauty and begin again to wonder anew."[2] These two godly men knew that Jesus Christ himself will be the centerpiece and cornerstone of our eternal heaven.

## HEAVEN EXISTS FOR GOD

We are selfish even in how we think about the final estate of heaven. We tend to ask, "What will I *get* out of it?" Questions people have about the final heaven are frequently stated: "Will I know my husband there? What about my friends and my pets? What will I *do* all the time in heaven?" Such questions are natural, but they demonstrate that as we look toward eternity, we remain wrapped up in the cocoon of self. People have a way of discussing what heaven will be like that never reckons with the fact of the Triune God being present and enthroned, as we behold him there. If you are not interested in the glory of God, you really can have no true interest in heaven.[3] Thus, we turn to consider what will seem a novel concept to many—the final heaven exists for God more than it does for us. The main goal of heaven is not simply to spare us from hell or to make us happy—although it will do those things infinitely. Heaven exists for God, to make his glory visible and elicit our praises. Apart from him, eternal life has no meaning at all.

First Corinthians 15:28 sets this theme: "When all things are subjected to him, then the Son himself will also be subjected to him who put all things in subjection under him, that God may be *all in all*." Our everlasting condition will be consumed by the glory of our God: basking in it, reflecting it, growing toward his wondrous splendor until it warms the marrow of our bones and gleams from our eyes. Both Edwards and Rutherford pined in their large souls to discover *who* God really is. In glory we shall be so taken outside of concern for our puny selves that ego, pride, and vanity will be swept aside. God himself will be our sun, moon, and sky!

## THE COVENANT OF GRACE CONSUMMATED

We read in Revelation 21:1–5 of the entire church of saved people from all the ages being presented to Christ as his bride at her wedding. Historically, a bride gave up her individuality to discover a new identity in union to her husband, and thus in most cultures she took on his name. This bride, the church, is said to be "adorned" (v. 2) in her wedding costume. The dress is borrowed, for the church wears Jesus's own righteousness, given to clothe all who believe upon him as Lord. We who have been justified and cleansed by Christ's sacrifice in our place shall thus be brought into the final heaven and presented to Christ, our Bridegroom.

It is strange for our ears to be told there is no longer a sea (Rev. 21:1). Beach lovers find this disconcerting. We need to know that for Israel the sea was always a place of heaving unrest and dangerous storms. The Mediterranean Sea was a path by which enemy fleets arrived to plunder God's people. So the absence of a sea is a symbol indicating that the curse and threat of sin is cancelled as God meets his people in a fresh new world where enemies like Egyptians or Phoenicians cannot approach with armadas of war.

We now focus on Revelation 21:3, where a loud voice from God's throne makes a momentous announcement: "Behold, the *dwelling place of God* is with man. He will dwell with them, and they will be his people, and God himself will be with them as their God." If you can recall the central importance of God's covenant with Israel and mankind generally, bells should peal in your head as you read those words. Back in Genesis 17:7 the Lord told Abraham, "And I will establish my covenant between me and you and your offspring after you throughout their generations for an everlasting covenant, to be God to you and to your offspring after you." The root of the historic covenant of grace was God's intention to draw from all nations a *people* set apart to himself, meant to dwell with him forever. This became the Lord's central task in human history. God promised this people an eternal dwelling where his shalom and his presence would overwhelm them. In the cross of Christ, entry to this covenant was secured for believing Gentiles as well as Jews. The biblical covenant of grace was always intended for persons beyond the ethnic Israelites (Rom. 4:16–17; Gal. 3:7–9, 28–29). Christ died to establish God's unending dwelling in the midst of an elect people from every nation. The covenant reaches its long-intended end when God-knowledge is most direct and immediate.

David prayed in Psalm 63:1, "O God, you are my God; earnestly I seek you; my soul thirsts for you; my flesh faints for you, as in a dry and weary land where there is no water." Augustine's famous prayer declared, "You have made us for yourself, O Lord, and our hearts are restless until they find rest in thee." God's greatest gift to us is *himself*.

## FROM "IN CHRIST" TO "WITH CHRIST"

Today we grope to envision this. Yet 1 John 3:2 promises believers, "Beloved, we are God's children now, and what we will be has not yet appeared; but we know that when he appears we shall be like him, because we shall see him as he is." It is Christ Jesus whom we will "see" in an altogether new way. Nowhere in Scripture are we told that the final beatific vision means gazing on the essence of God the Father, any more than we could presently stare into the sun for an hour without searing our retinas. Moses asked to see the face of God, and he was told, "You cannot see my face, for man shall not see me and live" (Ex. 33:20). Jesus was appointed to be God's visible representation in human form: "Whoever has seen me has seen the Father" (John 14:9). Scripture implies that in heaven Christ does not abandon his glorified body. It is the face of Jesus Christ that will dazzle us with glory.

My family once took friends who had never visited Niagara Falls to see this wonder of nature. It was early morning, and a heavy fog supplemented by mist from the falls surrounded us as we walked from our car through Victoria Park on the Canadian side to a railing just above the Horseshoe Falls. We experienced a strange ten minutes there because the falls were thundering immediately in front of us—our ears confirmed that we were in the right place, yet we could barely see twenty feet ahead. I assured my friends I had not deceived them about the existence of Niagara Falls, since I'd viewed them from that spot numerous times, and they said they trusted me. In short order, the warming sun burned off the fog and the panorama came into full view; I could not have orchestrated a more dramatic scene. The sight before us fulfilled every expectation and was rendered more delightful by the manner of its unveiling.

Think what it will mean to no longer just talk about Christ Jesus, but to *see him*, unobscured by the fog of our sin. Our knees will not support us in that moment! Every unsettled question will be answered and all arguments against God's mysterious ways shall cease.

It will surprise some to hear that the Bible's consistent description of eternal life and Christian immortality is not to say that we "go to heaven." A child's understanding can grasp that in the New Testament the terminology for heaven is simply being "*with* Jesus." He said, "I will come again and take you to myself, that where I am you may also be" (John 14:3). In John 17:24 Jesus prayed, "Father, I desire that they also, whom you have given me, may be *with me* where I am, to see my glory." These texts ring true with Revelation 21:23, which tells us that in the new earth, sun and moon are rendered superfluous: "The glory of God gives it light, and its lamp is the Lamb."

Believers are already "in Christ" today, bound in unbreakable spiritual union. But only in the final heaven will we see him clearly for the first time. We will gaze on his face in the manner that visionaries like Jonathan Edwards and Samuel Rutherford rhapsodized about. Then will the prophecy be fulfilled: "Your eyes will behold the king in his beauty" (Isa. 33:17).

## THE LAMB IS ALL THE GLORY

Samuel Rutherford is responsible for my all-time favorite Christian hymn. (Probably few people join me in this choice, but that is their loss.) My memorial service plan is on file with family members, and the first hymn of the service is one compiled from several paragraphs in Rutherford's writings. The hymn is known either by its first line, "The Sands of Time Are Sinking," or by its last phrase, "In Emmanuel's Land." The third stanza says, "O Christ, he is the fountain, the deep sweet well of love! The streams on earth I've tasted, more deep I'll drink above: there to an ocean fullness his mercy doth expand, and glory, glory dwelleth in Emmanuel's land."[4]

Everyone knows that a bride regards her wedding dress as the most beautiful outfit she is likely to wear in her lifetime. A woman's attention is fixated on that garment while she selects its design and has it fitted; she preens herself in that dress before a mirror. But Rutherford believed, when she walks down the aisle on her father's arm, no bride is entirely conscious of her dress any more. As the fourth verse expresses: "The bride eyes not her garment, but her dear Bridegroom's face. I will not gaze at glory but on my King of grace. Not at the crown he giveth, but on his nail-pierced hand: the Lamb is all the glory, of Emmanuel's Land."

In heaven every Christian's union with Christ will expand beyond limits. Thomas Boston said, "The union of Christ and the saints is never dissolved, but they continue to be his members forever and the members cannot draw their life but from their head . . . therefore Jesus Christ will remain the everlasting bond betwixt God and the saints, from which their eternal life shall spring."[5] God the Father is not visible to our eyes now, nor do we expect him to be in the future. But Jesus will be. His glorified resurrection body will be the form of divinity we are finally permitted to behold. In eternity, John Owen wrote, "the immediate object of our faith is the manifestation of the excellencies of Christ. And that faith will be turned into sight. . . . As Christ is the principal revealer of God in heaven, we shall see God supremely in him."[6]

## TO ENJOY GOD FOREVER

The famous first question of the Westminster Shorter Catechism asks, "What is man's chief end?" The answer: "To glorify God and enjoy him forever." There is no temple in the final heaven because we shall have unimpeded access to Christ. A temple or church today is only an architectural symbol for God's presence. In the weakness of remaining sin, we believers must worship God from a distance in liturgical exercises of hymns and prayers and by hearing preaching. Or we struggle to discipline ourselves alone, to conduct personal time with the Bible and prayer. We take our rebellious flesh in hand—fighting drowsy distractedness. Worship today is nearly always a bit of a *chore*; we just don't do it very well. How can we imagine an endless experience when the very air of heaven we breathe will taste of worship? Praise will not be a formal activity we must "perform," the way a student buckles down to complete homework. The aroma of Christ will fill the air. His visible glory will naturally and effortlessly draw forth from us all that is due him. God's glory displayed in the splendor of Christ will never be far from our line of sight. "No sin-induced stupor, no failure of hearing, no blindness of our vision will obscure the beauty of God from our knowledge. Though believers will still be creatures, limited in a capacity to know God as he knows himself, their knowledge of God will be pure and undiminished by sin. . . . Believers will see God as they have never seen him before."[7] Heaven and Christ are synonymous. Knowing him there, we shall be drenched, absorbed, and transformed by God's holy presence.

In a trying time early in my ministry, I met Psalm 73:25–26 with new eyes: "Whom have I in heaven but you? And there is nothing on earth that I desire besides you. My flesh and my heart may fail, but God is the strength of my heart and my portion forever." What an overflowing "portion" Christ will be to his people! Paul's prayer in Ephesians 3 shall be fulfilled. We will "comprehend with all the saints what is the breadth and length and height and depth, and to know the love of Christ that surpasses knowledge, that [we] may be filled with all the fullness of God" (vv. 18–19).

If you and I could blend into a single experience the thrills we obtain from a favorite sports team winning a championship and pleasures derived from hobbies, friendships, and births of children and grandchildren—

then add the sweetness of Christmas morning in the midst of family—it would not come close to the thrill of meeting Christ our Lord. No wonder Paul said in Philippians 1:23, "My desire is to depart and be with Christ, for that is *far better.*"

## THE FACE OF THE GIVER IS THE GIFT

Two important symbols appear at the beginning of Revelation 22: the river of life and the tree of life. The latter is described as something more like a whole orchard. In Middle Eastern lands, refreshing water from a flowing stream was life-bestowing. And if you enjoyed delicious fruit like a peach picked from a tree—imagine accessing it not for one brief season but any time you desired it. These symbols inform us that God's gifts to his people in the final heaven will refresh and satisfy all our needs. We will never want for sustenance. But the text does not intend to dwell on what we shall eat or drink. Its aim is to convince us that God's greatest gift will be himself.

One writer pictures John the apostle as if he is on a ladder peering over a high wall to see into heaven. In the throne vision of Revelation 5, John turns back to all of us from atop his ladder and shouts, "God is here!" Then as he sees the new heavens and new earth in Revelation 22, he shouts back to us again, "They are all about Jesus up here!" This is true, since Jesus is the focus of the worship of the saints in the final heaven.[8]

In J. M. Barrie's play *Peter Pan*, Peter at one point declares, "To die will be an awfully big adventure." Can you see why, for a Christian whose security is fixed upon Jesus as Lord, this adventure never ends? The final heaven is not a vaporous land of clouds. It is our home—where Christ awaits us. Hear Samuel Rutherford once more: "You have only these two shallow brooks, sickness and death to pass through; and you also have a promise, that Christ shall do more than meet you, even that he shall come himself and go with you, foot for foot, yea and bear you in his arms. O then! For the joy that is set before you, for the love of the Man that is standing upon the shore to welcome you: Run your race with patience."[9]

You can hardly take young children on a long car trip without at some point hearing from the back seat, "Are we there yet?" In a sense, that is the longing cry raised by Christ's church each Sunday morning. As we pray and serve him, we must ask, "Are we *there* yet? Are we there *yet?*"

Let an unnamed Puritan lead us in prayer: "May I be daily more and more conformed to thee, with the meekness and calmness of the Lamb in my soul, and a feeling sense of the felicity of heaven, where I long to join angels free of imperfections, where in me the image of my adored Savior will be completely restored, so that I may be fit for his enjoyments and employments. I am not afraid to look the king of terrors in the face, for I know I shall be drawn, not driven, out of the world. Until then, let me continually glow and burn out for thee, and when the last great change shall come let me awake in thy likeness, leaving behind me an example that will glorify thee while my spirit rejoices in heaven, and my memory is blessed upon earth, with those who follow me praising thee for my life." Amen.[10]

# PART SIX

# THE SECURITY OF A BELIEVER'S HOPE

Therefore my heart is glad, and my whole being rejoices;
    my flesh also dwells secure.
For you will not abandon my soul to Sheol,
    or let your holy one see corruption.
You make known to me the path of life;
    in your presence there is fullness of joy;
    at your right hand are pleasures forevermore.

**PSALM 16:9-11**

So we do not lose heart. Though our outer self is wasting away, our inner self is being renewed day by day. For this light momentary affliction is preparing for us an eternal weight of glory beyond all comparison, as we look not to the things that are seen but to the things that are unseen. For the things that are seen are transient, but the things that are unseen are eternal. For we know that if the tent that is our earthly home is destroyed, we have a building from God, a house not made with hands, eternal in the heavens. For in this tent we groan, longing to put on our heavenly dwelling, if indeed by putting it on we may not be found naked. For while we are still in this tent, we groan, being burdened—not that we would be unclothed, but that we would be further clothed, so that what is mortal may be swallowed up by life. He who has prepared us for this very thing is God, who has given us the Spirit as a guarantee. So we are always of good courage. We know that while we are at home in the body we are away from the Lord, for we walk by faith, not by sight. Yes, we are of good courage, and we would rather be away from the body and at home with the Lord.

**2 CORINTHIANS 4:16-5:8**

*CHAPTER EIGHTEEN*

# MY FLESH DWELLS SECURE

☼

*THE LATE JOSEPH BAYLY DESCRIBED* leading a nursing home worship service at which he spoke on the resurrection of Jesus as our hope in death. He reported, "Men and women were in wheelchairs, some listened from their beds in adjoining rooms. One lady was almost a hundred. She was weeping before the service began; as I leaned over to speak to her, she whispered, 'I'm afraid to die.' When I spoke, I asked a question: 'If I could promise to take you from this home to a beautiful spring-like place where you would be forever free from all your aches and pains, where you could walk and even run, hear and see, and never have any more loneliness or sorrow ever again; but if I had to take you first through a dark tunnel to get you there: how many of you would want to go?'" The question was rhetorical, yet almost every one of the seniors present raised their hands. The speaker explained, "Death is that tunnel. It is not to be feared if we trust Jesus, for he will take us through it to heaven."[1]

As we deal with the Bible's teaching on what lies beyond death, we need to stay grounded in knowledge that these are not abstract doctrines. Our established hope or lack thereof will write the tone and content of our funeral plans, and guide us in how we grieve for the passing of fellow believers. The subject affects pending medical decisions for extraordinary life-support like a feeding tube. It also colors a potentially memorable testimony to others as the gospel is declared by a calm demeanor as death approaches.

During the time in which I have been writing these pages, quite remarkably my pastoral ministry has included an all-time record of thirteen funerals occurring in our congregation—in just a three-month period. I presided at many of these, and my associates led others. All of the deceased were people I had known to some degree; each was a professed disciple of Jesus. Visiting the halls of our local hospice center and reading familiar Scripture passages at gravesides has made it impossible for me to forget that death is a real intrusion of devastating loss, as much-loved people pass away. One day they are conversing, laughing, or crying. The next day, all communication ends; their arms no longer embrace us; their eyes do not see the patch of sun at the foot of their bed. A familiar face we cherished becomes a motionless mask.

Biblical Christianity does not teach that your soul is important but your body is worthless. That was Plato's creed, not the teaching of Jesus. Scripture teaches that human beings woven in the image of God are a unity of soul and body. Death temporarily snaps the union, separating the soul from your physical self. However, God's power will reunite your soul with a new body, when Jesus Christ returns to consummate history.

## BODY AND SOUL REUNITED

The gospel claim is that no human beings are ever annihilated. John 5:28–29 says, "All who are in the tomb will hear his voice and come out." We all shall face eternity in bodies that are somehow like those on which God stamped his original image. The general resurrection for all the dead portends God's power to reconstitute your unique bundle of genetic codes, making you whole again. As a child of God, you will be whole as you have never been before. Regarding bodies of those who are not in Christ—the lost raised up only for judgment and eternal desolation—the Bible is mainly silent. I think we really do not want to know more about them.

God does not despise our physical nature. How could he? He created us in bodies: capable of language, able to worship, and eager for sexual intimacy. The magic of a first kiss was his design. Directed by his animating Spirit, we are made for hard work, mathematical calculations, and artistic expression. We are wired for Olympic sports and tears of delirious joy. Although my flesh deteriorates with depressing steadiness until it filters back to dust, God designed me so that once my justified soul obtains his gift of immortality, I shall be embodied once more. The next time around my body/soul radiance will shine forth without interruption or diminution. More than any other world religion, Christianity values persons alive in a casing of transfigured flesh.

Think how much time and energy is spent in this life to physically tone, dress, feed, massage, and photograph a human body. I was an adult before I ever gave any thought to the notion of what is called "body-image." Now, I realize that the temptation to think about this day and night is particularly strong for young women. Everyone desires their body to be better than it is—driving adolescent girls into miserable habits of anorexia and bulimia. In the early 1960s Marilyn Monroe and Bridgette Bardot were celebrated as the world's most enticing images of female beauty. Where is their voluptuousness now? Marilyn died tragically at age thirty-six. And if you have seen a picture of Ms. Bardot in her late seventies—let us be kind—modeling agencies and film casting directors long ago lost her phone number. The few who do inherit eye-catching beauty of physical form in their twenties and thirties possess it only for a brief shining hour. Is it possible that there will be another standard altogether for beauty in our resurrection bodies, which arthritis, sagging flesh, or baldness will not disrupt?

The pattern for the Christian's everlasting body is not a sultry young model sauntering along a Paris fashion runway. Nor is it the muscle boy with his oiled six-pack abs and three-days-without a razor stubble on his squared chin. The spiritual body of resurrection will be more permanent and attractive to behold than its weak physical predecessor could ever be, because its prototype is the risen form of Jesus. A new mode of attractiveness is seen in him. Paul wrote, "There are heavenly bodies and earthly bodies, but the glory of the heavenly is of *one kind*, and the glory of the earthly is of another" (1 Cor. 15:40). The pathway to a perfect body in heaven is not the health club, the plastic surgeon, or the beauty salon. A body endowed with what the Bible calls "glory" will be ours. Paul said, "We await a Savior, the Lord Jesus Christ, who will transform our lowly body to be like his glorious body, by the power that enables him even to subject all things to himself" (Phil. 3:20–21). The difference between "lowly" and "glorious" is about an entire transformation to a higher existence. Resurrection involves not a temporary facelift but a miracle.

## NOT ABANDONED TO THE GRAVE

Among several Scripture passages I always read at a graveside burial service is Psalm 16:9–11. David exulted: "Therefore my heart is glad, and my whole being rejoices; my flesh also dwells secure. For you will not abandon my soul to Sheol, or let your holy one see corruption. You make known to me the path of life; in your presence there is fullness of joy; at your right hand are pleasures forevermore." In his Pentecost sermon (Acts 2:25–28), Peter referenced this passage as evidence that God had long ago predicted Christ's resurrection. We are given to understand from this text that Christ's resurrection was a down-payment in earnest of our own.

The bitter emotion of a cemetery committal service is that, as family draws around an open wound in the earth, the casket is already closed and you know a beloved face will not be seen again. I have had to help a funeral director gently lift a sobbing widow who threw herself upon the mahogany veneer box, moaning in desolation. As a widow is escorted to the funeral director's car, anonymous men in coveralls who had stood to one side move in to efficiently lower the casket until what remains of her husband is sealed inside a concrete vault and covered with earth. The same man's body that held her in his arms or wrestled with his son now lies inert, just beneath the frost line, in a military alignment with dozens of strangers whose unseen physical forms have deteriorated in ways we do not let ourselves think about. A graveside committal service is the hard-as-granite sequel to the wedding ceremony's vow, "til death do us part." No wonder we ask, "If a man die, shall he live again?"

King David foresaw in Psalm 16 that while the body of flesh was under God's protection in the ground, the redeemed soul already revels in "fullness of joy" with the Lord. There is nothing more solid I can offer to a grieving person than this text. Here, David weighed all his blessings from God against many difficulties and trials. He saw that nothing could shake his position in the Lord. His God was the reality of realities. He reasoned that God would not, could not let go of him, even in a dimly-seen future life. The sheer boldness of David saying, "You will not abandon me to the grave," ought to take our breath away! Apart from assurance from on high, only a madman could consider all the generations of people dying around him and still declare, in effect, "God will not let death ruin me."

David knew his physical body must die; "corruption" would in fact devour his flesh. But he told us this really does not count as corruption, since it cannot touch his soul. The resurrected body of a man called David—the part that mattered eternally—would be united to his immortalized soul and would live forever. Exactly *how* God would achieve this was not David's concern. It only mattered that the God who would accomplish it was *his* God!

## MORE THAN CELLULAR REASSEMBLY

You may recall from biology class that all the cells in a human body are constantly dying and being replaced by duplicates. The estimate is that in less than seven years nearly every cell you have is replicated. This means that in the years I have been pastor of my present congregation, members are actually on their third entirely different senior pastor with the same name. (And I'm sure they wonder why each succeeding version looks worse than the one they hired in 1994.) Even in this world I can still be "me," with a completely different amalgamation of cells providing the vehicle of my identity.

Ignorant people mock the doctrine of resurrection because they say God could never resurrect someone killed in the nuclear blast at Hiroshima, or raise a sailor lost at sea whose body disintegrated at the bottom of the ocean centuries ago. Let's not sell God short. He is not dependent on physical DNA samples stored in his tissue laboratory. His resurrection work never relies crudely upon getting your "knee bone connected to your thigh bone" again. He requires no dental records, blood samples, or photographs to remake you, as *you*. Christians can afford to be realists about what happens to a human body. If not embalmed rather quickly, bacteria will voraciously consume our skin and organs. We deteriorate all too quickly, and we stink. A human body exposed in the woods for three days is not something you want to stumble upon during a weekend pleasure hike. But final resurrection is unaffected by survival of a material body.

## IS CREMATION A CHRISTIAN OPTION?

This leads into some practical issues about how we might dispose of our bodies after death. Christians can choose cremation without concern as to how that will affect God's practical ability to work his miracle on Resurrection Day. No clear biblical principle stands against cremation. Yes, it is true, as some have argued, that in certain Old Testament passages after a battle, the Israelites reverently gathered and buried the bodies of their own fallen warriors, while corpses of their foes were stacked and burned. From these historical descriptions, the implication is sometimes drawn that burning human remains was a dishonorable treatment—a way to heap insult upon a defeated enemy—while burial was deemed noble. We might just as readily consider that a mass funeral pyre was a quick and practical way for an army on the march to manage battlefield cleanup.

It also is true that all examples we are given about disposal of a body in the New Testament are burials: Lazarus of Bethany and Jesus, as well as the early martyrs James and Stephen. None were cremated. It would seem that whenever possible, early Christians reverently buried an intact body, in token of preparedness for the future resurrection. Yet nowhere does the Bible draw a moral judgment against cremation, and the silence seems significant. It is a decision to be based on culture, not theology. My own pastoral wisdom, for which I claim no special inspiration, is to tell people I personally prefer burial for my loved ones. However, I can see no sound reason to advise against cremation—especially in light of increasingly scarce and expensive cemetery space in large urban areas. Burial versus cremation is a personal decision with no moral or doctrinal issue involved.

When a human body is lost due to natural disaster, warfare, or murder, relatives always want to recover the body to bring their loved one home for burial. They speak about obtaining "closure," once they can know that the remains of a fallen soldier or kidnapped and murdered child have been respectfully laid to rest. Be assured of this: the miracle-working God of resurrection does not require closure with your cells and teeth and bones in order to raise you up on the day of Christ. Surely, the God who created the entire cosmos out of his spoken word of power is able to make every human being whole again. He wrote the original chromosome code that patterned a unique physical vessel for each one of us—can he not write it once more? The difference is that next time the strain of God-rebellion and the leukemia of sin will not intrude to smear his image written upon us.

In our human weakness, we are prone to forget the exact appearance of a beloved grandparent who died forty years ago, unless photographs call them to mind. The Lord has no such memory problem. "For he *knows* our frame; he remembers that we are dust" (Ps. 103:14). God's elect believers are "the apple of [his] eye" (Ps. 17:8). It is not too much for a Creator who saw us in our mother's womb to perfectly replicate everything that makes you and me ourselves. He shall refabricate us according to that template at the final day.

Can we therefore be liberated from clinging desperately to our remaining lives in these mortal bodies? Unique resurrection confidence should motivate every adult Christian to have a living will, or preferably a durable power of attorney, in place. This is absolutely vital today, since medicine is able to preserve your body much longer than was possible a few decades ago. Every state has its own laws about what legal instrument is needed, so you should by all means consult an attorney and your physician about these documents.

Since 1981, many states have adopted the Uniform Determination of Death Act. Death is now certified in either of two circumstances: (1) irreversible cessation of circulatory and respiratory function; (2) irreversible cessation of all functions of the entire brain, including the brain stem.[2] Technology is now at such a stage that its intervention can prolong the process of dying. Your body could be left in a vegetative condition beyond your desires, and without planning, no one could order hospital apparatus to be disconnected.

Be sure the person who holds decision-making power of attorney for you is one who knows you well and shares your Christian hope. There are differences between ordinary and extraordinary care that you need to understand, and expert advice is required to know the best legal instruments to employ in your state. I have witnessed situations where, for instance, a husband and his adult Christian daughter were of one mind regarding the wife/mother who suffered a devastating stroke. She was being given only palliative care, because it was her legally stated desire that exceptional or heroic measures should not be taken to prolong her life in such a situation. Yet along came the unbelieving prodigal son, after years of a guilt-laden and tense relationship with his parents and no trust in eternity's promise. He demanded to know why Mom was not being given a feeding tube or other medical measures that could only prolong her death, not restore her to a life with quality.

There are times when death should be allowed to take its course—never unduly hastened or artificially induced, of course. But the Christian should not desire long-term life support entirely by artificial means when restoration of health is not in sight.

## CONFIDENCE TO FACE THE END

I encourage you to know Paul's writing at the end of 2 Corinthians 4 and the beginning of chapter 5. There he recorded some of the most personal and endearing words of anywhere in all his writings. Paul bared his soul, allowing us to see what kept him going near the end of life, with prison and hardship as his daily lot. He wrote, "So we do not lose heart. Though our outer self is wasting away, our inner self is being renewed day by day" (2 Cor. 4:16). Personal resurrection was so sure in Paul's mind that he could say it was already going on within him while he remained in this world.

A little further, in 2 Corinthians 5:4, Paul groaned with spiritual longing, desiring "that we would be further clothed, so that what is mortal would be swallowed up by life." This is a 180-degree reversal of the way worldly people think. They cling piteously to their last days in a material body, no matter how wasted they might be by pain or disease. Not Paul! What he anticipated would swallow him up was not death, but *life*. The essence of God's eternal life cannot be experienced in the body we have today, only tasted. Thus we understand the apostle writing in 2 Corinthians 5:8, "Yes, we are of good courage, and we would rather be away from the body and at home with the Lord." Far from being a dirge sung by a suicidal man, this was the clarion call of a Christ-satisfied man.

God gave us our physical bodies, and he intends for us to use and enjoy them as long as we can, in ways that conform to his will. Just bear in mind that every single superb Winter Olympic athlete you may watch on TV, with lean muscular bodies encased in spandex—all so swift and agile—will go down to a grave one day. What will be inscribed on their tombstones? Will their best claim from a lifetime be "I won two Olympic gold medals"? That seems a grand achievement now. But a century of grave-moldering will obliterate the memory of athletic medals entirely. How much better if a headstone paraphrased David, saying, "Because of Jesus Christ who rose, my body rests secure. He will not abandon me to the grave" (see Ps. 16:9–10).

It is a privilege to hear the words of dying Christians who *know* they are dying and can tell us they are ready to go to the Lord. So I offer two examples of Christian courage where men "died well."

In the spring of 2000, Dr. James M. Boice had advanced cancer. He knew it, and so did his congregation. On May 7, the senior pastor was too weak to preach, but he appeared (for what would be his last Sunday on the podium) to give the call to worship and a brief informal update on his health condition. Here are some excerpts of what he said that morning: "Should you pray for a miracle? Well, you're free to do that, of course. My general impression is that the God who is able to do miracles—and he certainly can—is also able to keep you from getting the problem in the first place. Although miracles do happen, they are rare by definition. . . . Above all, pray for the glory of God. . . . God is in charge. When things like this come into our lives, they are not accidental. It's not as if God somehow forgot what was going on, and something bad slipped by him. . . . God is not only the one in charge; he is good. Romans 12:1–2 says we have the opportunity to actually prove what God's will is. 'His good, pleasing and perfect will.'"[3]

Those personal remarks, sealed by his death five weeks later, were a pastor's benediction on his ministry. For three decades at Tenth Presbyterian Church, Jim Boice preached the gospel of Christ's cross and resurrection, leading hundreds into the way of life. In his last two months, without specifically preaching on the subject, he taught his people by a submissive example how to die in the faith.

The Welshman Dr. Martyn Lloyd-Jones was another model of pulpit power and spiritual, Christ-centered ministry. He urged the necessity of a Christian's thoughtful preparation for death, if it were possible by one's circumstances: "We do not give enough time to death and to our going on. It is a very strange thing this: the one certainty, yet we do not think about it. We are too busy. . . . People say about sudden death, 'It is a wonderful way to go.' I have come to the conclusion that is quite wrong. I think the way we go out of this world is very important and this is my great desire now, that I may perhaps be enabled to bear a greater testimony than ever before." Dr. Lloyd-Jones continued, "We hold on to life so tenaciously—that is so wrong, so different from the New Testament! . . . The hope of a sudden death is based on the fear of death. But death is not something to slip past, it should be victorious."[4]

Lloyd-Jones was a physician before he became one of the great preachers of the twentieth century. So, when he lay dying in the winter of 1981, he had the doctor's advantage (some might say disadvantage) of fully understanding his condition. He also thought keenly about the new body awaiting him. He asked visitors to "pray that I enter heaven in the full-sail of faith." His doctor wanted him to take more antibiotics for his congested lungs, but he refused. He had no more use for his worn-out house of flesh. By February 26 Dr. Lloyd-Jones had lost the ability to speak, but he wrote for his wife with a shaky hand on a scrap of paper, "Do not pray for healing. . . . Do not hold me back from glory!" Lloyd-Jones's daughter Ann testified that he breathed his last that morning shortly after she had read to him from 1 Corinthians 15: "Thanks be to God, who gives us the victory in our Lord Jesus Christ."[5]

Only trusting Christ, who died and rose for you, can give you such unshakeable confidence in the face of physical death realized. I can have no greater prayer than that you live right now in that secure embrace of Jesus. Then you, too, may die well.

Precious in the sight of the Lord
    is the death of his saints.

**PSALM 116:15**


For Sheol does not thank you;
    death does not praise you;
those who go down to the pit do not hope
    for your faithfulness.
The living, the living, he thanks you,
    as I do this day;
the father makes known to the children
    your faithfulness.

**ISAIAH 38:18-19**

# CHAPTER NINETEEN

# PRECIOUS IN THE SIGHT OF THE LORD

☼

*DID YOU EVER THINK THAT* in your grief at the loss of a loved one, you might mismanage the situation to your own detriment, and that in the course of misguided grieving you could cause harm to others? For a glaring example of grief managed badly, we might look to Queen Victoria in nineteenth-century England. Victoria married a distant cousin, as royals often do. Prince Albert of Saxe-Coburg and Gotha was an intelligent man of high character who as Prince Consort proved to be a useful advisor in affairs of state. Together Victoria and Albert had nine children in twenty-one years of marriage. Theirs was a very happy union until Albert's rather sudden death, apparently caused by typhoid, in 1861, when he was forty-two years old.

Victoria's reaction was a total paralysis of sorrow. She made no public appearances for three years and withdrew from most affairs of state. She was called "the widow of Windsor." It was rumored that laughter was forbidden in her immediate presence. She wore only black dresses for the remaining forty years of her life. Every night at the Queen's dining table a place was set for Albert. His royal uniform was laid out in his bedroom by a valet, as though he would wear it the next morning; aside from this his suite of rooms was left undisturbed. The Queen built various architectural monuments in Albert's name all over England and commissioned florid biographies to extol his virtues. For a long time, many in England felt they had lost their Queen's attention and full interest. As various state decisions were resolved, she was heard to say, "I am sure this is what Albert would have me do." Queen Victoria's love for her husband was commendable, and we should not malign that, but she was obsessively preoccupied for the second half of a long life with a wound of grief that proved unhealthy for her and everyone around her.

This causes us to ask some questions: How will gospel faith in Christ help us to think and act at the time of a believer's departure from this life? When we hold a funeral for one who was justified in Christ, shouldn't the service sound a different note from the crushing sorrow and maudlin sentimentality given voice in many funerals for worldly people with no effectual hope? In a nutshell, can Christians grieve for a believer in ways that make it clear we truly do not "grieve as others do who have no hope" (1 Thess. 4:13)?

## GOD'S VIEW OF THE BELIEVER'S DEATH

It will help us tremendously to know how a believer's death is uniquely viewed by God our Father. Psalm 116 is by an anonymous author. It is a highly personal prayer, employing "me," "I," or "my" in almost every verse. This psalmist experienced deliverance from a sickness so severe he thought he would die (116:3). Amid his abject helplessness, the Lord had untangled "snares of death" from around his neck. Thus he penned a song of thanksgiving to God, who heard his cry for healing. As he wrote, the psalmist knew he would continue to "walk before the LORD in the land of the living" (v. 9) for more days to come.

Since the writer had escaped death, we could wonder about the meaning of the phrase in verse 15: "*Precious* in the sight of the LORD is the death of his saints." It seems abruptly placed and out of context. Why would the psalmist comment on death this way if he was celebrating a return to life? Apparently by a near-death experience, this Israelite discovered that death is not an evil monster waiting to claim a sick man's body. On the brink of death, he saw as never before that a heavenly Father's joyous homecoming for a prized child awaited him. Those who belong to him in bonds of grace, the Father will sovereignly choose either to bring to himself or return to earthly health. Either option is now understood as God's wise and loving choice. If the Lord chooses not to heal, he has not broken any promise. From our standpoint, death looks terrible. Yet this psalmist now understood that the Lord watches the believer's death out of great love for one he cherishes.

## BIBLICAL FUNERALS

Can you recall the first recorded funeral in the Bible? Genesis 23 tells it. Landless Abraham needed to bury his beloved wife Sarah, and out of deep respect for him the Hittites offered for him to choose any of their finest tombs. But Abraham chose "the cave of the field of Machpelah east of Mamre (that is, Hebron) in the land of Canaan" (Gen. 23:19). Then he insisted on paying full price for this land even though it was offered as a gift. In the cave he reverently buried Sarah. Later, the site received the bodies of Abraham and other patriarchs.

Another passage early in Bible history tells of Jacob setting up a memorial stone to mark Rachel's grave along the road to Bethlehem, after she died giving birth to Benjamin (Gen. 35:20). Then at the end of Genesis, chapters 49 and 50 narrate the deaths of Jacob and later his son, Joseph. Jacob pleaded to be buried with his forefather Abraham. So Joseph had his father's body embalmed by morticians of Egypt in a ritual that required forty days to complete; this is the first mention of embalming in Scripture (Gen. 50:2–3). Jacob's body was then transported to Hebron to lie with his ancestors. Closing statements of the book of Genesis tell of Joseph's death at 110 years of age. He too was embalmed and buried with a state funeral in Egypt. However, he had predicted to his children: "God will surely visit you, and you shall carry up my bones from here" (Gen. 50:25). His prophecy was remembered, because Exodus 13:19 tells of Moses taking Joseph's bones with him on the wilderness exodus, so his remains could be buried many years later in the Promised Land at Shechem, as reported in Joshua 24:32.

Before the New Testament era, certain funeral customs had evolved. Burial was the respectful way Jews dealt with a body. Cremation was not the norm, but neither was it explicitly forbidden. Burial had to be accomplished quickly in a hot climate. In the case of Lazarus of Bethany, this friend of Jesus was quickly sealed in his tomb before Jesus arrived. Long periods were customarily given to a formal wake of mourning, in which friends joined in a family's sorrow. Jesus himself was unashamed to weep before the tomb of Lazarus (John 11). The wrapping of a body with linen grave clothes impregnated with aromatic spices (as described in Jesus's burial after the cross) was done not for embalming, but to make the stench of putrefaction less offensive. The neighbors of Lazarus were blunt in protesting the opening of his grave: "Lord, by this time there will be an odor, for he has been dead four days" (John 11:39). (No former little boy can forget his Sunday school delight upon discovering the frank wording of the King James translation: "Behold, he stinketh!")

New Testament people expected a physical body to disintegrate to dust. They did not hold the Egyptian belief that physical remains must be preserved for a journey into an afterlife. Although early Christians prized hope in a future resurrection, they did not assume that the physical body needed to be intact in order to experience this miracle. Later, when bodily remains were mere bones, these might be reverently collected and placed for permanent keeping in a stone ossuary chest.

Acts 8:2 provides a very brief picture of another New Testament funeral. Following the martyrdom of Stephen we read this simple report, "Devout men buried Stephen and made great lamentation over him."

Overall, we gather from scenes of believers' deaths in the Bible that full allowance was made for profound grief and tears. Yet we do not hear about the more outlandish displays of wailing often observed today as a custom in some Middle Eastern lands. The body of the departed was treated with respect and dignity, but was buried without undue delay.

## LIFE CELEBRATION VS. CHRIST EXALTATION

Moving forward, we should ask how we might align our contemporary farewells to a departed believer so that they capture the attitude of our God and Father as he gathers in someone who is precious in his sight.

I assume a trend which I have observed in recent years is not peculiar to my local area. Funeral homes now designate the funeral as a "life celebration." It seems inevitable that we should come to this humanistic innovation. I have genuine respect for many professionals in the funeral industry, and I realize that their marketing terminology merely concedes to what the masses want. Before this vocabulary change came in vogue, many American funerals already were more about glorification of the departed's noble character, his life accomplishments and his family ties than about gospel hope, with Christ being the focus. "Life celebration" might be an appropriate term if it meant that the funeral was a proclamation of the true life of the soul that begins by a new birth of the Holy Spirit. But we all know that the life being celebrated these days is the human personality of the departed. That is what unredeemed people want to glorify.

Once I was having lunch in a restaurant with another pastor. We could not easily ignore a loud conversation in the next booth as three men discussed the recent funeral of someone we quickly realized was the father of two of them. One son declared his strong dissatisfaction with the minister who had presided at the funeral. He complained, "I wanted to hear more about Dad and his good life, not all that Bible stuff." (I have edited the profanities that preceded the words "Bible stuff.") My pastor friend and I exchanged knowing looks, realizing that this gripe might have been made about either of us. We were relieved that those in the next booth were not recognizable as family members from any funeral at which we had recently presided.

A decision must be made: is a funeral or memorial service primarily intended to exalt Christ and the Bible's realities about eternity, or is it an opportunity to showcase a human life, exalted beyond recognition in a flood of sentimental remembrances? In cases where the deceased was known to be a Christian and the service is planned by Christians, we need to demonstrate how the Savior was seen in this life, to the glory of God. Actually, I have had some individual Christians go overboard by giving advance instructions for no eulogies, no open casket—nothing that might suggest any spotlight on themselves when they are gone.

I have had occasions to smile when I meet with a new widow or other Christian relatives to arrange particulars for a funeral service and to be told firmly, "Now pastor, we will have unsaved relatives at this service, so be sure you give the gospel out loud and clear." I am glad for their concern, and I can put them at ease. No funeral I have ever conducted has failed to have the good news of eternal life by way of Jesus's cross and resurrection as its focal point. Apart from that, I am not sure what else I would talk about.

## PRACTICAL FUNERAL CONSIDERATIONS

An important aid to shaping a Christian funeral is advanced planning. People generally have some views about how they want their own funeral to be arranged, yet millions fail to tell anyone, so nothing is recorded to guide survivors or pastor. Our church provides a funeral planning guide, which can be filled out and returned to me to be kept in a permanent file. Yet fewer than ten percent of our members make use of it, although the forms are constantly available on a prominent literature rack. Such written expression of wishes should be left in the keeping of younger family members who are likely to outlive you, whose voices will be respected after your death. May I also suggest you include your pastor among those who get a copy of written plans. Quite often these days pastors are brought into the discussion only after family members have already met with a funeral director and certain options have already been decided, such as whether to have a church-based service versus the more sterile atmosphere of the funeral home. When I arrived at my present pastorate, funeral-home services were the norm. Now it is rare not to hold the service in our sanctuary, because people know we encourage this.

I discuss with our people two options they might consider. One is what we will call a traditional funeral: a service at either the church or funeral home followed immediately by travel to a cemetery and burial (except in the case of cremation when there is no burial). A second option has come to be favored by many Christians—though neither option is superior to the other. This option breaks the funeral into two steps: first, a private burial service is held at the graveside—usually in the morning—only for family and invited guests. That graveside committal can be as large or small in attendance as you determine. Then the same afternoon or evening—or perhaps on a subsequent day of greater convenience—a memorial service is scheduled, open to all who might come. Many Christians prefer this option because it separates the wrenching emotional goodbye at the cemetery from the later appointed time of worship. Grieving family members who have already been to the grave then have hours or even days to refocus on worship and thanksgiving. They are better prepared emotionally to praise the God of life. The comfort of Christ and notes of joyful hope often will resonate better once the cemetery farewell is behind you, not looming at the conclusion of worship. From long experience with both options, this latter one has become my personal preference in most circumstances, unless the service is likely to involve only a small number of guests—then the traditional pattern of funeral-to-burial is more practical.

What about embalming and viewing of a body? In my state of Pennsylvania the law does not require embalming; but if it is not done, the body cannot be viewed publicly and must be buried or cremated within five hours of removal from refrigeration. Other state laws will vary; any funeral director can answer your questions about this. Some Christians express very firm wishes "not to be put on display when I am dead!" Of course you may exercise a "no viewing" preference. What concerns me is when someone implies that viewing the body is unspiritual or that it serves no purpose. I cannot agree. You ought to consider carefully the emotional closure that a time for visitation with family and viewing of the deceased provides. Visualizing death is a step toward accepting it. Especially in the case of a sudden death, there is a sense of unreality present when someone has died and people cannot confirm it by their eyes and brain. It is not ghoulish or macabre for our minds to need this last brief goodbye.

I take exception to a view some people hold, which says children should not view a body in the casket. Parents definitely should keep youngsters from disrupting a prefuneral visitation time with loud behavior; their visit should be brief. But here is a prime opportunity to instruct a child and implant lifelong memories. Children are realists and should not be talked-down to about death. A parent may say, "We are going to see Grandpa's body. He has died, and the living part of him called his soul has gone to heaven to live with Jesus. We are sad to have him leave us, and we want to say goodbye to his body, so Mom and Dad might be sad while we are there. It's all right if you feel sad too. But one day we are going to see him again." This will inevitably provoke questions, which should be answered as straightforwardly and truthfully as possible. It is all right for the adult to admit there is a great mystery about death, but we can teach a child that God holds the answers. Most children of kindergarten age or older are ready for this experience—sometimes at younger ages, as a parent may decide. They will not be traumatized by viewing a body, as some imagine. It is better for them to experience a funeral home visitation than to be told half-truths like, "Grandpa is gone away." That only creates confusion. At some point in their lives, they will view a dead body. It is beneficial if a parent can make their first experience instructive and as positive as possible.

The eulogy or personal tribute is a key funeral service element that often separates a Christian service from the secular version. These tributes should not be unbridled exaltations of human virtue. Psalm 1 and Proverbs 31 are classic Scripture tributes to the life of a believer well lived, with godliness as the main theme. The focus should be on telling how Christ and the Holy Spirit were visible in the departed one's character and actions. Some humor can be helpful but should not be contrived. Ability for mourners to laugh at foibles or comments from the deceased is fine, as long as there is no attempt at ribald comedy.

A current trend I find to be nearly always *unhelpful* at memorial services is the offer of an "open microphone" for anyone present to step up and say an impromptu word. Based on bad experiences of this and almost no good ones, I cringe when attending services where it is done. In the service planning phase I advise against it, unless a family insists on it. Half of those who come forward tend (innocently of course) to make this time a "can you top this" exercise in storytelling. Or, the remarks really are more about the speaker than the deceased. Instead of this emotion-driven chaos, plan ahead to invite one to three trusted family members or close friends of the deceased to speak—ideally mature Christians. They need not be orators; sincerity and authenticity go a long way, and they will have time to prepare. I advise them to write out their remarks. Their names are printed in the order of service so it is clear that they are speaking by invitation, and no others. These personal eulogies usually counterbalance and introduce the pastor's sermon to follow. He is then free to shine the spotlight primarily on a biblical message of hope in Christ.

Music is another way to underscore a balanced Christian message at a funeral or memorial service. Avoid songs or musical solos that major on sentimentality. You should seek the doctrinal strength of classic songs or hymns that affirm salvation by the cross and the resurrection of Jesus and that speak of God's sovereign rule over death and sorrow. Without intending to catalog the many possibilities, some great hymns that cannot miss are: "Be Still My Soul"; "When I Survey the Wondrous Cross"; "Great Is Thy Faithfulness"; "It Is Well with My Soul"; "The Sands of Time Are Sinking"; "Amazing Grace"; "Jesus Lives and So Shall I"; etc. The modern classic "In Christ Alone" by Keith Getty and Stuart Townend is superb. This is only a small sample of many possibilities. The essential thing is for all funeral service music to be God-exalting and Christ-centered. Resurrection triumph over the grave must be the theme, not schmaltzy sentimentality. I hope you know the difference.

## HE WILL CATCH YOU

On June 17, 1963, five months before his own death, C. S. Lewis wrote a pastoral letter to a Christian woman who feared that her death might be imminent. He wrote: "Can you not see death as the friend and deliverer? . . . What is there to be afraid of? You have long attempted a Christian life. Your sins are confessed and absolved. Has this world been so kind to you that you should leave it with regret? There are better things ahead than any we leave behind. . . . Our Lord says, 'Peace child, peace. Relax. Let go. Underneath are the everlasting arms. Let go, I will catch you. Do you trust me so little?'" Lewis, who knew he, too, was in poor health, signed this letter of hope with the words, "Like you a tired traveler, near the journey's end. Jack."[1]

On the foundation of Psalm 116:15, we can know that our strong, expectant Father stands just inside death's door, waiting to welcome his redeemed one home. If the Lord brings one of his children to heaven, that event shall be marked with a blessed welcome, like the prodigal son received in Jesus's parable. Passing through death's door, each son or daughter is precious in God's sight! Jesus affirmed this when he reminded disciples that no sparrow dies and falls to the ground without the Father's awareness and care. He said, "You are of more value than many sparrows" (Matt. 10:31).

Once we have joined the psalmist in grasping that a believer's death is "precious in the sight of the Lord," we can move past maudlin sentiment to authentic hope expressed in spite of our tears. What a difference it makes to have a heavenly Father, who, as Lewis wrote, is ready to catch us! Our safe passage is guaranteed, as we fall into his everlasting arms.

Of all people on the earth, Christians are best prepared to understand Solomon's admonition: "A good name is better than precious ointment, and the day of death than the day of birth. It is better to go to the house of mourning than to go to the house of feasting, for this is the end of all mankind, and the living will lay it to heart" (Eccles. 7:1–2).

He was despised and rejected by men;
a man of sorrows, and acquainted with grief;
and as one from whom men hide their faces
he was despised, and we esteemed him not.

Surely he has borne our griefs
and carried our sorrows;
yet we esteemed him stricken,
smitten by God, and afflicted.

ISAIAH 53:3-4

When Jesus saw [Mary] weeping, and the Jews who had come with her also weeping, he was deeply moved in his spirit and greatly troubled. And he said, "Where have you laid him?" They said to him, "Lord, come and see." Jesus wept. So the Jews said, "See how he loved him!" But some of them said, "Could not he who opened the eyes of the blind man also have kept this man from dying?"

JOHN 11:33-37

*CHAPTER TWENTY*

# HE HAS BORNE OUR GRIEFS

☼

*MY WIFE AND I BOUGHT* an antique secretary-type desk manufactured from solid hardwood in a day when things were built to last. Two men at the store loaded it into the back of my vehicle, so I did not realize its full weight until I tried to grapple it from the back deck of my SUV to the garage floor. Somehow it traveled that far, with gravity doing the main work. At that moment, I thought I heard this desk laughing at my inane presumption that I was strong enough to move it into the house alone; I could not shift its ponderous bulk at all. Feeling like a weak old man, I asked a younger friend to lend some muscle to the task. Between us, the desk was carried to its new home without incident. But without a willing load bearer to support the task, this desk would still be standing in my garage like a stack of bricks, a monument to my weakness.

Jesus Christ is the only capable mover of a weighty object that lodges itself firmly in millions of lives every day: the five-ton elephant called *grief* that we face at the death of any loved one. Grief parks itself in the front room of your life and resists most human efforts to suggest that it move on to dwell elsewhere. Demographic studies say that at any given time, within the last year about 10 percent of all people have had someone close to them die: a spouse, sibling, parent, friend, or child. One person in ten will encounter this ponderous visitor in the coming year. If it has been a long time since your home has been affected by serious personal bereavement, know this: your turn is coming.

Biblical counseling has much help to offer in dealing with sorrow in the face of death, but that must be found in other books. Our main concern here is to know what Scripture has to teach us in this area. Is the aftermath of anyone's death truly made more bearable because of Christian faith?

John 11 tells of Jesus sobbing at the tomb of a close friend. The greatest antidote Christ offered to Mary and Martha to assuage their sorrow over their deceased brother Lazarus was the power of his own resurrection, which was foreshadowed in his raising of Lazarus on that very day. Yet, despite his own advanced knowledge that he could summon the power of God to raise Lazarus (who, by the way, had to die another day, for the second time), Jesus still "wept" for his friend (v. 35). His spirit raged against the desecration the foeman death had wrought. God's Word displays here a Savior who *"has borne* our griefs and carried our sorrows" (Isa. 53:4). Jesus Christ shoulders an impossible weight we cannot carry alone.

## GRIEFS EASED BY GROANS

There is a mistaken idea among Christians that disciples of Jesus should not vent their grief at all. The Archie Bunker school of grief counseling says, "Stifle it, Edith." We're sometimes told that to cry openly, to feel bereft or depressed in our losses supposedly does not honor God, and at worst may be a denial of our faith. This results in "stiff upper lip" behavior, in which sharp emotions are suppressed and we feel guilty if they are indulged.

C. S. Lewis temperamentally was not constituted to have a "stiff upper lip" when he lost his wife Joy Davidman Gresham to cancer, after a rather short marriage. In 1961, Lewis penned the sixty-page monograph *A Grief Observed*, which some of his friends thought was an inadvisable publication. In it, this mere Christian indulged his woe almost without restraint. He wrote, "There is a sort of invisible blanket between the world and me. . . . Grief still feels like fear. Perhaps more strictly like suspense. Or like waiting; just hanging about waiting for something to happen. . . . Her absence is like the sky, spread over everything."[1]

It troubled some reviewers that in the first pages of his little journal of grief, Lewis the evangelical Christian almost sounded agnostic: "Meanwhile, where is God? This is one of the most disquieting symptoms. . . . Not that I am (I think) in much danger of ceasing to believe in God. The real danger is coming to believe such dreadful things about him."[2] He continued a requiem for his Job-like loss. His prose was frank and biting: "It is hard to have patience with people who say . . . 'Death doesn't matter.' There is death. And whatever *is* matters. . . . And whatever happens has consequences, and they are irrevocable and irreversible. You might as well say birth doesn't matter . . . She died. She is dead. Is the word so difficult to learn?"[3]

A reader's benefit drawn from this book, as with some of the darker psalms in Scripture, comes by discerning how Lewis slowly turned toward a resolution, with a determination to hold on to the Lord through it all. His messy mourning was never all tied up neatly with a bow. *A Grief Observed* was more like a slow awakening with definite progress markers left along the path. "And so perhaps, with God I have gradually been coming to feel that the door is no longer shut and bolted. Was it my own frantic need that slammed it in my face?"[4] He began to see himself "like a drowning man who can't be helped because he clutches and grabs. Perhaps your own reiterated cries deafen you to the voice you hoped to hear. . . . God has not been trying an experiment on my faith or love in order to find out their quality. He knew it already. It was I who didn't."[5]

By grieving while stubbornly grasping Christ's resurrection, C. S. Lewis realistically saw that you don't simply "get over it." He wrote, "To say the patient is getting over it after an operation for appendicitis is one thing; after he's had his leg off it is quite another. . . . At present I am learning to get about on crutches. Perhaps I shall presently be given a wooden leg. But I shall never be a biped again."[6] I have given copies of *A Grief Observed* to mature Christians who wallow in grief and bear the additional burden of blaming themselves for succumbing to it. More than once this has led toward a therapeutic pastoral discussion.

This chapter is not intended to be a course on navigating the dark tunnel of grief. Others have filled volumes with the subject. I simply wish to contend that we must acknowledge the reality of this beast and determine to grapple with it in persevering faith and resurrection hope. Christians do themselves no benefit by attempting to lock grief into a closet. It will always break out when your back is turned. Facing it with patience and prayer as Lewis did is the only way through the morass to a place of new peace with God.

In Genesis 37, Jacob the patriarch had a settled trust in Jehovah, yet when he was told of the alleged death of his beloved Joseph in a cruel deception, we read that Jacob "mourned for his son many days" (v. 34). He was pierced by tumultuous grief over his favored son and could not be comforted. I see a more positive plan for dealing with sorrow from Jacob's earlier days, when he camped beside the river Jabbok, and being deeply troubled, wrestled by night with an angel (Gen. 32:22–31). We need to grope and pray through grief as a process, determining prayerfully to tell the Lord as Jacob did, "I will not let you go until you bless me" (v. 26).

In 1674, two years after his second wife's death, Puritan minister John Flavel published *A Token for Mourners*, a helpful study in biblical experience with grief. Flavel's insights were shaped by Scripture, not secular psychology. He declared, "It is much more becoming a Christian ingenuously to open his troubles than sullenly to smother them. There is no sin in complaining to God, but much wickedness in complaining of him. Griefs are eased by groans and heart pressures relieved by utterance."[7]

## LEARN THE DIRGES OF GOD'S PEOPLE

The prophet Jeremiah wailed for the loss of an entire nation. He wrote in Lamentations 1:12–13, "Is it nothing to you, all you who pass by? Look and see if there is any sorrow like my sorrow, which was brought upon me, which the LORD inflicted on the day of his fierce anger. From on high he sent fire; into my bones he made it descend; he spread a net for my feet . . . he has left me stunned, faint all the day long." Many grief images from Lamentations will resound to any mourner. There is carryover from Jeremiah's sorrow for a whole nation to poignant individual symptoms of grief, such as: "He has walled me about so I cannot escape; he has made my chains heavy; though I call and cry for help, he shuts out my prayer" (Lam. 3:7–8).

Numerous psalms also open a window on heavy scenes of grief. David cried out, "I sink in deep mire, where there is no foothold; I have come into deep waters, and the flood sweeps over me. I am weary with my crying out; my throat is parched. My eyes grow dim with waiting for my God" (Ps. 69:2–3). Anonymously written Psalm 88 is famous for its unrelieved darkness and pessimism, with the psalm ending with this sentence: "You have taken my companions and loved ones from me; the darkness is my closest friend" (v. 18 NIV). This is the only psalm that ends with no suggestion of resolution to its complaint. However, the one and only consolation justifying Psalm 88's inclusion in the Bible is that for all his bitter darkness, the psalmist was still *praying* to the Lord! Though he had not rediscovered the light and comfort he sought—by the very act of recording his pessimistic prayer, he hoped against hope for the Lord to meet him in the midnight of his soul. He prayed to a God he could not momentarily see.

## JESUS WEPT

In John 11, Jesus reached the tomb of Lazarus his frequent host. Meeting the dead man's sisters Martha and Mary already had painfully twisted the Lord's heart, since each woman in so many words accused him: "Where were you, Jesus? You might have prevented this!" Imagine arriving at a funeral home, burdened with your own sadness, only to have your dead friend's family openly blame you for not arriving sooner to prevent the tragedy!

Narrow the camera angle down for the scene of verse 33. When Jesus saw the lamentations of everyone present, "he was deeply moved in his spirit and greatly troubled." It is hard to capture his deep emotion. Jesus was "agitated, confused, disorganized, fearful, surprised . . . thrown off his horse as it were."[8] Then verse 35 further reports that at the tomb, "Jesus wept." Of the four Gospels, John's report is unique in exposing the depth of human woe that Jesus expressed. Do not imagine restrained or silent weeping here. More likely Jesus sobbed heavily—what some would call "losing control." Commentators point out a rare Greek verb used here: *embrimasthai*, which is used only a few times in the New Testament and carries a note of angry rage combined with distress. A comparison is to visualize a shudder passing over Jesus in the manner of a war horse snorting at smells of blood and gunpowder before charging into battle. Overpowering anguish was unleashed in Jesus as he saw fiendish death smiting humanity. Here—out of all other moments—is Jesus seen as the polar opposite of Greek mythical gods, with their cool apathy toward human beings. Our Savior proved that the heart of the true God is deeply touched by our griefs. Jesus was hot with a rage of indignation; he trembled and groaned at how Satan by death vandalizes God's glorious designs for men and women. Here, behold the Author of Life abhorring physical death as creation's ultimate obscenity.

## OUR UNDENIABLE HUMANITY

Once again, recognize that a strange evangelical expectation has harmed many Christians in their times of grief: the idea promoted by some that a positive, hope-filled facade is required at all times by a grieving disciple. They would send C. S. Lewis into a long time-out in the penalty box for his mawkish public display. Showing any public breakdown is deemed unworthy of us and an affront to our Lord. Where do these ideas come from? Neither Jesus in John 11 nor those who buried Stephen in Acts 8, nor the Psalms, nor Jeremiah, nor Job subscribed to stifling emotions in the face of grief. Christianity does not bestow an antigrief inoculation to banish tears, no matter how firm your grasp upon the resurrection to come.

A basic psychology course can teach you the phases of grief common to most human beings, with variations based on individual temperament and circumstance. Basic stages follow roughly this progression: (1) shock or numbness, in which you are emotionally anesthetized; (2) a strong wave of sorrow; (3) depression; (4) an unholy trio composed of fear, guilt, and anger doing a dance on your heart; (5) lingering apathy and depression; (6) gradual acceptance and healing. Any Christian who thinks he will bypass these universal reactions entirely is not dealing with reality. The Stoic ideal that says we should never break down, show impatience with God, or be depressed is neither biblical nor humane. Those who piously advocate that we should perform such a charade are as bad as Job's so-called "friends."

After acknowledging our humanity and allowing ourselves to process undeniable feelings, we are ready to claim the reminder that "you may not grieve *as others* do who have no hope" (1 Thess. 4:13). The cross and resurrection of Jesus put solid ground underfoot. Our experience of grief need not be like swimming in bottomless quicksand that always pulls us down. Think of it as like the procedure recommended for escaping an undertow current near an ocean beach. The advice I have always heard for that situation asks the swimmer to acknowledge the current rather than fight it in a panic. You are told to swim parallel to the beach until you move out of the hardest undertow, and you should eventually be able to stroke toward shore again. Believers in Christ most likely will pass through all of the classic grief stages, but we may do so more quickly than most people, not getting stuck in black despair.

## THE GRIEF-CARRIER

Grief cannot cancel the truth of what Jesus accomplished in dying for sin as our Savior and returning to life as Lord of heaven and earth. In the amazing drama of the cross, the Father *"put him to grief"* (Isa. 53:10) on our behalf. Jesus did more than just shudder in sympathetic horror beside the cold tomb of Lazarus. He was put into a tomb; but then by the power of God he broke free. He did this on our behalf—so when we trust in him, his death cancels our spiritual death.

Who but Jesus has a deeper background of experience in the tangled realms of human sorrow? In Isaiah 53:3, Jesus was appointed from of old to be the "man of sorrows, and acquainted with grief." Isaiah went on to predict that Christ would be "as one from whom men hide their faces." Jesus was an extreme sufferer—his pain so contorted his features on the cross that people would turn away from the grotesque nature of his sufferings, much as we might shun a dead raccoon by the side of the road. Yet we are asked to see that the sorrows of death he endured also qualify Jesus as the One *toward* whom we must turn our faces. We come to him, asking this remarkable One sent from God to carry off from us what we cannot lift for ourselves. He is qualified by his supreme strength demonstrated in history. And he deeply cares for us in our weakness, as no other could.

Samson comes to mind as a wonderful prophetic picture of Christ's carrying away a believer's grief. Philistine enemies were camped out at the city gates of Gaza, conspiring to take Samson captive as he left the city. Aware of the plot, Samson arose in the middle of the night while his enemies slept. Scripture reports: "He arose and took hold of the doors of the gate of the city and the two posts, and pulled them up, bar and all . . ." (Judg. 16:3). Samson carried the city gates away to a distant hill. From there he mocked his would-be captors.

By the exertion of God's supernatural power, Jesus died our death and rose to new life. The prison house which grief tries to build around us has no locked door, precisely because Jesus smashed the lock and carried the city gates completely away! If you are grieving for someone today, Christ who groaned and wept at the devastation death causes knows your situation right well. His tears show the compassion of a true friend. He does not need to say, "I know how you feel." His very presence with us says it all. "The eyes of the LORD are toward the righteous and his ears toward their cry" (Ps. 34:15).

This load bearer is also God incarnate, uniquely able to cancel the final effect of death. Robert Dabney said, "The God-man alone can sustain us; he has felt the mortal blow, for he is a man; he has survived it and returns triumphant to succor us, for he is God. Unless this divine guide be with us, we must fight the battle with the last enemy alone and unaided."[9] Psalm 30:5 gives a promise that Christians of all people can best understand: "Weeping may tarry for the night, but joy comes with the morning." There is a place for tears now, but that phase of grief can in time move off center stage of our souls, into the wings.

One of the Bible's final promises guarantees that when we are gathered to Christ in the new heaven and new earth, "[God] will wipe away every tear from their eyes, and death shall be no more, neither shall there be mourning, nor crying, nor pain anymore, for the former things have passed away" (Rev. 21:4).

Christian friend, let me guarantee this to you in the face of your sadness: when God himself wipes your tears from your eyes, they will forever stay dry!

[David] said, "While the child was still alive, I fasted and wept, for I said, "Who knows whether the LORD will be gracious to me, that the child may live?" But now he is dead. Why should I fast? Can I bring him back again? I shall go to him, but he will not return to me."

2 SAMUEL 12:22–23

You are he who took me from the womb;
    you made me trust you at my mother's breasts.
On you was I cast from my birth,
    and from my mother's womb you have been my God.

PSALM 22:9–10

# CHAPTER TWENTY-ONE

# IS MY CHILD IN HEAVEN?

☼

*LET ME TELL YOU ABOUT* Rebecca Leigh Wilson, who was born August 22, 1982, in Michigan. Becky is our niece; her mother is my wife's sister. Based on her birth date, you might assume she is now an adult and perhaps a wife and mother of her own growing family. Not so. Becky's earthly race ended in February 1989 when she was six and a half years old. This little girl was born with a rare cluster of neurological problems; we were told that less than a handful of children in the United States were likely to have this same disorder at any one time. Becky was blind and deaf; she had cerebral palsy; and she never grew normally. The most she ever weighed was about twenty pounds, the size of a toddler. She never sat up by herself or spoke a word—so there was no *Sesame Street* or singing along with Elmo. Yet she responded to touch and smiled when you hugged her or stroked her arm. She brought joy to her parents and everyone who encountered her. Physicians said Becky would not live to see her second birthday, but her family blew out six candles on a cake before her home-going to heaven finally came.

Yes—I deliberately said home-going to *heaven*—and that is not just an uncle's sentimental indulgence. My attempt in this volume has been to remain a biblical theologian. Considering Becky in that role, I believe the best deductions drawn from God's revealed Word and confident hope in Jesus Christ as risen Lord permit an expectation that I will greet her one day, when I too am done with this earth. Her mom said to me, "Our comfort is that when we do see Becky again, she will be *whole*." This mother's hope is biblically sound.

## A WRENCHING SUBJECT

In our consideration of the Bible's teaching on life after death, we turn to a most difficult topic. No subject contains more raw emotion than the death of a child—any parent's worst nightmare. Many who will read this have had a personal stake in the matter. On a Sunday morning, roughly half of the worshipers at our church are women, and a large number of them are above childbearing age. When I address this subject from my pulpit, I naturally speak to scores of women who have had miscarriages. Miscarriage leaves a unique scar upon a parent's heart because rarely is there a funeral to mark the passing of a child whose face and voice will be unknown in this world. Even best friends avoid speaking directly about your loss. Other worshipers on a given Sunday have lost a child to disease or accident. Add in millions of American children aborted before drawing their first breath. Then as you consider children worldwide who are dying of starvation, acts of war, adult neglect, or abuse—you begin to realize this is no theoretical subject. At one time in history about half of all children conceived did not reach adulthood. Even with improved infant mortality rates today, millions still die at a young age.

The topic is difficult for another reason. Doctrinal teaching about a dying child's salvation is not as clearly stated in God's Word as we might hope. The subject is not missing, but texts addressing it are rare and relatively oblique; we do not find the comprehensive summary we desire. Therefore, drawing conclusions on this subject resembles Bible debates on a topic like baptism: we must reason from God's mind expressed via indirect texts and by inferences more than from direct and indisputable statements. This will be a longer chapter than others by necessity, as we carefully weave together some scattered biblical threads. Please read with patience.

If you asked any sane person attending a child's funeral, "Do you think this child is in heaven?" he will answer, "Why, of course!" Natural compassion and general respect for children elicit this response. Those who accept the Bible's view of hell as mankind's default destination normally conclude that some out-of-the ordinary rulebook must be in effect for children who die. Every human impulse strains in that direction because no one can imagine a small child suffering eternal woe. However, it is not enough just to *will* this to be so; we must identify a scriptural basis for it. We cannot say a child is in heaven merely because children are naturally sweet or supposedly "innocent." That does not ring true with God's Word. Furthermore, we must weigh this matter while holding under consideration Bible truths like original sin and divine election. Children inherit

Adam's fall, and God owes no living person salvation merely for possessing a cute face and chubby legs.

So we ask, what happens at death to an unborn child, a six-month infant, or a seven-year-old? Add to the equation adults who are always childlike due to developmental problems: the mentally handicapped adult whose capacity to comprehend Christ will never be more than infantile. We need sound Bible principles to answer the poignant cry of thousands who ask: Is my child in heaven?

## GOD'S VIEW OF CHILDREN

The pivotal text for this chapter is 2 Samuel 12:22–23. But before examining it, we must trace several background issues to inform our understanding. First, Scripture gives insight into God's view of children even before they are born. Psalm 139 is David's paean of praise for divine care as God hovered over his life from his conception. The psalm declares, "For you formed my inward parts; you knitted me together in my mother's womb. . . . My frame was not hidden from you, when I was being made in secret. . . . Your eyes saw my unformed substance; in your book were written, every one of them, the days that were formed for me, when as yet there was none of them" (vv. 13, 15–16). David extolled God at work preceding his earthly life. He was enfolded in comprehensive care every hour he had lived and hours yet destined for him. His mighty God even knew his thoughts before they became words on his tongue. God our Creator is in complete, sovereign control of everything that happens to us, including our death, at any age.

David spoke similarly in Psalm 22, "You are he who took me from the womb; you made me trust you at my mother's breasts. On you was I cast from my birth, and from my mother's womb you have been my God" (vv. 9–10). His salvation was predestined—set in motion by action of the Spirit in his infancy. At minimum this indicates God's early redemptive watchcare over a life made in his image. Jeremiah said that the Lord told him by his Spirit, "Before I formed you in the womb I knew you, and before you were born I consecrated you; I appointed you a prophet to the nations" (Jer. 1:5). Becoming a prophet was not a career Jeremiah chose with the aid of his high school guidance counselor, or at a community job fair; he was compelled toward it by God's appointment. Add a New Testament word about John the Baptist in Luke 1:15. John's father Zechariah heard an angel predict John would be "filled with the Holy Spirit, even from his mother's womb." Thus, we have composite evidence that says David, Jeremiah, and John the Baptist were subjects of God's saving influences from conception in the womb.

Clearly, then, at least some infants are saved *in utero*. This hardly proves that God acts with saving intent this way upon every infant for all time, but it proves that by his sovereign will he *can* and he *has* done so for some. Reformed scholar Herman Bavinck wrote, "For God no door is locked, no creature unapproachable, no human heart inaccessible. With his Spirit he can enter the innermost being of every human, with or without the Word, by way of or apart from all consciousness, in old age or from the moment of conception."[1] God is fully aware of every child at conception—he knows its ultimate destiny for good or ill. Every life conceived in the womb is a person made in the image of God: a true *soul*! He knows his plans for us prior to our first birth-cry. No one escapes the Lord's all-comprehending supervision: "Where shall I go from your Spirit? Or where shall I flee from your presence? If I ascend to heaven, you are there! If I make my bed in Sheol, you are there!" (Ps. 139:7–8). We can say that the eternal destiny God plans for any child cannot be nullified by the child's untimely death before reaching full maturity, when he or she could make a conscious decision regarding justifying faith or condemning unbelief.

## KNOWING THE RIGHT HAND FROM THE LEFT

Another introductory issue is the unique way the Old Testament sometimes speaks of young children in a moral and spiritual category set apart from adults whom God judged as fully responsible for their unbelief and sin. Take note of Ezekiel 16:20–22. There the Lord indicts the people of Jerusalem for practicing child sacrifices. "And you took your sons and your daughters, whom you had borne to me, and these you sacrificed to them to be devoured. Were your whorings so small a matter that you slaughtered my children and delivered them up as an offering by fire . . . ?" The emphasis is that even if God's idolatrous people would not cherish their children because they had given them birth, the Lord called these babes "my children." God emphasized his ownership of them. And in other references he calls them "guiltless" and "the innocents" (Jer. 2:34; 19:4). Although these children were indeed born under the fall, they were innocent of the cold-blooded unbelief shown by their parents, and thus the Lord looked on them with compassion.

Jonah 4:11 offers another example, dealing this time with pagan children outside Israel's covenant. God's Spirit reasoned with reluctant Jonah to go to Nineveh as an evangelist, knowing the notorious godlessness of the population. The Lord said, "Should not I pity Nineveh, that great city, in which there are more than 120,000 persons who *do not know* their right hand from their left?" This appears to say that God's heart was uniquely compassionate toward the *children* of Nineveh; he knew the tally of them, implying perfect divine care even over young souls of pagan Ninevites who were hostile to Israel. In Deuteronomy 1:39 the same Hebrew expression is translated "children who . . . have no knowledge of good or evil." The phrase also occurs in Isaiah: "For before the boy knows how to refuse the evil and choose the good, the land whose two kings you dread will be deserted" (7:16). This reference is not only about a child not yet knowing good from evil; it more specifically states he cannot *choose* it with a rational will. The existence of some moral/spiritual threshold for fully accountable choices—a developmental landmark for souls, with its onset known only to God—is implied in such passages.

Another issue to note briefly is how the Lord drew a separation between sinful Israel and their young children on the Exodus journey. Due to their multifaceted unbelief repeated on many occasions, God forbade all adults who wandered with Moses for forty years from entering the Promised Land. However, the Lord said, "And as for your little ones . . . your children, who today have no knowledge of good or evil, they shall go in there. And to them I will give it, and they shall possess it" (Deut. 1:39). Clearly Israel's young children were not held accountable for unbelief they were incapable of committing before the Lord, but their parents were.

## CHILDREN AND ORIGINAL SIN

Now we look at a third background issue. All children are born under the dark shadow of mankind's great fall and the curse of Adam. "I was brought forth in iniquity, and in sin did my mother conceive me" (Ps. 51:5) applies to all living persons without exception. What we call "original sin" teaches that we are not sinners only by performing acts of sin; we sin because we are natively born sinners. Having inherited Adam's rebellion, we are bound to repeat it, and we justly deserve all the consequences thereof (Rom. 5:12–

20). We all are born "by nature children of wrath" (Eph. 2:3). This innate culpability to sin is true for all children. This doctrine absolutely must not be deemphasized as we consider the question before us.

Without letting go of original sin and its ultimate penalty of hell for every child born apart from Christ, it is still possible for God in his infinite mercy to decide that any or all young children who die could be exempted from the default penalty of condemnation before they have *opportunity* to produce willful decisions of rebel unbelief. If a child dies before taking full ownership of his sin nature and before intentionally naming Jesus as Lord, could we not conclude that God may apply redeeming grace to him or her, out of the mystery of his own good counsel? That grace must be the same imputed righteousness procured by Christ at Calvary—no other will suffice! Since the child was born under sin's curse, we cannot label him "innocent" of having a sin nature; that is a serious inaccuracy. Yet he could be accounted by the Lord as *judicially* innocent of committing willful acts of unbelief. Do you see the critical distinction? Even though the child is born under the curse, the Lord could in his sovereign mercy "count" electing grace and justification on behalf of one who has not yet taken active ownership of the rebellion that his nature would later exhibit if that soul survived to maturity.

This line of reasoning leads some theologians to discuss an "age of accountability." That is a notoriously difficult concept, and we should be clear that there is a veil of silence over this idea in Scripture. Existence of an age of accountability may be inferred by such passages as we have already mentioned, but it is nowhere stated explicitly. Only the Lord can possibly know a moment in the life when a person *does know* his right hand from his left, and is held spiritually and morally accountable. All endeavors to set an arbitrary age of accountability for divine judgment are the height of folly. We cannot say when a child crosses an invisible line in the sand in God's moral universe. Still, it seems broadly biblical to form this conclusion: the Lord in his own mercy surely may and can choose to apply his gracious salvation to the very young who die. Therefore, let us proceed to see if this tentative hypothesis may be bolstered by more evidence and might even be expanded.

## DAVID'S ASSURANCE ABOUT A DEAD SON

We finally come to our lead text from 2 Samuel 12:23—a passage unique within the Bible because of its firm statement regarding one specific dead child of a believing parent. On each of about five occasions in my pastoral ministry when I have had to preach at the funeral of an infant or young child, I have spoken from this text because it is God's clearest beam of sunlight on the subject. Here is David the grieving father, acting as a prophet by the voice of the Spirit. David knew his own solid hopes of enjoying the eternal presence of God in heaven. Now he boldly declares beyond doubt that he expects to share that eternity with his dead infant son.

Our passage comes on the heels of the tragic story of David's adultery with Bathsheba and his connivance to cause the death of her husband Uriah (see 2 Samuel 11–12). Following a stern rebuke from the prophet Nathan, the king made a swift, sincere repentance before the Lord. David immediately received assurance through Nathan that his life would be spared: "The LORD also has put away your sin; you shall not die. Nevertheless, because by this deed you have utterly scorned the LORD, the child who is born to you shall die" (2 Sam. 12:13–14). Despite God's sure forgiveness, the child's death was only the first stage of other painful consequences that would cluster around David's throne. Adultery with Bathsheba led to his house being entangled in fratricidal infighting and endless strife for following generations.

Some people foolishly complain that God appears to be a "monster" here. They ask why a little infant had to suffer for his father's crime. The simple answer is that the infant did *not* suffer. After a brief visit to earthly life, he was snatched into the arms of the Lord to dwell in eternal bliss. This unnamed first son of David and Bathsheba was spared sorrows of a mortal life—especially the inevitable stress he would have faced as a prince in David's line and target of throne competition with his step-brothers. Since we are told by David's prophecy that the baby could expect eternal life, there is little valid reason to pity this child! If he did suffer physical pangs in dying, they ended quickly. It was David and Bathsheba who suffered the great grief of losing their child, along with many subsequent woes within the Davidic dynasty.

In 2 Samuel 12, the king's servants were astonished to observe how calmly David took the child's death, since he had wrestled in prayer and fasted for days before the Lord, pleading for the baby's life. David explained himself in these crucial sentences: "Now he is dead. Why should I fast? Can I bring him back again? *I shall go to him*, but he will not return to me" (12:23). Here was a repentant believer in a right condition of chastened faith before his God.

Some interpreters speculate that the king's declaration, "I shall go to him, but he will not return to me," may indicate only that David's body would one day lie in a cemetery vault beside that of his son. That interpretation is highly unlikely. How could such a cold scrap of comfort have worked transformational change in David? It makes more sense to understand that the *place* in which David envisioned joining his son was not merely a graveyard, but the heavenly destiny described in Psalm 23:6: "Surely goodness and mercy shall follow me all the days of my life, and I shall dwell in the house of the LORD forever." How could David have envisioned a joyful father-son reunion in a lesser destination than he proposed in Psalm 16:11: "In your presence is fullness of joy; and at your right hand are pleasures forevermore"?

It is important to see that this trust in a heavenly reunion was not something David would or could have said about all his children. Compare a very different reaction from the King of Israel at the death of another, fully mature son. When handsome, charismatic Absalom rebelled against his father with an army and was killed by Joab's spear in an act of civil war, David wailed aloud in 2 Samuel 19:4, "O my son Absalom, O Absalom, my son, my son!" The King could not be comforted by any human means. Do you see the lesson implicit here? David *stopped* mourning when Bathsheba's baby son died; but he *started* deep mourning when Absalom died. The difference had to be that a no-name baby son was secure in God's heavenly presence, but Absalom presumably was not and never could be redeemed. David had no hope at all of seeing the face of Absalom in eternity.

## CAN WE SHARE DAVID'S HOPE?

How much can be generalized from this passage? When David spoke his 2 Samuel 12:23 insight about an after-death reunion with an infant son, was he speaking about a special divine providence afforded only to him as Israel's king? We must challenge someone to show us why this should *not* be generalized to include at minimum all redeemed *believers* who similarly lose children prematurely! It would be odd indeed to interpret this as a once-only act of the Lord, withholding similar confident hope from all believing parents. I am unaware of any commentator who argues to limit 2 Samuel 12:23 as an isolated blessing for an exceptional parent. If our reasoning in the matter is correct, David's declaration stands forth like a shining beacon to any parent whose trust for eternal life is also in David's Lord.

John MacArthur authored a small but unique book on this subject, titled *Safe in the Arms of God*.[2] MacArthur affirms his main conclusion this way: "For our loved ones in heaven, including the little ones, the day of perfection has already come. . . . Everything we can envision as the wholeness and perfection of Christ is the wholeness and perfection being experienced by our loved ones who dwell with him in eternity."[3] This includes babies. Our confidence of this rests upon the bedrock of the goodness and justice of God: "Shall not the Judge of all the earth do what is just?" (see Gen. 18:25).

Another pastor/scholar, John Piper, similarly expresses confidence in the salvation of all children who die in infancy. Piper emphasizes that God does not judge us in the end merely for bearing original sin, but for the sinful *deeds* done in our body, according to 2 Corinthians 5:10. We are justified entirely by grace through faith; however, Scripture asserts that we are judged according to our rebel deeds.[4] Piper bases his case primarily on Romans 1:18–20, where Paul states that God's wrath is visited against mankind universally, since the basic truth of God's creatorship is displayed in the world and is known by all men. People are "without excuse" for ignoring or suppressing this obvious knowledge of God in the natural creation. Piper states, "If a person does *not* have access to understand the revelation of God's glory in this world, if he lacks natural capacity to understand it, then Paul can be taken to imply they *will have an excuse* at the Judgment. God only executes wrath on those who have capacity to see his glory and *refuse* to embrace it. Infants, I believe, do not have this capacity."[5] An infant cannot "suppress the truth" in unrighteousness; so he cannot become "futile" in his thoughts. This leads to a conclusion that the nonelect, that is, all nonredeemed reprobates really must survive spiritual infancy in order to have opportunity to demonstrate in later actions the culpable deeds that mark their condemnation.

## HOW JESUS REGARDED CHILDREN

We move to another crucial strand of thought. Is there any evidence that Jesus Christ ever spoke about children in such a way as to make us think he saw the kingdom of heaven being populated by many of them? I believe there is such evidence, yet we can easily look right past it if we are not careful—I believe I did so for years. In Matthew 18:1–5, Jesus answered the disciples' question, "Who is the greatest in the kingdom of heaven?" by drawing a child into their midst. He stated, "Truly, I say to you, unless you turn and become like children, you will never enter the kingdom of heaven. Whoever humbles himself *like this child* is greatest in the kingdom of heaven. Whoever receives one such child in my name receives me." Jesus used a living child for a teaching analogy primarily to emphasize that a main characteristic of becoming his disciple was helplessness, the total dependency of hanging upon him by faith. Benjamin B. Warfield wrote, "The children of the kingdom enter it as children enter the world, stripped and naked—infants for whom all must be done, not who are capable of doing."[6] Jesus made a literal human child the archetype for all recipients of the kingdom of God.

The Lord did not set out in this passage to discuss the eternal status of young children; he was teaching on the utter helplessness required of adult disciples. Jesus said a similar thing in Luke 18:15–17. There he received "infants" who were brought to him for a blessing, and his purpose for rebuking his disciples for turning these little ones aside as if they were unimportant was to show how every disciple must be "like a child" to enter the kingdom (v. 17).

However, while correctly taking that main lesson from these passages, we should not miss this implied but vital secondary fact: using a child for purposes of analogy presupposes that the actual child in Jesus's presence had the qualities being commended. If that warm, breathing child embraced by Jesus was not a recipient of God's saving grace, what kind of an example did he provide? Reading Luke 18:16, for instance, I for years brushed aside the importance of the Lord saying, "Do not hinder them, for *to such* belongs the kingdom of God." It would be a great contradiction for Jesus Christ to commend characteristics of childlikeness as prerequisites for salvation while slamming the door of heaven upon the very immature soul he chose as the exemplar of these qualities! There were real children present as Jesus spoke; he did not refer to some vague idealization of childhood. Thus, John MacArthur stated, "An analogy works only if it is rooted in truth! If children are not readily and fully received into the kingdom of heaven (as they already are) then the analogy comparing them to spiritual conversion would be a poor one. As it is, the analogy is a great one because children are readily accepted into the kingdom."[7]

The analogy Jesus employed was valid because actual "infants"—spiritually as well as physically helpless there in his arms—already possessed qualities needed by a recipient of God's grace in salvation. But hear a caution: this cannot mean that *all* currently living children are inevitably saved. That would call for universalism, which is patently unbiblical. Reality teaches us that many young children will grow older to demonstrate that they are reprobates when they are thirteen years old, or twenty-five—or sixty-two or eighty-three. Our concern here deals only with children who *die* while still a child. If a youngster dies before attaining full spiritual maturity and accountability, his soul exhibits to God the precise "childlike" helplessness Jesus required from adult disciples. What would logically hinder that dying child's salvation?

Consider the pointed Gospel sequel in Matthew 18:10: "See that you do not despise one of these little ones. For I tell you that in heaven their angels always see the face of my Father who is in heaven." (This does not establish literal existence of guardian angels for children, as popularly supposed; the Bible knows nothing of guardian angels in any other text. It has been well argued that the words "their angels" in 18:10 could mean the same as "their disembodied souls." That makes good sense.) Jesus used a figure of speech about "angels" here, to emphasize that young children in death are beyond question the objects of the heavenly Father's tender regard. Then we add the powerful words Christ spoke in Matthew 18:14: "It is not the will of my Father who is in heaven that one of these little ones should perish." Some commentators point out that the "little ones" Jesus spoke about in Matthew 18:10 and 14 includes childlike adult disciples. I believe this is correct, but the term absolutely must also include among its antecedents the actual children upon whom Jesus based his teaching analogy.

Jesus declared that if childlike adult disciples who consciously trust in him *or* the actual children in his presence were to die momentarily, they could not "perish." All "little ones"—whether a disciple like Peter or John or a sticky-fingered infant squirming in his arms—are under the protection of our Lord's watchful love. There is a flash of parental fire in Christ's demeanor in these passages against anyone who would interfere with this special bond of kingdom adoption. You sense from Jesus the roar of a mother grizzly toward anyone who would try to harm her cub. He said, "Whoever causes one of these little ones who believe in me to sin, it would be better for him to have a great millstone fastened around his neck and to be drowned in the depth of the sea" (Matt. 18:6; see Mark 9:42; Luke 17:2)!

Jesus also put hands of blessing on young children (Matt. 19:13). Was his blessing a mere hollow gesture? Would the Son of God pronounce personal blessing on souls who might later turn out to be cursed or eternally condemned? John Calvin commented: "From this we gather that his grace reaches to this age of life also . . . it follows that they (the children before Jesus) were regenerated by the Spirit in the hope of salvation . . . that he embraced them was testimony that Christ reckoned them in his flock."[8]

John Newton, eighteenth-century Reformed pastor and beloved author of the hymn "Amazing Grace," commented on the several passages of Matthew 18 and 19 that I have mentioned. In a sweeping conclusion, Newton wrote, "I am willing to believe, till the Scripture forbids me, that infants, of all nations and kindred, without exception, who die before they are capable of sinning after the similitude of Adam's transgression, who have done nothing in the body for which they can give an account, are included in the election of grace. They are born for a better world than this." He further said, "The number of infants who are effectually redeemed to God by his [Christ's] blood, so greatly exceeds the aggregate of all adult believers."[9] Note this well: Newton was prepared to say that *all infants* who died in a state of spiritual infancy must be considered elect. He included children of Islam, of Hinduism, Buddhism, and pagans of no faith at all. Not everyone is ready to agree that God's decree extends this widely, but Newton is hardly alone, as we shall hear shortly.

## THE WESTMINSTER CONFESSION SPEAKS

Early seventeenth-century British church fathers who gathered in Westminster Abbey demonstrated scrupulous wisdom in writing the Westminster Confession of Faith. They were determined that this should be a thoroughly biblical creed. Chapter 10 of the Confession ("Of Effectual Calling") contains a masterful statement from this Puritan super-committee: "Elect infants, dying in infancy, are regenerated and saved by Christ, through the Spirit, who worketh when, and where and how he pleaseth: so also are all other elect persons who are uncapable of being called outwardly by the ministry of the Word."[10] Read that over again. Those three lines are packed tight with truth that proceeds as far as Scripture allows, but refuses to delve into further speculation. The

Westminster Confession says that God certainly *can* and he *may* work salvation apart from the normal "means of grace"—outside normal boundaries of outward faith and intellectual profession. It also states that God will save all "*elect* infants" who die before maturity and all elect mentally incompetent persons. However, this creed carefully stops short of speculating as to whether *all* infants and *all* mental incompetents in the world—or even *all* such progeny of professed believers—should be considered elect. The Westminster divines left unanswered how extensively this special case in election might apply. Thus the Westminster Confession echoes a view on this subject concluded by an early church scholar named Voetius, who said about salvation for *all* deceased infants, "I would not wish to deny it, nor am I able to affirm."[11]

Many, but not all, Reformed and Presbyterian scholars adhere to a strict interpretation of the Westminster Confession, judging that any more sweeping conclusion about the elect status of all children who die regardless of whether they have parents in the faith goes too far. They would say that the views of John MacArthur, John Piper, and John Newton state too much.

In a magisterial summation Herman Bavinck wrote, "At bottom, the Reformed confession is more magnanimous and broader in outlook than any other Christian confession. It locates the ultimate and most profound source of salvation solely in God's good pleasure, in his eternal compassion, in his unfathomable mercy, in the unsearchable riches of his grace, grace that is both omnipotent and free."[12] Ironically this means that only Calvinism—which is so often caricatured as the severe doctrinal system—has anything to say to parents who are grieving a dead child. God's sovereign decree of election in Christ is our one source of hope in this area!

## VOICES OF THE UNBORN

Thus far in our discussion, it seems that, at minimum, believing parents can trust God for a sure reunion with children we conceive, who die in infancy or early youth. Our departed little ones rest safe in God's merciful arms when they cannot be sheltered in ours. They have not *lost* their lives. They have gained eternal life.

What about lost little ones whose faces the mother and father never even behold? Those who never utter a single audible cry? Can we include infants who are miscarried or aborted in what we are saying here? The main issue is whether human life begins at conception. If it does, which nearly all pro-life people conclude is the safest and most logical concept, then we must also give account for the eternal state of children who never draw a breath outside the womb. Given infant mortality rates throughout human history and the prevalence of abortion today, we know that millions upon millions of children have not enjoyed life as we know it.

A rather shocking passage in Ezekiel 16 has the Lord describing Israel as if it were a newborn baby who survived an attempt to destroy it. "As for your birth, on the day you were born your cord was not cut, nor were you washed with water to cleanse you, nor rubbed with salt, nor wrapped in swaddling cloths. . . . But you were cast out on the open field, for you were abhorred, on the day that you were born. And when I passed by you and saw you wallowing in your blood, I said to you in your blood, 'Live!'" (vv. 4–6). God symbolically took up Israel as an abandoned child left to die in a field. The Lord then tells how he cleansed, fed, and clothed his people with tender care. However, in Ezekiel 16:20 and following, the Lord sternly indicts the Israelites because "you took your own sons and daughters, whom you had borne to me, and these you sacrificed for them to be devoured." This refers to child sacrifices some Israelites had stooped to perform before Canaanite idols like Moloch. Clearly, God reserves compassionate love for the child who is discarded, unloved, or even unseen by the eyes of careless-living men and women of this world.

## CORROBORATING TESTIMONIES

Now let us briefly survey what various other theologians and preachers of the Word have concluded about the eternal salvation of children who die. An early voice, the church father Irenaeus once commented about "all who by (Christ) are born again to God, infants and children, and boys and young men and old men."[13] Many early church fathers linked the salvation of a dying child directly to its baptism, even without biblical warrant for that. Augustine defended the idea that baptized infants were certainly to be regarded as redeemed at their death, but he further said that the unbaptized child might at least be regarded by God's softer mercies in some way, which he did not define.[14]

Martin Luther, Melanchthon, and other Lutheran theologians held to the assertion in the Augsburg Confession that baptism is necessary to salvation (article 9). The Lutheran confessional stance therefore holds no clear hope for unbaptized children. Yet B. B. Warfield quotes Luther as conceding this much about unbaptized children of Christians who die: "The holy and merciful God will think kindly upon them. What he will do with them he has revealed to no one . . . but has reserved to his own mercy; God does wrong to no one."[15] The Church of England's official confessional views closely resemble the Lutheran view, requiring baptism for confidence about a child's salvation.[16]

In the Reformed view, membership in the kingdom of heaven is not restricted by the rigid fence of baptism. The absolutely free grace of God in election alone determines who is saved. But most Reformed scholars show primary confidence in the heavenly status of the children of believers, holding to the covenant promise: "for you [baptized believers in Christ] and your children and for all who are far off, everyone the Lord our God calls to himself" (Acts 2:39). Also see Acts 16:31: "Believe on the Lord Jesus, and you will be saved, you and your household." And when Paul in 1 Corinthians 7:14 says, "otherwise your children would be unclean, but as it is, they are holy," his distinction is drawn on the basis of these children having at least one believing parent. So we can concede there is some evidence for the Lord showing special regard for a believer's child over others in the vast population.

Among the more broadly Reformed, Ulrich Zwingli stood out in his time by maintaining that the death *of any* young child must be indicative of its election by grace.[17] And those who mistakenly imagine John Calvin to be the dour prophet of the doctrine of predestination probably surmise that he consigned dying infants to hell, as sinners without the benefit of Christ. Calvin certainly believed that children are born in original sin, however he also did not believe a reprobate person could die while an infant. If an infant were to die (as did Calvin's only child, a son), the pastor of Geneva assumed that death to be proof of the child's election by grace. It must be admitted that there is some vagueness about Calvin's views on this subject. Yet in all Calvin's writings, nowhere does he plainly say that anyone dying in infancy is lost.[18]

The historic view of Reformed Bible scholars was typified by the Puritan John Owen. He said that God saves infants first and foremost "by interesting [including] them in the covenant, if their immediate or remote parents have been believers."[19] However, Owen also conceded that God may act for some infants "by his grace of election which is most free, and not tied to any conditions, by which I make no doubt but God takes many unto him in Christ whose parents never knew, or had been despisers of, the gospel."[20] It seems Owen did not say that baptism for a believer's child was always required in order for a dying infant to be redeemed, although he never diminished the importance of covenant baptism. He did not go out of his way to apply grace to all dying children, but seemed to at least allow for it.

In summary, most Calvinists historically have held to something rather close to the Westminster Confession of Faith statement that says we can be confident of the eternal state of dying children of believers, and mental incompetents, while leaving the matter open regarding the dying children of unbelievers. Although Reformed thinkers still dispute whether God's electing grace applies to all young children who die in the world or only to children of professed believers, it should be noted that both parties stand together on a platform of divine salvation based on sovereign grace alone.

We should point out that the so-called Arminian (or Pelagian) gospel concept, which is based entirely upon human choice, offers no word of hope on the subject of children who die. Arminianism insists that the decision of the human will is the final arbiter for personal salvation. So logically, that system grants no reprieve to an immature will that is incapable of choosing Christ. If even one dying infant who cannot use mental abilities to select faith in Christ would prove to be saved, that one represents a glaring, illogical exception to the entire Arminian system! How will the Arminian explain David's hope regarding his son in 2 Samuel 12:23? He can have no hope in the matter, if he wants to be consistent with his exaltation of unfettered human choice. If you see human free will entirely in the driver's seat of salvation, "You must abandon [billions] of infants who die to damnation. In the final analysis, it remains a riddle what Pelagianism can have against God glorifying his efficacious grace in the lives of sinners."[21]

## THE BROAD VIEW DEFENDED

We have already heard John MacArthur, John Piper, Ulrich Zwingli, and John Newton promote a very broad view of the salvation of *all* infants who die, with Martin Luther, John Owen, and John Calvin seeming to allow at least for its possibility. In further testimony, here is part of a letter Newton wrote to friends whose young child had died, offering these consoling words: "I hope you are both well reconciled to the death of your child. I cannot be sorry for the death of infants. How many storms they escape! Nor can I doubt, in my private judgment, that they are included in the election of grace."[22]

Charles H. Spurgeon was known for definite opinions on most subjects relating to God's Word. Defending his views against those who claimed his Calvinism damned infants to hell, Spurgeon did not speak mildly: "Among the gross falsehoods uttered against Calvinists is that we believe in the damnation of little infants. A more base lie was never uttered! . . . Scripture saith but very little, and therefore where Scripture is scant it is for no man to determine dogmatically. But I think I speak for the entire body [of Calvinists], or certainly with exceedingly few exceptions, when I say that all infants who die are elect of God and therefore saved. . . . We do sometimes hope that the multitude of the saved shall be made to exceed the multitude of the lost. . . . I believe the Lord Jesus who said, 'of such are the kingdom of heaven' does daily receive into his loving arms those tender ones who are snatched away from us to heaven."[23]

Benjamin B. Warfield was the premier theologian of old Princeton Seminary in the late nineteenth and early twentieth centuries. No man had greater concern for a systematic theology that was at every point firmly Bible-based, or was more a champion of the Westminster Confession of Faith. Yet Warfield took a step beyond the more cautious stance of the Confession. He held that it was entirely within the logical inference of Scripture that *all infants who died, without exception*, should be regarded as elect. Warfield concluded, "Is [this] the Scriptural answer? It is as legitimate and logical an answer as any, based on Reformed postulates. . . . But if it stands, it can stand on no other theological basis than the Reformed. If all infants dying in infancy are saved, it is certain they are not saved by or through the ordinances of the visible church . . . it can only be through the almighty operation of the Holy Spirit who worketh when and where and how he pleaseth, through whose ineffable grace the Father gathers these little ones to the home he has prepared for them."[24] Warfield's brilliant Princeton colleague Charles Hodge was known to hold the same view, as did Augustus Toplady, Philip Doddridge, Robert Candlish, and Loraine Boettner—all from the Reformed camp.

I have already shown that author John MacArthur takes a firm stand on this issue. Hear him once more: "Fallen, sinful, guilty and depraved children who die with no spiritual merit—no personal, moral or religious merit—are welcomed by God into glory. On what basis? Solely by God's grace! How were you or any other person saved? By law? Or by grace? None of us had any more to do with regard to the accomplishment of our own salvation than the youngest and most helpless infant. We have all been saved by grace."[25]

My own view in this matter will hardly influence anyone. Having considered this subject carefully for decades, I choose to stand with those named above, by leaning into the broader view that says *all* dying infants may be considered elect. This seems biblically consistent and not out of keeping with God's known character. I remind myself, as Spurgeon stated, that we cannot be dogmatic where God has not given us a clear lead. And along with Warfield, I am submissive to the formulas of the Westminster Confession. Yet as Warfield put it so well, the broader view seems to be as legitimate and logical an answer as any, set against the broad picture of Scripture.

## CONSIDER THE VAST OUTCOME

If we are correct in this view, pause to consider the stupendous wonder that *billions* now populate heaven whose souls were gathered to Christ as infants! Surely this calls to mind John's inspired vision in heaven, where he was allowed to see "a great multitude that no one could number, from every nation, from all tribes and peoples and languages, standing before the throne and before the Lamb . . . crying out with a loud voice, 'Salvation belongs to our God who sits on the throne, and to the Lamb!'" (Rev. 7:9–10).

Be clear in your mind once more, so there is no misunderstanding: neither I nor any theologian cited here imagines that children are saved simply by virtue of a false doctrine of a universal salvation that is equally received by every human being, nor by being blanketed in a sentimental, humanistic notion of so-called sinless innocence. Only God sovereignly saves a child by his mercy. In order to do so, he must apply the righteousness of Jesus Christ to young children as a special act of divine grace. Very young children truly need Christ as their Savior, just as all sinners do. God remains sovereign and unhindered in his inscrutable designs. He does not choose someone to salvation in advance merely because he foresees they are going to die in infancy. It is more accurate to say that a child who dies at a young age must have been one of those Jesus claimed as his "little ones," foreordained to eternal life from the foundation of the world.

There is a gravestone in the churchyard of Winchester Cathedral marking the resting place of one Susannah Taylor who died at four years of age. In Latin the inscription reads: "Amicis chara. Parentibus charior. Deo charissima." Translation: "Dear to her friends; dearer to her parents; dearest to God."[26]

We do not own our children. They are loaned to us on trust from the Father of us all. Christian, I firmly believe your deceased child or infant is in heaven. You will greet him or her, whole and splendid in glory when you, like King David, "go to him." Your absent child is safe within the care of him who does what is just and merciful. If you are a mother or father who has buried, miscarried, or aborted a child in this world, I hope that with bright-eyed hope you will join many other Christian parents who have learned to say, "We have many children, some on this earth and some safely in God's arms."

## TO BECKY

Becky, my dear niece, I hardly knew you. You who could not see, or hear, or speak on this earth—today you comprehend the length, the breadth, the depth, and the height of unspeakably grand truths about Christ. How privileged you were to precede me! Our appointment for a renewed relationship will come one day. Then you shall be my instructor.

It is my eager expectation and hope that I will not be at all ashamed, but that with full courage now as always Christ will be honored in my body, whether by life or by death. For to me to live is Christ, and to die is gain.

**PHILIPPIANS 1:20-21**

# CHAPTER TWENTY-TWO

# TO LIVE IS CHRIST, TO DIE IS GAIN

☀

*EVEN IF YOU HAVE READ* every preceding page to this point, you could contend that I have not "proved" the existence of heaven to anyone. And I cannot do so. We accept heaven's shining reality entirely on the evidence of faith alone—faith based in the excellence of trusting the living Christ yesterday, today, and tomorrow.

Consider this situation: "If I were a twin in the womb, I doubt that I could prove the existence of earth to my mate. He would probably object that the idea of an earth beyond the womb was ridiculous, that the womb was the only earth we'd ever know. If I tried to explain that earthlings live in a greatly expanded environment and breathe air, he would only be more skeptical. After all, a fetus lives in water; who could imagine its being able to live in a universe of air? To him, such a transition would be impossible. It would take birth to prove earth's existence to a fetus. A little pain, a dark tunnel, a gasp of air—and then the wide world! Green grass, lakes, the ocean, horses (could a fetus imagine a horse?), rainbows, walking, running, surfing, ice skating. With enough room that you don't have to shove, and a universe beyond."[1]

How is it possible for anyone to live with a firm and lively focus upon that next world while we are still well rooted in this one? Has anyone succeeded in doing this, except Jesus? But he, after all, had already been a dweller in the world of his Father's glory before coming into the cow stall, the carpenter's shop, and that gruesome way station called Golgotha. He had an advantage on us in visualizing what was yet to come after his tomb. Perhaps, after Jesus, the apostle Paul came closest to having his mind and soul dwell in heaven before he got there. Before we check in with Paul on this, I want you to meet a twenty-first-century friend who now occupies the immediate heaven with Christ. I introduce him because his soul also drank deeply from the atmosphere of his new eternal home before he slipped away from here to there.

## CHRIST THE CENTER, ALL ELSE CIRCUMFERENCE

I share excerpts from a letter written by the late Dr. J. Alan Groves. Al was a beloved professor of Old Testament at Westminster Seminary in Philadelphia whose body succumbed to cancer in his fifties. As an academic, his skills in Hebrew made a notable contribution to that field of study. But Al was the rare combination of first-rate scholar and warm-hearted disciple of Jesus. He wrote this letter while desperately ill. He planned it to be read at his memorial service, offering his testimonial about the very essence of life. Dr. Groves said, "As I have walked through the valley of the shadow of death, I have walked hand-in-hand with Jesus, the one who has already walked through that valley and come out the other side, alive, raised from the dead. And as I hold his hand and trust him, I too am raised with him, for this was his purpose in walking that path: to raise those who trusted in him. . . . Now as I have died, I come before God, the King of the universe, and I come in Christ. He chose to suffer and die on the cross in my place so that on account of him I might have forgiveness from sin and victory over death. And now I have received the resurrection and eternal life that has been my only hope, past, present and forever."

He continued, "I have led a truly blessed life. At a young age, I realized that Jesus was not just a story in a comic book, but that he was real and I could actually know him. I wish I could describe to you what a powerful moment of understanding that was. I have thought about it many times over the years, marveling over and over at the truth of this central fact. . . . Through all my life, Christ has been constant. Even as I have grown and changed, he is still the one whom I loved that first day. And nothing ever changed in how I came to him; every day of my life the story is the same: I come to God in Christ. His love for me has been steadfast, and he has pursued me through every time I have turned away from Him and every time I have returned. The constant prayer of my heart for my own life and the lives of those around me has been that we would see Jesus, and that He would be welcome and present among us."

Alan Groves ended with a pastoral exhortation: "If you struggle with faith, let me encourage you that in the hardest moments I have faced, he has been there. Death has been defeated. I am in Christ, as you are in

Christ. So let us live out of the grace we have received. Let us live out of Christ. . . . For most of my Christian life I have wanted to see Jesus face-to-face, to join in with the heavenly chorus in his presence around his royal throne and declare his praise in new ways. . . . He is good. From the beginning, his steadfast love has endured. It endures forever. He is a gracious God, slow to anger, abounding in steadfast love. Trust in him with all your heart, for he is faithful."[2]

We have now considered together many aspects of the Bible's view of death and eternity. In several unblinking chapters we weighed terrible facts of judgment and hell that the Scriptures prescribe for unbelief. Then we sketched the incredible destination of heaven for those who belong to Christ. We've reviewed Scripture's forecast of solid certainty that a Christian's soul is with the Lord immediately at death and that we have joyful expectation of resurrection bodies and a new creation when Christ returns to conclude earth's present age.

As we wrap up these studies—much as Dr. Groves's letter sought to do—the final word will be an attempt to leave us facing heaven unafraid and joyfully expectant. Once more we look to Scripture, this time for a provocative summary from the apostle Paul in the brief sentence of Philippians 1:21: *"For to me to live is Christ, and to die is gain."* Of this verse James Boice commented, "This text cuts like a surgeon's scalpel, right into the heart of Christianity."[3] John Stott reinforces that claim, adding, "The person and work of Christ are the foundation rock upon which the Christian religion is built. . . . Take Christ from Christianity and you disembowel it; there is practically nothing left. Christ is the center of Christianity; all else is circumference."[4]

I propose to examine Philippians 1:21, "to live is Christ, and to die is gain," which I have left instructions to have engraved on my own tombstone. We will cast this summary statement into past, present, and future applications, hoping you can connect to Jesus at each point.

## LIFE AND DEATH IN THE PAST TENSE

First, sincerely saying, "for me to live is Christ and to die is gain," requires that somewhere in your *past* you bowed low and placed your soul's full trust in the Christ of Calvary and Easter. In the words of Al Groves, "At a young age, I realized Jesus was not just a story in a comic book. He was real and I could know him. I wish I could describe what a powerful moment of understanding that was." We are called to a historic encounter with the Christ of history.

A martyr for the faith in World War II, Dietrich Bonhoeffer wrote, "Let us seek the wealth and splendor which are vouchsafed for us in Jesus Christ. . . . His grace is costly because it costs a man his life, and it is grace because it gives a man the only true life. . . . The old life is left behind and completely surrendered. . . . When we are called to follow Christ we are summoned to an exclusive attachment to his person. . . . The first Christ-suffering which every man must experience is the call to abandon the attachments of this world. . . . When Christ calls a man, he bids him to come and die."[5]

I said earlier that when you have died the first death with Christ, you give up absorption in your sins—you die to materialism, pride, and building your own kingdom in this world. Then physical death awaits you only as a passage to the fullness of life. The second death of spiritual devastation for unbelief cannot touch you, since you already died vicariously through Christ.

An incident has been told about missionaries traveling in the mid-nineteenth century to their field of service at a South Sea island. The ship carrying them to their assignment was captained by a compassionate man who felt he ought to do his best to warn the missionaries that they were headed into very real danger because the natives were notoriously violent. The captain told the head of the missionary party words to this effect: "Look, Reverend—I don't like to interfere, but did your mission board make it clear to you that the native tribes of your new island settle everything with knives and spears and some are headhunters? They won't spare you. I wonder if you can survive there more than a few weeks. They will kill you all." The head of the missionary delegation looked thoughtful for a moment but then he replied, "Captain, thank you for your concern. But I'm sure it will be all right. You see, we all died before we left home."

Saul of Tarsus was as proud and headstrong a young man as ever lived in his time. Extremely intelligent, he was self-reliant and abounded in arrogance. In human terms the young Saul bowed to no man alive. One day on the road from Jerusalem to Damascus, carrying letters of authorization from temple authorities to hunt down Christians, Saul was blinded by a blazing vision of Jesus. The risen Savior appeared, and a self-sufficient religious career-climber was not only knocked from his horse; his entire existence teetered from its mooring and came crashing down. If Saul had ever previously dwelt upon the question "What is life?" he probably would have said, "Life was given to me to obey God's law and build up my own righteousness as far as my efforts can achieve that." We know from his own testimonials (see Phil. 3:4–7) that in early life he was consumed by attaining the greatest heights of influence he could reach within official Judaism. But after the Damascus Road, a new man (soon to be called Paul) stated, "For me, to live *is* Christ." Everything else now was "counted as loss . . . because of the surpassing worth of knowing Christ Jesus my Lord" (Phil. 3:7–8).

Many years later, writing the letter we call Philippians, Paul was acutely aware that his earthly life was closing down. He was under Roman arrest and could estimate that his execution was likely as soon as a court finished its protracted business. Expecting to die really puts everything into crystal clear focus. You ask yourself, "What has this whole business of living been about, anyway?" Paul stated with confidence that living is all about Christ. He is the only reason we have to go on breathing. Paraphrasing him, the apostle told his friends in Philippi, "I could go on living twenty more years, and if I did, it would mean fruitful gospel work, more people being won and built up as Christian disciples. However, I could also die right now with no regrets, no qualms. In fact, dying is the best thing I can imagine, because it means being immediately with Christ."

We are not apostles, and God is unlikely to grant us a searing vision of Jesus comparable to Paul's. And it is better that God does not have to confront us that way—it may indicate we are not such hard cases as Paul. In 1 Peter 1:8 Peter praised folks who bowed to Christ without having physically seen him at all: "Though you have not seen him, you love him." Can you say at this present moment that no matter how much less dramatically Christ took hold of you, you know with certainty that you have saving faith in him? Can you claim that everything that has permanent meaning to you comes from God through Jesus Christ? Every Christian must consciously surrender self in trembling faith to Jesus Christ as Lord. We drive a stake in the ground and tell Almighty God, "I take my stand with your wonderful Son. From this hour forward, do unto me, O Lord, whatever you graciously plan to do for all who belong to Jesus."

A boy named Alan Groves, who would become a seminary professor, met Jesus decisively in the mid-twentieth century, and at his funeral his boyhood faith mattered far more than all his scholarly attainments. In the first century, a self-consumed persecutor of the church named Saul met Jesus, and he died to self and worldly success. A young German Lutheran pastor was so consumed by obedient faith in Christ that he put his life on the line to oppose Hitler and was hanged for it. Each of these men was an intellectual leader in his generation. Each bowed intellect and will and pride to Jesus, who became his *all*. Does your life record a similar encounter with Christ in which you died to self and came alive in him? I pray you know that there is such a landmark in your past, when the Author of Life took hold of you, transforming you with heavenly hope.

*[handwritten margin note: 1995 the worst and best year!]*

## LIFE IN THE PRESENT TENSE

Second, we weigh the present dimension of "to live is Christ." This means walking now, in deep union with him who is the Lord of life. Every man and woman holds some innate worldview that supplies meaning to each day. For millions of poor in the third world, their subconscious worldview requires simply existing day to day; basic survival consumes all their energies. Their life is not far above the animal pursuit of subsistence by a deer in the Pennsylvania woods or a lion prowling the Serengeti. Human beings can "exist" without living as God created them to live. Americans at all economic class levels may pursue life in an elemental, brutish manner as they live paycheck to paycheck, or cycle mindlessly each week from one drug fix to the next.

Others in developed countries have sufficient resources to follow the Epicurean life: "Eat, drink and be merry, for tomorrow we die." Immediate pleasure is their goal. Still others adopt the Stoic ideal that dictates life is hard and the main thing is to grit your teeth and push on through inevitable pain. Then there are Cynics. Shakespeare spoke for them in *Macbeth* when he wrote, "Life is a tale told by an idiot, full of sound and fury but signifying nothing." Cynics have not lived as God created them to, yet they have decided the endeavor is futile. They know not what they reject. Epicurean, Stoic, or Cynic: ancient Greeks delineated each of these basic worldviews long before people in our times adopted them. The problem with all such philosophies is that none of them even pretends to stand up against the threat of looming death.

Hebrews 2:14–15 correctly analyzes the uniqueness of Christ over against all other worldviews: "He himself likewise partook of the same things [our flesh and blood] that through death he might destroy the one who has the power of death, that is, the devil, and deliver all those who through fear of death were subject to lifelong slavery." If you ever discover some rival worldview to Christianity that effectually unlocks universal human bondage to the craven fear of death the way that Jesus did, please do let the rest of us know!

Christian disciples are bound in vital union with Christ today, even before we die. Galatians 2:20 summarizes: "I have been crucified with Christ. It is no longer I who live, but Christ who lives in me. And the life I now live in the flesh I live by faith in the Son of God, who loved me and gave himself for me." Another way Paul described it was to say, "Therefore, if anyone is *in Christ*, he is a new creation" (2 Cor. 5:17). To be "in" Christ is not about mysticism; it is a fundamental union of our spirit and God's Spirit, mediated by his Son.

Not long ago I preached through the book of Colossians and was thrilled anew to explore the mind-expanding way Christ is exalted in Colossians 1 as cosmic Lord. He is called: "The image of the invisible God, the firstborn of all creation" (v. 15); "He is before all things, and in him all things hold together" (v. 17). Christ Jesus *is* the epitome of the so-called "unified field theory" that Albert Einstein sought to identify on his mathematician's blackboard strewn with formulas. The living Lord Christ is the source, the head, the goal, the heartbeat, the climax of everything that exists. He is Creator, Redeemer, and Sustainer. Knowing Christ becomes the heartbeat of a disciple's daily existence.

Union with the risen Jesus transformed eleven defeated disciples into world-changers. After the crucifixion they were huddled behind a locked door in Jerusalem for fear of the Jews (John 20:19). In a matter of weeks, you could threaten the same men with prison for preaching—even lock them up—and as soon as they were released, the resurrection of Jesus was spilling again from their tongues in any available marketplace (Acts 5:40–42). The vitality of Jesus was their internal dynamo. It could truly be said, "It was not the church that mothered the resurrection, the resurrection mothered the church."[6]

A married couple in their midnineties was critically injured in a car accident in their Midwestern state. They survived to reach the hospital, where they were placed on adjacent gurneys in the emergency room. The gravely injured but conscious wife reached out to grasp tightly the hand of her husband of more than seventy years. Sadly, he soon expired from his injuries. A physician sought to certify his death and was at first confused because a pulse was being registered on the electronic monitor attached to the man, despite all bodily signs indicating he was dead. Then, someone realized that the pulse detected by the monitor was the secondary heartbeat of the wife, as she clung to her dead husband's cooling hand.[7] That will be our destiny in Christ, as our heavenly Father detects the life of Jesus pulsating in you and me.

Apart from Christ no one properly lives; we only exist. When we say "for me to live is Christ," we declare that the risen Lord Jesus is the pulse of our present existence. We grasp him who died in our place, and his supernatural life is communicated to us. The day is coming when my heartbeat shall at last be stilled beyond detection, while his indefatigable life force beats on as mine.

## LIFE IN THE FUTURE TENSE

We are not finished with Philippians 1:21 until we add its future dimension. Beyond the words "to live is Christ" comes "to die is gain"—a phrase which must qualify as one of the most paradoxical statements in God's Word. A Christian's confidence fixes on one day receiving the greatest possible *gain* through what is (in the eyes of all humanity) the ultimate catastrophic *loss*. I wonder if the apostle Paul had heard people at first-century funerals shaking their heads over the body of the departed one and muttering, "What a loss . . ." If so, he corrected this sentiment before it could be spoken at his own death. When Paul died, he wanted it known that his life's balance sheet would only display *a gain* of the highest order. He was not talking of some slight enhancement a notch above wretched disappointments this life hands you—but of gain beyond our best and most satisfying joys on earth. James Boice said that "death for the Christian is never pictured in the Bible as gain over the worst in this life. Instead it is an improvement on the best."[8]

On December 31, 2011, Americans were frustrated by slow progress nationally in crawling out of the slough of a worldwide economic recession. On that date the Dow Jones Industrial Average finished the year less than one point from the numerical level of that index on the past January 1. You might have earned something on individual investments which performed better during that year, but if all your money was in a stock index fund that simply shadowed the Dow Jones performance, your earnings had simply run in place for 365 days. The stock market is supposed to be a prime economic engine of "gain" in our society. Yet for that year taken as a whole, the market produced no numerical overall advance even after trillions of dollars changed hands back and forth and millions of stock shares soared and plunged. Evidently real gain must originate from somewhere other than national economic power generators.

Paul's gospel of life in vital union to Christ declares that by knowing your Creator God through justifying faith and being indwelt by his living Spirit, you can be sure that physical death will only mean *more* of Christ than you already possess. You will pass from this shadow-world experience of spasmodic, momentary tastes and glimpses of the Savior into direct access to his fullness. A noted New Testament scholar wrote that Paul's personal dilemma in Philippians 1:23 of being "hard pressed" about whether he preferred to live or die "was a dilemma between Christ and Christ; between Christ much and Christ more; Christ by faith and Christ by sight. It was resolved ultimately by a perfect union with him."[9]

In 1970, when people still used printed encyclopedias to research information, I bought the entire set of the *Encyclopedia Britannica*. After owning this bulky set for thirty years and moving them around numerous times with the rest of my library, in 2002 I sadly carted these books to the curb for trash pick-up, victims of computer search engines. I recall that in volume 1, at the very beginning of *Britannica's* tens of thousands of pages, was a publisher's preface filling maybe a dozen pages. Do you realize your present life in union with Christ on this earth barely exceeds that tiny preface statement, in comparison to hundreds of thousands of pages of rich experience yet to be written about you and me, in heaven with Christ?

When we claim Paul's theme "to die is gain" as our own, by adding up all things that could possibly be counted valuable to us, Christ is still more valuable than the sum. Death will bring all of myself to Christ and all of himself to me. Enmeshed in matter and time, we behold him only, as the King James version put it, "through a glass, darkly" (1 Cor. 13:12). At last, all our relations will be transparent and "face to face." Heaven will *be* Christ, and Christ himself will *be* heaven!

Pondering this, how can we who possess the Spirit of Jesus as down payment for what is to come (Eph. 1:13–14) ever speak of our death as a *loss*? Even those who die young in the Lord do not miss anything essential to them. Truly—what is their tragedy? Paul estimated his own options between continuing life on earth versus his death as being finely balanced. He told the Philippians he tilted toward remaining alive only because they needed him as instructor and pastor, not for his personal need to continue on earth. My first New Testament Greek professor told his class that this Christ-saturated man, Paul, was so passionate in writing Philippians 1 that despite his literary prowess in the Greek language, he used fractured grammar here. A strictly literal translation shows that in his excitement Paul said in Philippians 1:23, "To depart and be with Christ would be *very much more better*!"

Based on Paul's confidence, we may be equally sure that God will leave us in this world exactly as long as he has a useful role for us to play. The Lord's perfect plan for the duration of your life might differ greatly from death's timing as you plan for it. But in God's perfect providence, there are no incomplete lives or premature removals.

In an entry in his manuscript called the "Miscellany," Jonathan Edwards gave one of his many choice descriptions of Christ in heaven with these words: "The external heaven surrounds Christ not merely as a house surrounds an inhabitant or as a palace surrounds a prince or as stones and timber encompass a land. But rather as plants and flowers are before the sun—that have their life and beauty and being from that luminary."[10]

Alexander MacLaren summarized Philippians 1 saying, "One thought about the future should fill our minds as it did Paul's, which is to be with Christ. . . . To us as to him heaven should be Christ and Christ should be heaven. All the rest is but accident. Golden harps and crowns and hidden manna and white robes and thrones and all other representations are but symbols of the blessedness of union with him. . . . To be with Christ is all we need . . . . Let us not fritter away our imaginations and our hopes on the subordinate and non-essential accompaniments, but concentrate on the one central thought."[11] MacLaren the eloquent Scot concluded, "Brethren! There are but two theories of life. . . . The one says, 'To me, to live is Christ and to die is gain'; the other, 'To me to live is self, and to die is loss and despair.' One or the other must be your choice. Which?"[12]

# APPENDIX: IS THERE
# TIME IN HEAVEN?

*THIS MATERIAL IS NOT DESIGNATED* as chapter 23 for a reason. By labeling it as an appendix, I am making a statement. While the following pages certainly relate to topics covered in this volume (particularly to chap. 9, "The Immediate Heaven"), some will regard its foundation as less exegetical. Others could find the thinking presented here so alien sounding as to seem preposterous. Up to this point I have resisted a temptation to hypothesize about eternal life if I could not point to explicit texts of God's Word to defend my arguments. Now we delve into a side-road of eschatology that I freely admit is more tentative and theoretical by nature. I present this as an appendix because, as you will realize, the basis is more speculative; it is more a matter of asking "what if" than stating "thus says the Lord."

Nevertheless, if I believed that what I will unfold here were antibiblical, I would not venture in this direction. I ask you to let your mind range through a topic that uncorks the imagination and opens vistas on eternity that fulfill the promise, "No eye has seen, nor ear heard, nor the heart of man *imagined*, what God has prepared for those who love him" (1 Cor. 2:9).

## TIME-BOUND THINKING

Are any of us really able to think about human experience without framing our thoughts by *time*? We are time-bound, linear thinkers, required to conceptualize in terms of before and after, yesterday and tomorrow. Like water to a goldfish, time is our base medium of existence.

Let me try to sketch where I am leading you. Among my heroes in the Christian faith is Aurelius Augustine, who died August 28, 430, as an army of Vandals hammered at the gates of his North African city. On May 27, 1564, John Calvin breathed his last in Geneva, Switzerland, and was buried the next day in an unmarked grave. The Rev. Jonathan Edwards passed from this world March 22, 1758, in the second-floor bedroom of the president's house at the College of New Jersey, from a bad reaction to a smallpox inoculation. Those men are all giants of Christian history. Permit me to add to this group (for purposes of illustration only) my humble father, Paul A. Rogers, who went home to heaven February 12, 2004. These four individuals represent diverse periods of history and cultural backgrounds, though each lived for the same Lord Jesus Christ and each died in that Savior's embrace. Using our terminology, Augustine has now enjoyed the immediate heaven for almost sixteen centuries. Calvin has had four centuries of sweet heavenly fellowship with his fellow-Reformer Martin Luther (and we assume they solved their dispute over the Lord's Table moments after meeting at the feet of Jesus). Edwards has occupied the heavenly kingdom, which he preached about with his passionate heart, for over two hundred fifty years. Perhaps during his mere eight years of eternal residence, my father's soul has met these great men of the faith whose writings he admired.

But wait—am I correct in speaking about earth years of *time* applied to those who no longer dwell in a material world? Does time have a continuing claim on anyone after death? Is it possible that in slipping the surly bonds of earth, these four men of history, and all other saints, entered a timeless eternal "now" and "arrived" in heaven simultaneously? Then, to stir the pot some more, could it be that my own heavenly arrival will occur no later than any of those who, according to earth's calendar, have long preceded me? Maybe Abraham and Sarah have not been awaiting Christ's appearance for four thousand years after all.

Do I seem to be talking nonsense? Read on.

## IS THE "INTERMEDIATE STATE" UNNECESSARY?

Even though classic Protestant orthodoxy has long assumed an "interim or intermediate state," it is unclear from 2 Corinthians 5 that Paul definitely expected to endure any gap period (or "the immediate heaven") before receiving his "building from God," a resurrection body. You can conclude from this text that the apostle did not discuss the prospect of being a disembodied soul. Some scholars understand Paul's concept of being "naked" in 2 Corinthians 5:3 or "unclothed" in 5:4 to mean a soul existing without a body. But I remind you that a better argument can be made that "nakedness" in 2 Corinthians 5 means exposure to judgment—a soul after death is "naked" if it lacks its needed atonement covering for sin. Paul knew that he would never face "nakedness" as a man redeemed in Christ.

Paul also taught in 1 Thessalonians 4 that a final glorious body of resurrection will not be granted to anyone until Christ's final return. So we naturally tell ourselves that *logically*, there must be a calendar "interval" of centuries or even millennia during which souls await the last consummation. In chapter 9, I echoed the majority theology of classic Protestant orthodoxy: upon physical death our soul and our body part ways. Then the soul dwells with Christ in immediate heaven (or the "intermediate state"), awaiting bodily resurrection and the final heaven.

With all that spread on the table, now I present an alternative interpretation. Could it be that Paul was less than explicit about an "intermediate state" for disembodied souls in 2 Corinthians 5 simply because he saw no logical necessity for such a "gap" in our path to the final state? Second Corinthians 5 is the most pointed passage on the subject, and it is notoriously hard to pin down precisely *what* existence Paul anticipated next. He spoke about a "building from God, a house not made with hands, eternal in the heavens" (v. 1), which (apparently) would be received as soon as "the tent that is our earthly home is destroyed." "Building" implies a permanent dwelling, and it is termed an "eternal building" at that. What else could this be except the final resurrection body? Where does an "intermediate" state fit?

Perhaps Paul expected upon his death an *instantaneous* transport to the last day return of Christ! That need not conflict with 2 Corinthians 5, or Christ's coming in 1 Thessalonians 4. The big question is: what if Paul assumed, by the Spirit of God, that earth's *time* had no hold upon anyone's soul after death? You see, the knot in our thinking is our insistence upon a "passage of time" between any man's death and the final hour of Christ's return. Totally immersed in clock-regulated, calendar-framed humanity, we cannot help being time-bound. But why should time apply to departed souls? Only the assumption that the dead in Christ still experience linear time requires a hypothetical "intermediate state." The Bible nowhere conclusively demands this metaphysical way station.

## THE SCIENCE OF RELATIVITY AIDS THEOLOGY

Forty years ago as a theological student I was attracted to the idea that time is entirely relative beyond human death. Yet I felt I must be mistaken, because so few scholars seemed to take up that viewpoint. Then I encountered remarkable writings of the late Arthur C. Custance. Trained as both a scientist and scholar of biblical Greek and Hebrew, this Canadian's career dwelt at the intersections between biblical studies and the physical sciences. Custance first wrote about eternity apart from time in volume 6 of his *Doorway Papers*, titled *Time and Eternity*.[1] This gifted scientist and Bible scholar explored a wide array of matters like creation, evolution, early man, and other topics where science and Scripture are interwoven. Arthur Custance later expanded on the biblical issues surrounding time in *Journey Out of Time*.[2]

Custance stated his main thesis: "There is no direct pathway between time and eternity: they are different categories of experiences. The fundamental point to grasp in all this is that when we step out of time we step into eternity and we cannot be in both at once. But God can."[3] When we recall Jesus saying, "Before Abraham was, I am" (John 8:58), we realize that God is not held captive within time as we are. Further, 2 Peter 3:8 suggests that God dwells above time: "With the Lord one day is as a thousand years, and a thousand years as one day." God created time without being trapped in it. Isaiah 65:24 raises a tantalizing prospect, as the Lord said, "Before they call I will answer; while they are yet speaking I will hear." Assuming this is more than a mere figure of speech, the mystery of divine sovereignty in prayer declares that a sequential past, present, and future does not restrict the Almighty. He is prepared to answer prayer before it is even uttered at a moment in time because he knows what will be said and exactly what purposes he predestines to achieve.

As a nonscientist, my brain gropes to understand how Einstein's theory of relativity determined that time, as a fourth dimension, has no absolute existence apart from the physical universe—so it could not have existed prior to God's creation.[4] Somehow, in the language of quantum physics, past, present, and future events can exist *together* on a space and time continuum. Time belongs to the created order as much elephants, oceans, oak trees, and the Grand Canyon. Do not ask me to explain this as a hypothesis of physics—I trust Albert Einstein on this one. He wrote, "If we assume that all matter would disappear from the world, then, before relativity, one believed that space and time would continue existing in an 'empty' world. But according to the theory of relativity, if matter and motion disappeared there would no longer be any space or time."[5]

The genius of Princeton postulated that once we exit life in the physical creation, all handcuffs of time drop away from us. Before Einstein's revolutionary work, "the concept of absolute time—meaning time that exists in reality and tick-tocks along independent of any observations of it had been a mainstay of physics since Newton. . . . The same was true for absolute space and distance."[6] Einstein boldly cast off the mantle of Newtonian physics. From the development of his general theory of relativity beginning in 1905, physics no longer recognized the absolute existence of time apart from a relation to matter or space. "Einstein had shown that space and time did not have independent existences, but instead formed a fabric of spacetime."[7]

For all of us nonphysicists, the now widely accepted theory of relativity as it touches upon our ideas of time elicits responses of "Huh?" and "Wow!" deliriously blended. The cultural historian Paul Johnson said about the theory of relativity, "It formed a knife to help cut society adrift from its traditional moorings."[8]

## CUTTING OUR MOORINGS TO TIME

We may need our doctrinal mooring lines cut, to better think about being "present with the Lord" immediately at death. We imagine eternal life as a similar existence to this one, only much longer—perhaps 100,000,000,000,000 years, or any other number too large to handle. Wrong concept. Eternity is greater than any enormous number you can conjure by multiplying a hundred trillion by a thousand trillion. Eternity is a distinct realm, completely apart from time. Eternity is the dwelling place of God, better conceived of as an all-encompassing "now," not a line of historic years strung together like billions of tiny beads on a one-thousand-mile string. Linear ideas about time seem necessary when we speak about the dead in Christ, so we interpose a proto-heavenly waiting-room between each one's departure from this life and that last day when soul and body are rejoined in resurrection. Now, science says there may be no absolute time within which this so-called "interval" of "waiting" can occur.

Our final glorification to be with Christ in resurrection bodies is the great destination God prepares for every Christian soul. Is it impossible to think that the triumphant day of the Lord greets every believer the moment he or she dies? Arthur Custance wrote, "When any Christian dies, he passes from this realm of time and space into another realm of pure spirit, that is to say, out of time as we experience it into a state of timelessness, the ever-present of God. . . . Every event in God's scheduled program for the future, which as revealed in Scripture must come to pass before the Lord's return, must crowd instantly upon him. He does not 'wait' for the Lord's return; it is immediate . . . though the 'living' who survive him do await these events in the future. . . . Within the framework of time the general resurrection is future, but to the 'dying' Christian it is a present event."[9] Custance went on to theorize that at our death "the experience of each saint is shared with all other saints, by those who have preceded us and those who are to follow. . . . Each one finds to his amazement that Adam too is just dying and joining him on his way to meet the Lord: and Abraham and David, Isaiah and the Beloved John, Paul and Augustine, Hudson Taylor and you and I—all in one wonderful experience meeting the Lord in a single instant together, without precedent and without the slightest hint of delay, none being late and none too early."[10]

Those ideas from the fertile thinking of a brother in Christ stimulate my heart today just as they did when I first encountered them decades ago. Custance continued, "For us who remain (alive on earth) this event is still future, an event greatly longed for. For those who have gone on, it has already happened—but not without us."[11]

## SCRIPTURE CORRELATIONS

Hebrews 11:39–40 seems to support this concept, declaring about the Old Testament saints from the roll call of faith: "And all these, though commended through their faith, did not receive what was promised, since God had provided something better for us, that *apart from us they should not be made perfect.*" The inspired author of Hebrews described real solidarity between believers of old named in Hebrews 11 and believers today, based on the covenant of grace. He wrote of a climactic reunion when Christ appears and all believers from all ages of the universal church of Jesus together "receive what was promised."

One Bible passage that may seem opposed to what we are postulating is Revelation 6:9–10. John saw in a vision "under the altar the souls of those who had been slain for the word of God and for the witness they had borne. They cried out with a loud voice, 'O Sovereign Lord, holy and true, how long before you will judge and avenge our blood on those who dwell on earth?'" Remember, Revelation is almost entirely cast in symbolic imagery, so we are not devaluing this Scripture in a liberal manner when reminding ourselves that the scene is a metaphor, not an engineering drawing of heaven as a home for impatient martyrs in the intermediate state. The passage does teach vividly that there will seem to be a long historical wait from earth's vantage point, before God's justice appears. But it does not require making Revelation 6:9–10 into a literal snapshot of an intermediate state. John was a man like us, still restricted in categories of time.

We could also mention an apparent inversion of time in God's scheme of governing redemption by the cross. Jesus was called in Revelation 13:8 the Lamb slain "before the foundation of the world." The same expression occurs nine other times in the New Testament (Matt. 13:35; 25:34; Luke 11:50; John 17:24; Eph. 1:4; Heb. 4:3; 9:26; 1 Pet. 1:20; Rev. 17:8). Some view this as speaking only of God's foreknowledge, that Jesus would be slain in the future. But a plain reading implies a divine event determined outside of time in order that it might be implemented within time. A similar thing is stated when Jesus announced in John 5:25, "Truly, truly, I say to you, an hour is coming, *and is now here*, when the dead will hear the voice of the Son of God, and those who hear will live." Typical concepts of present and future seem to be blended within this "hour" of God's supernatural work.

## AUGUSTINE, LUTHER, AND LEWIS ON TIME

Long before Einstein, in fact just four centuries after Christ, Augustine contemplated the question, "What was God doing before he created the universe?" Augustine believed time began with the act of divine creation of the universe God made out of the word of his power. To use Augustine's words, "Beyond a doubt the world was made not in time, but together with time."[12] It is astonishing how closely Augustine, the ancient African theologian, anticipated Einstein.

Arthur Custance also believed he found some support for his theory in writings of Martin Luther. Luther spoke about the "sleep" of his body (not his soul) after death when he wrote, "For just as a man who falls asleep and sleeps soundly until morning does not know what has happened to him when he wakes up, so shall we suddenly rise at the Last Day. . . . We are to sleep until He comes and knocks on the grave and says, 'Dr. Martin, get up.' Then I will rise in a moment and will be eternally happy with him."

The telling portion of Luther's writing on the subject followed: "Here you must put out of your mind and know that in that world there is neither time nor a measure of time, but everything is one eternal moment. . . . It will seem to Adam and the patriarchs just as though they were living half an hour ago. There is no time there. . . . The patriarchs will not reach the Last Day before we do."[13]

I realize Clive Staple Lewis represents a different brand of theologian from either Augustine or Luther. But it is interesting to note that he also included a short chapter called "Time Beyond Time" in the middle of his classic *Mere Christianity*. He first spoke of the confusion some folk express about how God could hear the prayer of hundreds of thousands addressed to him in the same moment and suggested that time was the obstacle to our thinking correctly on the matter. "We tend to assume that the whole universe and God himself are always moving on from past to future as we do. . . . Almost certainly God is not in time. His life does not consist of moments following one another. . . . If you picture Time as a straight line along which we have to travel, then you must picture God as the whole page on which the line is drawn."[14] Lewis said further, "Suppose God is outside and above the Time-line. In that case, what we call tomorrow is visible to him in the same way as what we call today. All the days are 'now' for him."[15]

All these thinkers were suggesting that perhaps at the moment of death we believers are living souls in God's "now"—entirely apart from any calendar.

## CONCLUDING THOUGHTS

Arthur Custance said about the mind-expanding concept of no time after death: "If this seems a difficult concept, I agree!"[16] He readily acknowledged the difficulty many would have with the idea: "Speculating I am certainly doing. But going beyond the evidence: that is a matter of opinion—though all re-thinking is viewed as speculation by those who prefer established confusion to novel truth. . . . Speculation which may be anathema to the cautious theologian is the very life-blood of scientific progress, where it is called by another name—hypothesizing."[17]

To summarize once more, this tentative interpretation of what happens to us immediately after death asks us to imagine the possibility that your day of death on earth, and the death of every believer from all centuries before and after, is an instantaneous doorway by which you are present at the great last day of Christ (1 Thessalonians 4). You are no longer time-bound, as God is not. There is no conscious "in between" epoch required while a departed soul takes a number and "waits" in heaven's antechamber. We find ourselves present in the company of every other believer who has already died or is yet to die in earth time. Vast throngs of the church are simultaneously gathered into the glorious presence of returning King Jesus, who bestows glorified bodies upon us all, as promised in 1 Thessalonians 4 and 1 Corinthians 15. On my approach to Christ's throne I arrive beside my relatives and friends I lost years ago. Surrounding me in a welcoming convocation are scores of now perfected Christians whose funerals I presided over in my ministry. Over there is Moses, Peter, Augustine, Luther, Edwards, and Bonhoeffer. This stunning event fulfills Jesus's promise in John 14:3: "I will come again and will take you to myself, that where I am you may be also." This means my soul shall never be without a body for any time. We are transferred directly from this corruptible flesh into the incorruptible!

Arthur Custance concluded, "Over the years, I have often observed that minds less trammeled with education and more nurtured on simple Bible study will grasp the complexities of this situation and will go away rejoicing with a very real understanding."[18] Is this a sound alternative view of what happens immediately at death, conforming to biblical data? If so, it would replace the basis of all I wrote in chapter 9 about the more conventional idea of an "immediate heaven." Once your mind begins to wrap around it, the idea is impressive for its great simplicity. And I am pressed to find Scripture that obviously opposes the concept. However, I would say on the side of genuine caution that while I can see here a thrilling point of view, I am not prepared to dogmatize at this point. I only wanted you to consider it an option.

We are not decision makers regarding what is true in this matter. One thing is sure—we *will* find out! Meanwhile, as believers in the Risen Lord Christ we can sing with David, "Therefore my heart is glad, and my whole being rejoices; my flesh also dwells secure. For you will not abandon my soul to Sheol, or let your holy one see corruption. You make known to me the path of life; in your presence there is fullness of joy; at your right hand are pleasures forevermore" (Ps. 16:9–11).

Amen and amen. . . . Come, Lord Jesus!

# NOTES

*Preface*
1. Cornelis P. Venema, *The Promise of the Future* (Carlisle, PA: Banner of Truth, 2000).
2. Edward Donnelley, *Biblical Teaching on the Doctrines of Heaven and Hell* (Carlisle, PA: Banner of Truth, 2001); Anthony Hoekema, *The Bible and the Future* (Grand Rapids, MI: Eerdmans, 1979).

*Chapter 1: The Land of Deep Shade*
1. Stephen J. Nichols, ed., *Jonathan Edwards' Resolutions and Advice to Young Converts* (Phillipsburg, NJ: P&R, 2001), 18.
2. "Imagine," music and lyrics by John Lennon, Apple Records, catalogue, 1840, 1971.
3. Richard Baxter, *The Reformed Pastor* (repr. 1974; Edinburgh, UK: Banner of Truth, 1656), 113.
4. Martin Luther, "A Sermon on Preparing to Die," in *O Love That Will Not Let Me Go*, ed. Nancy Guthrie (Wheaton, IL: Crossway, 2011), 106.
5. Ibid., 107.

*Chapter 2: Death's Universal Reign*
1. Timothy J. Keller, "Rubbing Hope into Death," in *O Love That Will Not Let Me Go*, ed. Nancy Guthrie (Wheaton, IL: Crossway, 2011), 88.
2. Helmut Thielicke, *Death and Life* (Philadelphia: Fortress Press, 1970), 145.
3. Annie Dillard, *Pilgrim at Tinker Creek* (New York: Harper & Row, 1974), 89–90.
4. Thomas Goodwin in *Romans*, ed. Geoffrey Wilson (Edinburgh, UK: Banner of Truth, 1976), 86.
5. John R. W. Stott, *Romans* (Downers Grove, IL: Inter Varsity, 1994), 148.
6. D. Martyn Lloyd-Jones, *The Assurance of Our Salvation* (Wheaton, IL: Crossway, 2000), 83.

*Chapter 3: Death's Power Destroyed*
1. Harper Lee, *To Kill a Mockingbird* (New York: HarperCollins, 1960), 30.
2. Charles H. Spurgeon, "Concerning Death," in *O Love That Will Not Let Me Go*, ed. Nancy Guthrie (Wheaton, IL: Crossway, 2011), 149–50.
3. Saint Chrysostom, *Homily 4, The Epistle to the Hebrews* (Lynchburg, VA: Liberty University Christian Classics on-line). Emphasis added.

*Chapter 4: Because He Lives*
1. Paul L. Maier, *A Skeleton in God's Closet* (Nashville: Thomas Nelson, 1994).
2. Josh McDowell, *Evidence That Demands a Verdict* (San Bernardino, CA: Here's Life, 1972).
3. Frank Morison, *Who Moved the Stone?* (Grand Rapids, MI: Zondervan, 1977).
4. Paul Helm, *The Last Things* (Edinburgh, UK: Banner of Truth, 1989), 141.
5. Blaise Pascal in *The Mind on Fire*, ed. James Houston (Colorado Springs: Victor Books, 2006), 22.

*Chapter 5: The Default Destination*
1. Edward Donnelley, *The Biblical Teaching on the Doctrines of Heaven and Hell* (Edinburgh, UK: Banner of Truth, 2000), 10.
2. David Wells in the introduction to Robert Peterson, *Hell on Trial: The Case for Eternal Punishment* (Phillipsburg, NJ: P&R, 1995), x.
3. J. C. Ryle, *Expository Thoughts on the Gospels* (Cambridge, UK: James Clarke, 1865) 1:164.
4. C. S. Lewis, *The Great Divorce* (New York: Macmillan, 1946), 72.

5. Herman Bavinck, *The Last Things*, ed. John Bolt, trans. John Vriend (Grand Rapids, MI: Baker, 1996), 147.
6. Paul Helm, *The Last Things* (Edinburgh, UK: Banner of Truth, 1989), 109.
7. Ibid., 109–10.

### Chapter 6: The Strange Disappearance of Hell
1. "Hell's Sober Comeback," *U. S. News and World Report*, March 25, 1991, 52.
2. David Lodge, *Souls and Bodies* (London: Penguin, 1980), 113.
3. Martin Marty as quoted in "Hell's Sober Comeback," 57.
4. Westminster Confession of Faith, 3.7, emphasis added.
5. I acknowledge helpful summarizations from a variety of sources on the doctrine of reprobation, all from the classroom teaching of Dr. John S. Light of Lancaster, PA. See also Wayne Grudem, *Systematic Theology* (Grand Rapids, MI: Zondervan, 1994), 684–86.
6. Loraine Boettner, *The Reformed Doctrine of Predestination* (Philadelphia: Presbyterian and Reformed, 1972), 287–88.
7. Richard Niebuhr, *The Kingdom of God in America* (New York: Harper & Row, 1959), 193.
8. Rt. Rev. Bill Phipps, interview with *The Ottawa Citizen*, October 30, 1997.
9. Remembrance of this communion service and a best recollection of the words of James M. Boice were confirmed to me by Dr. Philip Ryken.

### Chapter 7: What Jesus Taught about Hell
1. Edward Donnelley, *The Biblical Teaching on the Doctrines of Heaven and Hell* (Edinburgh, UK: Banner of Truth, 2000), 31.
2. Bertrand Russell, *Why I Am Not A Christian* (London: 1976), 22–23.
3. Leon Morris, "The Dreadful Harvest," *Christianity Today*, May 27, 1991, 34.
4. Robert Peterson, *Hell on Trial: The Case for Eternal Punishment* (Phillipsburg, NJ: P&R, 1995), 200.
5. Paul Helm, *The Last Things* (Edinburgh, UK: Banner of Truth, 1989), 112.
6. C. S. Lewis, *The Great Divorce* (New York: Macmillan, 1946), 72.
7. Augustine, *The Works of Saint Augustine: A Translation for the Twenty-First Century*, trans. Edmund Hill, ed. J. E. Rotelle (Brooklyn, NY: New City Press, 1990–), pt. 3, 2:163.
8. Thomas Brooks, *The Works of Thomas Brooks*, ed. Alexander B. Grosart (Edinburgh: Banner of Truth Trust, 1980), 6:209–10.

### Chapter 8: Does Hell Last Forever?
1. Clark H. Pinnock in *Four Views of Hell*, ed. William Crockett (Grand Rapids, MI: Eerdmans, 1992), 39.
2. David L. Edwards and John R. W. Stott, *Essentials: A Liberal and Evangelical Debate* (London: Hodder & Stoughton, 1988), 320.
3. Clark H. Pinnock, "The Destruction of the Finally Impenitent," in *Criswell Theological Review* 4 (Spring 1990): 225.
4. Ibid., 246–47.
5. Harry Buis, *The Doctrine of Eternal Punishment* (Philadelphia: Presbyterian and Reformed, 1957), 49.
6. Scot McKnight as cited by Robert Peterson, *Hell on Trial: The Case for Eternal Punishment* (Phillipsburg, NJ: P&R, 1995), 165.
7. Peterson, *Hell on Trial*, 88.
8. Edward Donnelley, *The Biblical Teaching on the Doctrines of Heaven and Hell* (Edinburgh, UK: Banner of Truth, 2000), 14.
9. Ibid., 25.
10. Alec Motyer, *Life 2: The Sequel, What Happens When You Die?* (Ross-shire, Scotland: Christian Focus, 1996), 42.
11. Donnelley, *Heaven and Hell*, 27.
12. John Blanchard, *Whatever Happened to Hell?* (Wheaton, IL: Crossway, 1995), 117.
13. Ibid., 298.
14. Jonathan Edwards as cited by John Gerstner, *Jonathan Edwards on Heaven and Hell* (Grand Rapids, MI: Baker, 1980), 85.

*Notes*

### Chapter 9: The Immediate Heaven
1. Philip E. Hughes, *The Second Epistle to the Corinthians*, New International Commentary on the New Testament (Grand Rapids, MI: Eerdmans, 1962), 165.
2. Scott J. Hafemann, *2 Corinthians*, NIV Application Commentary (Grand Rapids, MI: Zondervan, 2000), 209.
3. Samuel Rutherford, *Letters of Samuel Rutherford* (Edinburgh, UK: Banner of Truth, 1984), 376.
4. John Calvin, *Second Epistle of Paul to the Corinthians*, trans. T. A. Small (Grand Rapids, MI: Eerdmans, 1964), 65.
5. J. R. R. Tolkien, *The Return of the King* (Boston: Houghton & Mifflin, 1955), 930–31.

### Chapter 10: Immortality Is Not Enough
1. Anthony Hoekema, *The Bible and the Future* (Grand Rapids, MI: Eerdmans, 1979), 86.
2. Herman Bavinck, *Gereformeerde Dogmatik*, IV, 567 as cited by Hoekema, *The Bible and the Future*, 89.
3. Ibid., 26
4. Jonathan Edwards as cited by Iain Murray, *Jonathan Edwards: A New Biography* (Edinburgh, UK: Banner of Truth, 1987), 35.
5. Philip Graham Ryken, *1 Timothy*, Reformed Expository Commentary (Phillipsburg, NJ: P&R, 2007), 36.
6. John Calvin, *First Epistle to the Corinthians*, trans. John Fraser (Grand Rapids, MI: Eerdmans, 1960), 340.

### Chapter 11: The Final Heaven Inaugurated
1. C. S. Lewis, *Mere Christianity* (New York: HarperCollins, 1952), 65.
2. Gregory K. Beale, *1–2 Thessalonians* (Downers Grove, IL: IVP Press, 2003) 138–39.
3. John Calvin, *Selected Works: Tracts and Letters* (Grand Rapids, MI: Baker, 1983), 3:414, 490.
4. Cornelis Venema, *Promise of the Future* (Carlisle, PA: Banner of Truth, 2000), 51.
5. Geoffrey Wilson, *I & II Thessalonians* (Edinburgh, UK: Banner of Truth, 1975), 63.
6. Leon Morris, *First and Second Thessalonians*, New International Commentary on the New Testament (Grand Rapids, MI: Eerdmans, 1959), 143.
7. John R. W. Stott, *The Gospel and the End of Time* (Downers Grove, IL: IVP, 1991), 105.
8. Arthur Bennett, ed. *The Valley of Vision: A Collection of Puritan Prayers and Devotions* (Edinburgh, UK: Banner of Truth, 1975), 203.

### Chapter 12: We Shall All Be Changed
1. Joni Eareckson Tada, *Heaven, Your Real Home* (Grand Rapids, MI: Zondervan: 1995), 39.
2. C. S. Lewis, *The Weight of Glory and Other Addresses* (Grand Rapids, MI: Eerdmans, 1949), 14–15.
3. C. S. Lewis, *The Great Divorce* (New York: Macmillan, 1946), 27.
4. Ibid., 30.
5. Cornelis Venema, *The Promise of the Future* (Carlisle, PA: Banner of Truth, 2000), 371.
6. Matthew Poole, *A Commentary on the Holy Bible* (Edinburgh, UK: Banner of Truth, repr. 1963), 3:507.
7. N. T. Wright, *Surprised by Hope* (New York: HarperCollins, 2005), 102.
8. Poole, *Commentary on the Holy Bible*, 597.
9. Anthony Hoekema, *The Bible and the Future* (Grand Rapids, MI: Eerdmans, 1979), 249.

### Chapter 13: The Day of the Lord
1. Ligon Duncan, *Fear Not!* (Ross-shire, Scotland: Christian Focus, 2008), 63–64.
2. See these concise critiques of dispensationalism: W. J. Grier, *The Momentous Event* (Edinburgh, UK: Banner of Truth, 1945), chaps. 6–7; Anthony Hoekema, *The Bible and the Future* (Grand Rapids, MI: Eerdmans, 1979), chap. 5; Cornelis Venema, *The Promise of the Future* (Carlisle, PA: Banner of Truth, 2000), chap. 10.
3. Paul Helm, *The Last Things* (Edinburgh, UK: Banner of Truth, 1989), 12.
4. Hoekema, *Bible and the Future*, 256.
5. Alec Motyer, *Life 2: The Sequel, What Happens When You Die?* (Ross-shire, Scotland: Christian Focus, 1996), 99.

6. Helm, *Last Things*, 69.
7. Ibid., 63–64.
8. Venema, *Promise of the Future*, 403.

### Chapter 14: Are Christians Judged for Rewards?
1. John Calvin, *Tracts and Treatises in Defense of the Reformed Faith*, trans. Henry Beveridge (Grand Rapids, MI: Baker, 1983), 3.152.
2. Paul Helm, *The Last Things* (Edinburgh, UK: Banner of Truth, 1989), 79. Emphasis added.
3. Cornelis Venema, *The Promise of the Future* (Carlisle, PA: Banner of Truth, 2000), 415.
4. Jonathan Edwards, *Works* (Edinburgh, UK: Banner of Truth, 1974), 2:618.
5. J. B. Wakely, *Anecdotes of George Whitefield (1875)*, as cited by Arnold Dallimore, *George Whitefield* (Westchester, IL: Cornerstone Books, 1979), 2:353. Remarkably some Internet sources reverse this quote, having John Wesley saying it about Whitefield. But it would be out of character for Wesley, and earlier sources seem to clearly indicate it was said by Whitefield.

### Chapter 15: New Heavens and a New Earth
1. Cornelis Venema, *The Promise of the Future* (Carlisle, PA: Banner of Truth, 2000), 457.
2. Randy Alcorn, *Heaven* (Wheaton, IL: Tyndale House, 2004), 81. A chief virtue of Alcorn's book is its strong emphasis on the new earth as our final home.
3. Edward Donnelley, *The Biblical Teaching on the Doctrines of Heaven and Hell* (Edinburgh, UK: Banner of Truth, 2000), 112.
4. Paul Helm, *The Last Things* (Edinburgh, UK: Banner of Truth, 1989), 142.
5. Anthony Hoekema, *The Bible and the Future* (Grand Rapids, MI: Eerdmans, 1979), 278.
6. Eugene Peterson, *Reversed Thunder* (San Francisco: Harper, 1988), 169.
7. Paul Marshall with Lela Gilbert, *This World Is Not My Home* (Nashville: Word, 1998), 249.
8. Edward Thurneyson, as cited by Hoekema, *The Bible and the Future*, 279.
9. Peterson, *Reversed Thunder*, 170–71.
10. Herman Bavinck, *The Last Things*, ed. John Bolt, trans. John Vriend (Grand Rapids, MI: Baker, 1996), 158.
11. Peterson, *Reversed Thunder*, 174.

### Chapter 16: A Sabbath Rest for God's People
1. James F. Roberts Jr., *Stonewall Jackson* (New York: Macmillan USA, 1997), 753.
2. 60 Minutes, "Transcript: Tom Brady, Part 3, June 2005, www.cbsnews.com/stories/2005/11/04/60minutes/main/015331.shtml.
3. Walter Chantry, *Call the Sabbath a Delight* (Edinburgh, UK: Banner of Truth, 1991), 35, 46.
4. Richard Baxter, *The Saint's Everlasting Rest* (Ross-shire, Scotland: Christian Focus, 1998), 4.
5. Robert Grant, "O Worship the King," 1833.
6. K. Scott Oliphint and Sinclair Ferguson, *If I Should Die Before I Wake* (Grand Rapids, MI: Baker, 1995), 93.
7. Edward Donnelley, *The Biblical Teaching on the Doctrines of Heaven and Hell* (Edinburgh, UK: Banner of Truth, 2000), 117.
8. Jonathan Edwards, *Works* (Edinburgh, UK: Banner of Truth, 1974), 2:209.
9. Randy Alcorn, *Heaven* (Wheaton, IL: Tyndale House, 2004), 443.

### Chapter 17: In Emmanuel's Land
1. Jonathan Edwards, "The Christian Pilgrim," in *Pressing into the Kingdom of God* (Morgan, PA: Soli Deo Gloria, 1998), 335–36.
2. Samuel Rutherford, *Letters of Samuel Rutherford* (Edinburgh, UK: Banner of Truth, 1984), 330–31.
3. Edward Donnelley, *The Biblical Teaching on the Doctrines of Heaven and Hell* (Edinburgh, UK: Banner of Truth, 2000), 77.
4. Anne R. Cousin, "The Sands of Time Are Sinking," 1857, based on writings of Samuel Rutherford.
5. Thomas Boston, *Human Nature in Its Fourfold State* (London: Banner of Truth, 1964), 453.

6. John Owen, *The Works of John Owen* (Edinburgh, UK: Banner of Truth Trust, 1965), 7:336–38.
7. Cornelis Venema, *The Promise of the Future* (Carlisle, PA: Banner of Truth, 2000), 488.
8. See Ligon Duncan, "The Eternal Glory" in *These Last Days,* ed. Richard Phillips (Phillipsburg, NJ: P&R, 2011), 74, 77.
9. Samuel Rutherford, *The Loveliness of Christ* (Edinburgh: Banner of Truth, 2007), 103–4.
10. Arthur Bennett, ed. *The Valley of Vision: A Collection of Puritan Prayers and Devotions* (Edinburgh, UK: Banner of Truth, 1975), 205.

*Chapter 18: My Flesh Dwells Secure*
1. Joseph Bayly, *The View from a Hearse* (Elgin, IL: David C. Cook, 1969), 84–85.
2. Anne Wyman, "Life or Death: Who Decides?" *Boston Globe*, April 25, 1983.
3. *The Life of James Montgomery Boice, 1938–2000,* memorial booklet (Philadelphia: Tenth Presbyterian Church, 2000), 40–41.
4. Iain Murray, *D. Martyn Lloyd-Jones: The Fight of Faith, 1939–1981* (Edinburgh, UK: Banner of Truth, 1990), 730–31.
5. Ibid., 747–48.

*Chapter 19: Precious in the Sight of the Lord*
1. C. S. Lewis, *Letters to an American Lady*, ed. Clyde S. Kilby (New York: Pyramid Books, 1967), 117–18.

*Chapter 20: He Has Borne Our Griefs*
1. C. S. Lewis, *A Grief Observed* (New York: Seabury Press, 1961), 7, 29, 13.
2. Ibid., 9–10.
3. Ibid., 16.
4. Ibid., 38.
5. Ibid., 42.
6. Ibid., 43.
7. John Flavel, *Facing Grief: Counsel for Mourners* (repr. 2010; Edinburgh, UK: Banner of Truth, 1674), 16.
8. Michael Horton, "Death's Sting Is Removed but Its Bite Remains" in *O Love That Will Not Let Me Go,* ed. Nancy Guthrie (Wheaton, IL: Crossway, 2011), 23.
9. Ibid., 140.

*Chapter 21: Is My Child in Heaven?*
1. Herman Bavinck, *Reformed Dogmatics*, vol. 4, ed. John Bolt, trans. John Vriend (Grand Rapids, MI: Baker Academic, 2008), 123.
2. John MacArthur, *Safe in the Arms of God: Truth from Heaven about the Death of a Child* (Nashville: Nelson Books, 2003).
3. Ibid., 113.
4. John Piper, "What Happens to Infants When They Die?" DesiringGod.com, compiled by Matt Perman, January 23, 2006.
5. Ibid.
6. Benjamin B. Warfield, "Children," in *Selected Shorter Writings* (Phillipsburg, NJ: Presbyterian and Reformed, 1970), 1:230.
7. MacArthur, *Safe in the Arms of God*, 59.
8. John Calvin, *A Harmony of the Gospels*, trans. T. H. L. Parker (Grand Rapids, MI: Eerdmans, 1972), 2:252.
9. John Newton, *The Works of John Newton* (Edinburgh: Banner of Truth Trust, 1985), 4:553, 552.
10. Westminster Confession of Faith, 10.3.
11. Voetius, as cited by Bavinck, *Reformed Dogmatics*, 4:275.
12. Bavinck, *Reformed Dogmatics*, 4:727.
13. Benjamin B. Warfield, "The Development of the Doctrine of Infant Salvation," *Studies in Theology* (repr. 1988; Phillipsburg, NJ: Presbyterian and Reformed, 1932), 411.
14. Ibid., 412–13.
15. Martin Luther in ibid., 423.
16. Ibid., 428–29.

17. Loraine Boettner, *The Reformed Doctrine of Predestination* (Philadelphia: Presbyterian and Reformed, 1972), 147–48.
18. Warfield, *Studies in Theology*, 431.
19. John Owen, *The Works of John Owen,* ed. William H. Goold (Edinburgh, UK: Banner of Truth Trust, 1967), 10:81.
20. Ibid.
21. Bavinck, *Reformed Dogmatics*, 4:85.
22. John Newton, *Works* (Edinburgh: Banner of Truth, 1985), 6:187.
23. Charles H. Spurgeon, "Expositions of the Doctrines of Grace," *Metropolitan Tabernacle Pulpit*, vol. 7 (London: Passmore and Alabaster, 1862), 300.
24. Warfield, *Studies in Theology*, 444.
25. MacArthur, *Safe in the Arms of God*, 76.
26. Robert Rayburn, "Preaching After the Loss of a Child," in *The Hardest Sermons You'll Ever Preach,* ed. Bryan Chapell (Grand Rapids, MI: Zondervan, 2011), 144.

### Chapter 22: To Live Is Christ, To Die Is Gain

1. Joseph Bayly, *The View from a Hearse* (Elgin, IL: David C. Cook, 1969), 88.
2. Letter by Dr. J. Alan Groves given to me courtesy of his wife, Elizabeth Groves.
3. James M. Boice, *Philippians*, An Expositional Commentary (Grand Rapids, MI: Baker, 2000), 74.
4. John R. W. Stott, *Basic Christianity* (Grand Rapids, MI: Eerdmans, 1958), 20.
5. Dietrich Bonhoeffer, *The Cost of Discipleship* (New York: Macmillan, 1949), 39, 47, 62–63, 99.
6. Murray J. Harris, *Raised Immortal: Resurrection and Immortality in the New Testament* (London: Marshall, Morgan, and Scott, 1983), 64–65.
7. As narrated in a sermon by Dr. Bryan Chapell (Lancaster, PA, November 13, 2011).
8. Boice, *Philippians*, 81.
9. H. C. G. Moule, *Philippian Studies* (Glasgow, UK: Pickering and Inglis, n.d.), 71.
10. Jonathan Edwards, "Miscellany 1122," as cited by John Gerstner, *Jonathan Edwards on Heaven and Hell* (Grand Rapids, MI: Baker, 1980), 16.
11. Alexander MacLaren, *Expositions of Holy Scripture*, vol. 14 (Grand Rapids, MI: Eerdmans, 1942), 14:227.
12. Ibid., 232.

### Appendix: Is There Time in Heaven?

1. Arthur C. Custance, *Time and Eternity*, vol. 6, *The Doorway Papers* (Grand Rapids, MI: Academie Books/Zondervan, 1977).
2. Arthur C. Custance, *Journey Out of Time: A Study of the Interval between Death and the Resurrection of the Body* (Brockville, ON: Doorway, 1981.)
3. Custance, *Time and Eternity*, 39.
4. See Ibid., 12.
5. Albert Einstein as cited by Philipp Frank, *Einstein, His Life and Times* (New York: Alfred Knopf, 1947), 178.
6. Walter Isaacson, *Einstein, His Life and Universe* (New York: Simon & Schuster, 2007), 125.
7. Ibid., 223.
8. Paul Johnson, *Modern Times* (New York: Harper & Row, 1991), 1–3.
9. Custance, *Time and Eternity*, 42.
10. Ibid., 43.
11. Ibid.
12. Augustine, *De Civitates Dei*, bk. 11, chap. 6, as cited by Custance, *Time and Eternity*, 19.
13. Martin Luther, as cited by Paul Althaus in Custance, *Journey Out of Time*, 240–41.
14. C. S. Lewis, *Mere Christianity* (New York: HarperCollins, 1952), 167–68.
15. Ibid., 170.
16. Custance, *Journey Out of Time*, 179.
17. Ibid., 194.
18. Ibid., 243.

# SCRIPTURE INDEX

# GENERAL INDEX